'I laughed out loud so many times my wife thought that I had Tourette's. It's so well written, full of detail, self-deprecating and funny. A seminal book – an intelligent, literate rock and roll memoir full of candour and wit' Alan Parker

'A real pleasure – a rich, funny and fascinating story. Nick is a wonderfully dry and laconic guide' Peter Gabriel

'The fact that this man can remember anything about the orgy he calls his career is a miracle – an amazing view of a life most of us would kill for' Ruby Wax

'With a wit drier than an AA clinic, and a charm more disarming than a UN peace-keeping force, Nick Mason gives us a literary drum solo par excellence' Kathy Lette

'There cannot be many stories left in rock that are as big as Pink Floyd's. And I doubt whether anyone could tell this story so well as the patient, witty man who watched it all unfold from his perch behind the drum kit'

Paul Du Noyer, founder of *Mojo* magazine

'Mason could very probably have plied a successful trade as a writer. He has a measured, uncluttered style which he leavens with a dry, original wit . . . he writes with the calm authority of someone who was act~~ually~~ ....)ne of the greatest stories in the .... *Guardian*

'A wise and witty a............... hile rock biographies' Ian Ran~~k~~

Nick Mason was born in Birmingham in 1944. He is – of course – best known as the drummer in Pink Floyd. When not behind the drums Nick's other passion is motor racing. He has raced extensively in both historic and contemporary cars and competed in five Le Mans 24-hour races. In 1998 he wrote, with Mark Hales, *Into the Red*, a celebration of 21 cars from his collection of classic sports and racing cars (the book, updated and enlarged, was republished as *Passion for Speed* in 2010). Nick has also written for a wide variety of publications including *The Sunday Times*, the *Independent*, *Time*, *Tatler*, *GQ*, *Autosport*, *Classic Cars*, *Red Line*, *Octane* and is a contributing editor to the official Ferrari magazine. He is the Chairman of the Advisory Committee of the National Motor Museum.

Philip Dodd is an author and editor who specialises in music and popular culture. He co-edited *The Rolling Stones: A Life on the Road* and, with Charlie Watts and Dora Loewenstein, *According to the Rolling Stones*. He was the interviewer and editor for *Genesis: Chapter and Verse*, and is the author of *The Book of Rock*.

INSIDE OUT

A PERSONAL HISTORY OF **PINK FLOYD**

NICK MASON
EDITED BY PHILIP DODD

WEIDENFELD & **NICOLSON**

First published in Great Britain in 2004
First published in paperback in 2005 and reissued in 2011
This edition first published in 2017 by Weidenfeld & Nicolson
an imprint of The Orion Publishing Group Ltd
Carmelite House, 50 Victoria Embankment
London EC4Y 0DZ

An Hachette UK Company

3 5 7 9 10 8 6 4 2

Text copyright © Nick Mason 2004, 2017
Edited by Philip Dodd

Picture research by Emily Hedges and Stephanie Roberts
Pages 4–5 of picture section 3 designed by Storm Thorgerson
Editorial by Jo Murray, Claire Wedderburn-Maxwell
and Jennifer Condell

Original hardback design direction David Rowley
Original hardback design David Eldridge at Two Associates

A CIP catalogue record for this book is
available from the British Library.

ISBN 978 1 474 60648 6

Printed in Great Britain by Clays Ltd, St Ives plc

www.orionbooks.co.uk

CONTENTS

VOX

POLY
DAYS
1

ROGER WATERS only deigned to speak to me after we'd spent the best part of six months studying at college together. One afternoon, as I tried to shut out the murmur of forty fellow architectural students so that I could concentrate on the technical drawing in front of me, Roger's long, distinctive shadow fell across my drawing board. Although he had studiously ignored my existence up until that moment, Roger had finally recognised in me a kindred musical spirit trapped within a budding architect's body. The star-crossed paths of Virgo and Aquarius had dictated our destiny, and were compelling Roger to seek a way to unite our minds in a great creative adventure.

No, no, no. I'm trying to keep the invention to a minimum. The only reason Roger had bothered to approach me was that he wanted to borrow my car.

The vehicle in question was a 1930 Austin Seven 'Chummy' which I'd picked up for twenty quid. Most other teenagers of the time would probably have chosen to buy something more practical like a Morris 1000 Traveller, but my father had instilled a love of early cars in me, and had sourced this particular car. With his help, I learnt how to keep the 'Chummy' operational. However, Roger must have been desperate even to want me to lend it to him. The Austin's cruising speed was so sluggish that I'd once had to give a hitch-hiker a lift out of sheer embarrassment because I was going so slowly he thought I was actually stopping to offer him a ride. I told Roger the car was off the road, which was not entirely true. Part of me was reluctant to lend it out to anyone else, but I think I also found Roger rather menacing. When he spotted me driving the Austin shortly afterwards, he had his first taste of my penchant for occupying that no-man's-land between duplicity and diplomacy. On a previous occasion, Roger had accosted Rick Wright, who was also a student in our class, and asked him for a cigarette, a request Rick turned down point blank. This was an early sign of Rick's legendary generosity. These first, mundane, social contacts – during the spring of 1963 – contained the seeds of the relationships we would enjoy and endure over the years ahead.

Pink Floyd emerged from two overlapping sets of friends: one was based around Cambridge, where Roger, Syd Barrett, David Gilmour and many future Floyd affiliates hailed from. The other – Roger, Rick and myself – came together in the first year of an architecture course at the Regent Street Polytechnic in London, which is where my recollections of our common history begin.

I had in fact already retired as a drummer by the time I arrived at the Poly (since rather grandly retitled the University of Westminster). The college was then based in Little Titchfield Street, just off Oxford Street in the centre of the West End. The Poly, in retrospect, seems to be from a bygone era, with old-fashioned wooden panelling reminiscent of a giant, utilitarian public school. As far as I can remember there were no real onsite facilities, other than some tea-making equipment, but the Poly – in the heart of the rag trade area around Great Titchfield and Great Portland Streets – was surrounded by cafés offering eggs, sausage and chips up to midday, when steak and kidney pie and jam roly-poly would be the *menu du jour*.

The architectural school was in a building housing a number of other related disciplines and had become a well-respected institution. There was still a fairly conservative approach to teaching: for History of Architecture a lecturer would come in and draw on the board an immaculate representation of the floor plan of the Temple of Khons, Karnak, which we were expected to copy, just as they had been doing for thirty years. However, the school had recently introduced the idea of peripatetic lecturers, and played host to some visiting architects who were on the frontline of new ideas, including Eldred Evans, Norman Foster and Richard Rodgers. The faculty clearly had a good eye for form.

I had strolled into studying architecture with no great ambition. I was certainly interested in the subject, but not particularly committed to it as a career. I think I felt that being an architect would be as good a way to earn a living as any other. But equally I wasn't spending my time at college dreaming of becoming a musician. Any teenage aspirations in that area had been overshadowed by the arrival of my driving licence.

Despite my lack of burning ambition, the course offered a variety of disciplines – including fine art, graphics and technology – which proved to deliver a good all-round education, and which probably explains why Roger, Rick and I all, to a greater or lesser degree, shared an enthusiasm for the possibilities offered by technology and visual effects. In later years we would become heavily involved in everything from the construction of lighting towers to album cover artwork and studio and stage design. Our architectural training allowed us the luxury of making relatively informed comments whenever we brought the real experts in.

For those interested in tenuous connections, my interest in the mix of the technical and visual probably came from my father, Bill, a director of documentary films. When I was two, he accepted a job with the Shell film unit, and so we moved from the Birmingham suburb of Edgbaston, where I'd been born, to North London, where I spent my formative years.

Although my father was not particularly musical, he was definitely interested in music, especially when it related directly to one of his films. In those instances, he could become quite passionate about music ranging from Jamaican steel bands to string sections, jazz or the wilder electric ramblings of Ron Geesin. He was also fascinated by recording equipment, stereo test records, sound effects and racing cars, in various combinations, all interests which I inherited.

However, there was some hint of a musical heritage within the family: my maternal grandfather, Walter Kershaw, played in a banjo band with his four brothers and had had a piece of music published, called 'The Grand State March'. My mother Sally was a competent pianist, whose repertoire included Debussy's now extremely politically incorrect 'Golliwog's Cakewalk'. The selection of 78s at home was even more eclectic, including classical pieces, Communist workers' songs performed by the Red Army Choir, 'The Teddy Bears' Picnic' and 'The Laughing Policeman'. Doubtless traces of these influences can be found somewhere in our music – I shall leave it to others more energetic to winkle them out. I did take some lessons on the piano, as well as the violin, but they failed to uncover a musical prodigy and both instruments were abandoned.

I will also confess to a mysterious attraction for Fess Parker singing 'The Ballad Of Davy Crockett', a single released in the UK in 1956. Even in those days the unholy relationship between music and merchandising clearly existed, since I was soon sporting a natty nylon coonskin cap exquisitely set off by its rakish tail.

I must have been about twelve when rock music first impinged on my consciousness. I can remember struggling to stay awake through Horace Batchelor's exhortations for his unlikely pools system on Radio Luxembourg, hoping to catch 'Rocking To Dreamland'. I helped Bill Haley's 'See You Later Alligator' reach the UK Top Ten in March 1956 by buying it on a 78 from the local electrical store, and later that year I splashed out on Elvis Presley's 'Don't Be Cruel'. Both of these were played on the family's new state-of-the-art gramophone that was electric and connected to a device resembling a cross between the cabinets made in the days of Louis XIV and a Rolls-Royce dashboard. At thirteen I had my first long-playing album – Elvis's *Rock 'N Roll*. This seminal album was bought as a first LP by at least two other members of the Floyd, and almost all of our generation of rock musicians. Not only was this fantastic new music, but for a teenage rebel it also had the additional frisson of receiving the kind of parental welcome usually reserved for a pet spider.

It was about this time that I set off with my satchel, and in short flannel trousers and school blazer – the latter pink with a black trim and an iron cross badge – to see Tommy Steele performing at a variety show in East London. I was on my own. Apparently none of my school friends was as enthused. Tommy was top of the bill, and the rest of the bill was dire. Comics, jugglers and other refugees from the English music halls vied to clear the hall before Tommy came on, but I stuck it out. I have to say he was terrific. He sang 'Singing The Blues' and 'Rock With The Caveman' and looked exactly like he did on *The Six-Five Special*, the original pop show on UK television. He wasn't Elvis, but he was certainly the next best thing.

Within a couple of years, I had gravitated towards a group of friends from the neighbourhood who had also discovered rock 'n' roll, and it seemed an excellent idea to put a band together. The fact that none of us knew how to play was only a minor setback, since we didn't have any instruments. Consequently allocating who played what was something of a lottery. My only link with drumming was that Wayne Minnow, a journalist friend of my parents, had once brought me a pair of wire brushes. After the failure of my early piano and violin lessons, this seemed a perfectly legitimate reason to become a drummer. My first kit, acquired from Chas. E. Foote of Denman Street in Soho, included a Gigster bass drum, a snare drum of indeterminate age and parentage, hi-hat, cymbals, and an instruction book on the mysteries of flam paradiddles and ratamacues (which I am still attempting to unravel). Equipped with this devastating armoury I joined my friends to form the Hotrods.

The group included Tim Mack on lead guitar, William Gammell playing rhythm, and Michael Kriesky on bass. We also boasted a sax player, John Gregory, though his sax, which pre-dated the standardisation of concert A at 440 cycles, was half a tone higher than a new model, and consequently unplayable with an ensemble. Michael, with help from the rest of us, had built his bass from scratch. Frankly, the Saxons building a space probe would have had more success, but we did achieve the vague outward appearance of an instrument. Although we had access to some amps, these were so shameful that when we posed for a group photo, we felt obliged to mock up a Vox cabinet using a cardboard box and a biro.

Thanks to my father's film work we had access to a brand new stereo Grundig tape recorder. Rather than waste time rehearsing we immediately launched into our first recording session. The studio technique involved a trial and error positioning of two microphones somewhere between the drums and amplifier. Regrettably these tapes still exist.

The Hotrods never really developed beyond endless versions of the theme from the TV show *Peter Gunn*, and my career in music seemed destined to falter. But now I had gone from prep school to Frensham Heights, an independent co-ed school in Surrey. Here there were girls (I met my first wife Lindy there), a jazz club, and you could wear long trousers after the third form. Yes, this was the sophisticated life I had been looking for.

Compared to being at prep school, I really enjoyed my time at Frensham – the school was in a large country house with extensive grounds, near Hindhead in Surrey. Although it was fairly traditional – in terms of blazers and exams – it had a far more liberal approach to education, and I have fond memories of both art and English teachers there. I also began to learn the skills of negotiation. Since the school was close to Frensham Ponds, I had managed to acquire a canoe, and in return for lending it to the games master, I was able to avoid ever having to play cricket. As proof of this the clothing inventory included an expensive cricket sweater; mine never emerged from its original cellophane wrapping...

The school used the ballroom in the country house for assemblies and other functions, but on a regular basis it was used for its original purpose, when we would dance waltzes, foxtrots and veletas. However, during my time at Frensham, the ballroom dances evolved into hops, although I am sure that we had to get special clearance to play the latest singles, an attempt by the school to limit the invasion of pop music. We did have a jazz club, though. This was not something created by the masters, but an informal gathering of pupils: Peter Adler, the son of the great harmonica player Larry, was at the school. I remember him playing piano, and we may have tried playing jazz together at some point. It was difficult even to listen to our own jazz records, since the school only had one LP player, and we would only have had our own players towards the end of my time there. The club was probably more of an opportunity to get out of doing something more arduous and less agreeable, but it did at least represent a nascent interest in jazz. Later on I would spend time in London going to places like the 100 Club to hear the leaders of the trad jazz movement in England, players like Cy Laurie and Ken Colyer. However, I never liked the paraphernalia of a lot of trad jazz – all the bowler hats and waistcoats – and I moved on to bebop. I still have a great enthusiasm for modern jazz, but as a teenager, the advanced playing techniques required were an insurmountable barrier. I went back to perfecting the drum part to 'Peter Gunn'.

After leaving Frensham Heights, and following a year in London spent improving my studies, I arrived at the Regent Street Poly in September 1962. I studied a bit, produced various pieces of work for my portfolio, and attended numerous lectures. I did, however, show serious application in attempting to cultivate the correct look, with a penchant for corduroy jackets and duffle coats. I also tried smoking a pipe. It was some time during my second term at college that I fell in with what the older generation used to call a 'bad lot', namely Roger.

Our first abortive conversation about the Austin 'Chummy' had perhaps surprisingly led to a growing friendship, based on shared musical tastes. Another bond in the friendship that developed between us was a common liking for anything that took us outside the school building, whether trawling up and down the Charing Cross Road looking at drums and guitars, going to matinée shows at West End cinemas, or heading off to Anello and Davide's, the ballet-shoe makers in Covent Garden who were then also making Cuban-heeled cowboy boots to order. The prospect of a weekend break at Roger's house in Cambridge also occasionally encouraged an early Friday departure from the rigours of class work.

Politically we came from fairly similar backgrounds. Roger's mother was an ex-Communist Party member and a staunch Labour supporter, as were my parents: my father had joined the Communist Party to oppose fascism, and then on the outbreak of war left the CP and became a shop steward in the ACT, the Association of Cinematographic Technicians. This kind of background was also shared by our respective girlfriends, and later wives, Lindy and Judy. Roger had been the chairman of the youth section of the Campaign for Nuclear Disarmament in Cambridge, and he and Judy took part in a number of CND marches from

Aldermaston to London. Lindy and I did join at least one CND march on the outskirts of London on the last day, and she later was part of the Grosvenor Square demonstration which the police broke up with a rather heavy hand. I would now tend to say that probably reflects quite accurately my own general commitment to politics – slightly to the left of half-hearted with only the occasional outburst of good behaviour.

Some of Roger's strength of conviction had probably been picked up from his mother Mary, a teacher who'd shown her personal toughness by bringing up Roger and his elder brother John single-handed after her husband Eric Waters (who was also a teacher) had been killed in Italy during the Second World War. Roger had attended Cambridgeshire High School for Boys at the same time as Syd Barrett – among their fellow pupils was Storm Thorgerson, who later on would play a major role in the band's history as our graphic designer for over three decades. The school also provided Roger with the raw material for a particular kind of bullying teacher who would later appear as a caricature in *The Wall*.

Roger's musical activities were not particularly different from any other teenager's at the time: a bit of guitar strumming, picking up riffs and ideas from old blues records. Like me he was an avid listener to Radio Luxembourg, as well as the American Forces Network. When he came down to college in London his guitar travelled with him. An early indication of putting our training to good use was the way he had used Letraset, then a specialist design tool, to print 'I believe to my soul' on the body of the guitar. To our eyes, it looked pretty smart.

Along with his guitar, Roger packed a particular attitude. Like a few of the others in the class, he had already had a few months' experience working in an architectural office before arriving at college. This had given him a slightly more sophisticated view of where all this training might lead, and he sported an expression of scorn for most of the rest of us, which I think even the staff found off-putting.

A fellow student, Jon Corpe, has a vivid memory of Roger's impact at the Poly: 'Tall, gaunt, with poor skin, he projected an image of the High Plains Drifter. He carried his guitar, which he played softly in the studio or firmly in the Student Players office [this was the office of the Poly drama club, one of our rehearsal rooms]. To me Roger will always be at a distance, singing songs of morbid loss.'

We were occasionally called upon to form teams to complete a work assignment and so sometime during our first year Roger and I joined forces with Jon Corpe to design a small house. Our building design was received rather well, despite the fact that it was totally impractical, but this was mainly because Jon was an excellent student who seemed happy to concentrate on the architecture while Roger and I unloaded his grant on curry and musical instruments.

Working with Roger was not easy. Typically I would travel from Hampstead in North London, where I was still living at home, across town, only to find a note from Roger pinned to the door – 'Gone to the Café des Artistes'. His living arrangements were usually unsettled; for a while he lived in a particularly rough squat just off the King's Road in Chelsea. With no hot water – baths were taken at the Chelsea bathhouse just up the road – no phone and some wildly unstable co-squatters, this experience probably gave him a head start in coping with life on tour, but on a practical level it was extremely difficult to set up a drawing board.

Although the sight, sounds and aromas of Roger's lodgings have stayed with me, I have few clear memories of Rick at this juncture, and he could never do much better. I think he realised as soon as he arrived at college that architecture was not for him – according to Rick this was a totally arbitrary choice suggested by a careers master – but it took the Poly a full year to arrive at the same conclusion. Once both parties reached this mutual understanding, Rick left to seek an alternative route, ending up at the London College of Music.

What history does record is that Rick had been born in Pinner, that his father Robert was the chief biochemist for Unigate Dairies, and that the family home was in Hatch End on the outskirts of London: from there Rick attended Haberdashers' Aske's Grammar School. Rick played trumpet as a schoolboy, and always maintained that he played the piano before he could walk... but would then add that he didn't walk until he was ten. In fact it was a broken leg at twelve years old – with two months spent in bed – that left him with a guitar for company but no tutor. Rick taught himself to play using his own fingering, and later, encouraged by his Welsh mother Daisy, used the same approach for the piano. This teach-yourself method produced Rick's unique sound and style, and probably prevented him from ever making a living as a professor of technique at a conservatoire.

After a brief flirtation with skiffle, Rick had succumbed to a trad jazz influence, playing the trombone, saxophone and piano. I'm sorry to say that he once confessed to using a bowler hat as a mute for the trombone. He went to see Humphrey Lyttelton and Kenny Ball at Eel Pie Island, and Cyril Davies, one of the fathers of British R&B, at the Railway Tavern in Harrow. He also hitched or cycled to Brighton at weekends before mods went on scooters and adopted the dress style of a raver (collarless shirt, waistcoat and, on the odd occasion, bowler hat). Before arriving at the Poly he had a brief stint as a Kodak delivery assistant, where work experience had been based on watching the drivers sidling off at midday to play golf before returning to the depot at eight o'clock in the evening to clock out and claim their overtime.

My impressions of Rick at college are of someone quiet,

introverted, with a circle of friends outside the Poly. Jon Corpe remembers that 'Rick was the possessor of manly good looks, with long, luscious eyelashes that made the girls curious about him.'

In our first year, Rick, Roger and I all found ourselves in a band constructed by Clive Metcalfe, another Poly student who played in a duo with Keith Noble, one of our classmates. I'm sure that Clive was the original motivator of the band: he could actually play the guitar a bit and had clearly spent many hours learning the songs. The rest of us were all recruited in the most casual 'Yeah, I used to play a bit' way rather than through any burning ambition. This first Poly band – the Sigma 6 – consisted of Clive, Keith Noble, Roger, myself and Rick, with Keith's sister Sheila occasionally helping out on vocals. Rick's position was a little tenuous since he had no electric keyboard. He would play if a pub venue had a piano, but without any amplification it was unlikely anyone could hear him over the drums and the Vox AC30s. If no piano were available, he would threaten to bring along his trombone.

Rick's girlfriend, and later wife, Juliette was more a guest artist with a repertoire of various blues pieces including 'Summertime' and 'Careless Love' that she sang particularly well. Juliette, who'd been studying modern languages at the Poly, left for university in Brighton at the end of our first year, at the same time as Rick went on to the London College of Music. However, by then we had found enough in common musically to continue our friendship.

I think the band stabilised around the worse rather than the better players. We briefly had one really capable guitarist (I know he was good because he had a nice instrument and a proper Vox amplifier) but he moved on after a couple of rehearsals. My memory is that we never tried to formalise the line-up: if two guitarists turned up it simply extended the repertoire, as undoubtedly one of them would know a song the rest of us hadn't learnt. At this point Roger was designated rhythm guitarist. He was only relegated to bass later when a refusal to spend the extra money for an electric guitar, combined with Syd Barrett's arrival, forced him to take a more lowly position. As he later remarked, 'Thank God I wasn't pushed down to the drum kit.' I have to agree with that sentiment. If Roger was drumming, I suppose I'd have ended up as the roadie…

Like most start-up bands far more time was spent talking, planning and coming up with names than rehearsing. Gigs were very few and far between. Until 1965 none of the gigs we did was strictly commercial in the sense that they were organised by us or fellow students for private rather than public functions. Birthday parties, end of terms and student hops were the norm. We rehearsed in a tearoom in the basement of the Poly, and along with songs suitable for student parties such as 'I'm A Crawling King Snake' and numbers by the Searchers we also worked on songs written by one of Clive Metcalfe's friends, a fellow student called Ken Chapman. Ken became our manager/songwriter. He had cards printed up offering our services for parties, and a major publicity drive for our – thankfully brief – manifestation as the Architectural Abdabs was mounted around a rather coy photograph of us, and an article in the student paper in which we expressed our allegiance to R&B over rock. Unfortunately, Ken's lyrics tended to be a little too far on the ballad-cum-novelty side for us with lyrics such as 'Have you seen a morning rose?' (set to the tune of 'Für Elise') and 'Mind the gap'. But he did eventually get an opportunity to demo them to a well-known publisher, Gerry Bron, who came along to audition the band and the songs. We rehearsed manfully for this opportunity but it was not a great success. Gerry liked the songs better than the band (well, that's what Ken told us anyway), but not even the songs made it.

By the start of our second year as students in September 1963, Clive and Keith had decided to strike out on their own as a duo, and so the next version of the band began to coalesce around a house owned by Mike Leonard. Mike, then in his mid-thirties, was a part-time tutor at the Poly, who, in addition to his love of architecture, was fascinated by ethnic percussion and the interplay between rhythm, movement and light, which he enthused about during his lectures. In September 1963, by now also teaching at the Hornsey College of Art, Mike acquired a house in North London and wanted some tenants to provide him with rent income.

39 Stanhope Gardens in Highgate is one of those comfortable Edwardian houses with spacious rooms and high ceilings. Mike was in the process of converting it into a flat on the ground floor with his own rather more exotic accommodation and drawing office above. He had opened up the substantial roof area and created a large space ideally suited as a rehearsal facility, but luckily for him the stairs were just too steep and we rarely had the energy to lug all the equipment to the top.

Mike also needed some part-time help in his office, where his work adding toilet accommodation to schools for the London County Council enabled him to finance the design and building of the light machines he was constructing at home; these used perforated metal or glass discs with perspex elements rotated by electric motors to throw out patterns of light onto a wall. Mike's suggestion that we become his tenants seemed an ideal arrangement, so Roger and I moved in. Over the next three years Rick, Syd and various other acquaintances all lived there at different periods; the mood of the place was captured by an early *Tomorrow's World* documentary on BBC TV, which showed one of Mike's light machines in action while we rehearsed downstairs (the programme bravely predicted that by the 1970s every living room in the land would have its own light machine).

Mike owned two cats called Tunji and McGhee – one a Burmese, the other a Siamese – that both he and Roger were particularly fond of. As a result Roger continued a cat relationship for years. I think he found their arrogant aggression comforting. The walls in the house were covered in hessian and after trailing a kipper across the fabric Mike would signal mealtimes to the cats by the use of an old motor horn. The cats would sprint back from terrorising the neighbourhood, leap through the letter box and then start a crazed trip up the walls and along the window ledges until they found the kipper, occasionally nailed to the drawing office ceiling.

Stanhope Gardens made a real difference to our musical activities. We had our own permanent rehearsal facility, thanks to an indulgent landlord: indeed, we used the name Leonard's Lodgers for a while. Rehearsals took place in the front room of the flat where all the equipment was permanently set up. Unfortunately, this made any study very difficult and sleep almost out of the question since it was also Roger's and my bedroom. The neighbours naturally complained, though the threatened noise injunction never materialised, but, just in case, we occasionally eased their pain by renting a rehearsal hall in the nearby Railway Tavern on the Archway Road.

There were never any complaints from Mike. In fact, he became an active participant. He was a capable piano player, and we persuaded him to purchase a Farfisa Duo electric organ and become our keyboard player for a while. Mike still has the Farfisa. The other great bonus was that Mike gave us access to the experiments in light and sound going on at the Hornsey College. Roger, in particular, spent many hours down there working with the light machines, and became a kind of de facto assistant to Mike.

So, throughout our second year at college, we lived at Stanhope Gardens, rehearsed, played the occasional gig, while we continued our studies in a fitful fashion. The next really significant change in our fortunes was the arrival of Bob Klose in September 1964. Bob, another product of Cambridgeshire High School for Boys, came to London with Syd Barrett, and enrolled in the architectural school two years below us. Bob was able to move straight into Stanhope Gardens since I'd moved out of the flat during the summer and back home to Hampstead. It had become quite obvious that if I was to stay at the Poly, which seemed to be a good idea at the time, I would have to do some more work, and studying at Stanhope Gardens was impossible.

Bob's reputation as a guitar player was well known and much deserved. Going into a guitar shop with him was a delight as even supercilious salesmen were impressed with his Mickey Baker jazz chords and lightning finger work, although from our point of view he did regrettably favour the more conservative semi-acoustic guitars over the Fender Stratocaster. With Bob we felt musically more confident, but as Keith Noble and Clive Metcalfe had both left the Poly and the band, we were desperate for a vocalist. The Cambridge connection worked again, and Bob supplied us with Chris Dennis. He was a little older than the rest of us, and had been part of some of the better bands on the Cambridge music scene. Chris was an RAF dental assistant stationed at Northolt. He didn't have a car (I was generally the driver – still driving the Austin 'Chummy') but he did own a Vox PA system consisting of two columns and a separate amplifier with individual channels for the microphones. When pressed we could put guitars through the PA as well. With all this equipment Chris was, of course, automatically guaranteed the position of vocalist.

As front man for the band – now called the Tea Set – Chris had an unfortunate tendency for making Hitler moustaches with his harmonica, saying 'Sorry about that, folks' and announcing each number ('with deadly aplomb' as Bob Klose puts it) as 'Looking Through The Knotholes In Granny's Wooden Leg'. Had Chris stayed with the band, I suspect this routine might have proved a liability when the Floyd became, so I am reliably informed, the darlings of London's underground intelligentsia.

We parted company with Chris after a short while, when Syd Barrett started to play with us on a regular basis. Roger knew Syd from Cambridge – Roger's mother had taught Syd at junior school – and we had been planning to add him to the band even before he arrived in London to study at Camberwell College of Art. It was very much a case of Syd joining us, rather than him recruiting a band. Bob Klose recalls the moment well: 'I remember the rehearsal that sealed Chris Dennis's fate. It was the attic at Stanhope Gardens. Chris, Roger, Nick and I were working over a few of the R&B faves then current. Syd, arriving late, watched quietly from the top of the stairs. Afterwards he said, "Yeah, it sounded great, but I don't see what I would do in the band".'

Although Syd was not sure where he might fit in, it felt right that he should join. As a result, the days of Chris Dennis and his PA system were numbered. Since Bob had been responsible for recruiting Chris, Roger decided that he should accordingly be in charge of handling the unrecruiting procedure, which Bob undertook from a payphone in Tottenham Court Road tube station. As it happened, Chris was being posted abroad in any case. And so partially by default Syd became the front man.

Having no childhood reminiscences of Syd I can only say that on first meeting him in 1964 he was delightful. In a period when everyone was being cool in a very adolescent, self-conscious way, Syd was unfashionably outgoing; my enduring memory of our first encounter is the fact that he bothered to come up and introduce himself to me.

Syd's upbringing in Cambridge had been possibly the most bohemian and liberal of us all. His father Arthur, a university and hospital pathologist, and his mother Winifred had always encouraged him in his music. They had allowed, even welcomed, rehearsals by Syd's early bands in their front room. This was advanced behaviour for parents in the early 1960s. Alongside music, Syd's interest in and talent for painting was evident during his time at Cambridgeshire High School, which he left to study art at Cambridge Tech, just after the death of his father. An old acquaintance of his, David Gilmour, was also there, studying modern languages. The two got along well – getting together at lunchtimes with guitars and harmonicas for a jam – and later spent a summer down in the south of France, hitch-hiking around and busking.

Syd was not always Syd – he'd been christened Roger Keith, but at the Riverside Jazz Club he went to in a local Cambridge pub, one of the stalwarts was a drummer called Sid Barrett. The club regulars immediately nicknamed this newly arrived Barrett 'Syd', but with a 'y' to avoid total confusion, and that's how we always knew him.

Storm Thorgerson remembers Syd as an interesting, but not necessarily the most interesting, member of a talented set of friends living in Cambridge, all enthused by the elegance and culture of the town and the countryside around. Syd was good-looking, charming, funny, played a bit of guitar and smoked the occasional joint. Certainly when he joined our band in London, there was no sudden transition in our musical tastes. Syd was quite comfortable with the Bo Diddley, Stones and R&B cover versions that formed the bulk of our repertoire. Storm also recalls that Syd adored the Beatles, at a time when most of his friends preferred the Stones.

Just as Stanhope Gardens solved our rehearsal problems, the Poly was a ready-made performance facility. The impression I have is that we actually had to do quite a lot of work at the college. The architectural course required significant amounts of studying outside the class, and evenings at home – and later in the flats we lived in – were spent working, or at least trying to despite any other distractions. There was little, if any, going out to clubs or bars during the week, but come Friday night we could relax in the pub, and at weekends there were regular events within the Poly. These took place in a large hall that had the feel of a gym. There was a stage at one end, where various functions and occasional theatrical productions took place. The hops were straightforward dances, with a record player blasting out the latest hit parade, but once in a while a live band would be booked.

As the only house band we managed on a few occasions to support the main act. This was quite a significant development for us, and we must have hustled hard to get the opportunity. We would probably have got paid, but not much; it was the prospect of playing that was exciting. We were not daunted by the thought of performing – in any case, we were only going to get up and do some cover versions for people to dance to – but we were overwhelmed by the professionalism of the full-timers. The way they did their set underlined what a gulf there was between a band playing regularly for a living and a part-time student group like ours.

I particularly remember supporting the Tridents, who at the time featured Jeff Beck on guitar. The Tridents was Jeff's first band of any commercial note, and they had established a reasonable reputation; more significantly when Jeff left the Tridents, it was to take over Eric Clapton's role in the Yardbirds, and enhance his reputation as one of the great blues rock guitarists, but one who was also able to create that dancing-round-the-handbag party classic 'Hi Ho Silver Lining'.

Around Christmas 1964, we went into a studio for the first time. We wangled this through a friend of Rick's who worked at the studio in West Hampstead, and who let us use some down time for free. The session included one version of an old R&B classic 'I'm A King Bee', and three songs written by Syd: 'Double O Bo' (Bo Diddley meets the 007 theme), 'Butterfly' and 'Lucy Leave'. These became our staple demo songs, on $^{1}/_{4}''$ tape and a limited vinyl pressing, and were invaluable since many venues demanded these prior to live auditions.

Curiously enough, around this time Rick had a song called 'You're The Reason Why' published and released as a B-side on a single called 'Little Baby' by an outfit known as Adam, Mike & Tim, and so he received a publishing advance of £75 years before any of the rest of us knew what 'rip-off' really meant...

We managed to land a residency later in the spring of 1965 at the Countdown Club, a basement at 1A Palace Gate, just off Kensington High Street. The Countdown Club was below a hotel or a block of flats, which of course led to problems about the level of noise emanating from the club. The Countdown had no particular thematic decor or moody ambience. It was a place set up for music, with a relatively young clientele, and the drinks were quite cheap. I think the idea was that, given the lack of advertising, the owners expected groups like ours to bring along a large bunch of friends for support, who would refresh themselves at the club's bar.

We played from about nine at night until two in the morning with a couple of breaks. Three sets of ninety minutes each meant we started repeating songs towards the end of the evening as we ran out of numbers and alcohol affected the audience's short-term memory. It was also the beginning of a realisation that songs could be extended with lengthy solos. We started to assemble a wider variety of songs as well as a small but loyal following. Although initially using amplification, we had only done two or three successful nights when the club was served with a noise injunction. We were so desperate for the work (this was our only paying gig at the time) that we offered to perform acoustically. Roger somehow acquired a double bass, Rick dusted off the upright piano, Bob and Syd played acoustic guitars and I used a pair of wire brushes. I know the repertoire included 'How High The Moon', one of Bob's showcase tunes, and 'Long Tall Texan', but the other numbers have long since been forgotten.

At the same time, we auditioned for two potential career openings. One was as a support act at a club called Beat City. They had advertised for bands in the *Melody Maker*, the weekly paper that – until it closed in 2000 – carried information on 'Musicians Available and Wanted' ('A Able Accordionist…' was the opener for years). We saw the ad for Beat City and along we went, performing a selection of our own songs. They turned us down.

Another audition was for *Ready Steady Go!*, which was the definitive music show of the day, where groovy young people could be seen dancing to groovy young bands. Broadcast on ITV, the still comparatively new commercial channel, it could be a little more radical than the BBC would have dared. Regrettably even the *Ready Steady Go!* producers found us rather *too* radical for the general viewer, and suggested they would like to hear us again, this time playing songs they were more familiar with. But at least they had shown some interest, and had the decency to invite us all back to be in the studio audience the next week. This gave me a good reason to head off to Carnaby Street and buy a pair of hound's-tooth black and white check, flared hipster trousers, as the audience were to be seen flouncing about in front of the cameras. It was also an opportunity to see bands like the Rolling Stones and the Lovin' Spoonful live.

Another cracking idea to launch our career was going in for rock contests. We entered two. One was a local event at the Country Club in North London. We had played here a couple of times, and had a small knot of fans, so we got through to the finals without too much difficulty. At this point however we hit a snag. We had also entered a grander event, the *Melody Maker* Beat Contest (Beat was a heavily over-used word that decade). Anxiously we had sent off our demo tape along with band photos taken in the back garden of Mike's house, and notable for our band uniform of tab-collar shirts and blue Italian knitted ties, all from Cecil Gee's in the Charing Cross Road.

The demo and the knitted ties seemed to do the trick. Having gained our entry to the contest we then found that our heat was to take place on the same night as the final of the Country Club contest. The final couldn't be changed, and nor could our heat, since the *Melody Maker* contest was an elaborate device allowing a promoter to make money by selling quantities of tickets to each band's supporters in an attempt to stuff the ballot box. Eventually we managed to negotiate with another band to let us go on first. This was without doubt the worst possible slot (and although it didn't make any difference, our banner was misspelt Pink Flyod). Our later slot went to the winners, the St Louis Union, who couldn't believe their luck – and who eventually won the national first prize. After playing, we rushed to the Country Club, only to be disqualified from any chance of first place by our late arrival. This left a band called the Saracens to take the honours and grasp the career opportunities.

Bob Klose left the band during the summer of 1965 at the insistence of both his father and his college tutors. He did surreptitiously play a few more times with us, but even though we were losing the person we considered our most proficient musician, it didn't seem like a major setback. This remarkable prescience – or sheer lack of imagination – was to become something of a habit.

I was about to start a year of work experience working for Lindy's father, Frank Rutter, at his architectural office near Guildford. I have Roger to thank for getting me this far through the course, since he coached me through the mysteries of structural maths when I was in danger of failing the exam re-take. Roger on the other hand was held back a year, and told to get some practical experience, in spite of receiving a commendation from an outside examiner. I think the staff were finally responding to long-term exposure to

Roger's disdain, coupled with his increasing lack of interest in attending lectures. Their decision was either pure revenge, or it could be that they simply needed a break from Roger.

Frank was a good, practical architect, but was also an admirer of the new movement, and had a strong sense of the culture and history of architecture. In a way, he represented something of a role model for what I might have aspired to had I stuck with architecture as a career. He had recently finished the university in Sierra Leone and was just starting work on a university in British Guiana, which was the project I worked on when I arrived as the most junior of juniors. Although my involvement was pretty low-grade, it brought home to me that I had completed three years of architectural training but had no idea about how to transform the plans on the drawing board into reality. It was something of a confidence blow.

I stayed at the Rutters' house in Thursley, south of Guildford, which was big enough to house the drawing offices for Frank's large practice, as well as extended family and guests. The substantial grounds allowed us the rather civilised option of playing croquet on the lawn during the lunch-break. By coincidence, Frank later sold the house to Roger Taylor, the drummer with Queen.

Throughout the autumn we played on, usually under the name the Tea Set, but we now had an alternative name, created by Syd. The name had come about under duress. We were playing, as the Tea Set, out at an RAF base, probably Northolt just outside London, when, lo and behold, we found that, extraordinarily, there was another band called the Tea Set booked to appear. I'm not sure if the other Tea Set had precedence because they were on first or later, but we rapidly had to come up with an alternative. Syd produced, with little further ado, the name the Pink Floyd Sound, using the first names of two venerable blues musicians Pink Anderson and Floyd Council. Although we might have been aware of them on some blues imports, the names were not ones we were particularly familiar with; it was very much Syd's idea. And it stuck.

It is extraordinary how a spur-of-the-moment decision can become a permanent, comfortable fixture, with long-lasting and far-reaching implications. The Rolling Stones came up with their name in a pretty similar situation, when Brian Jones had to give *Jazz News* the name of his band, and he looked down and saw the track 'Rollin' Stone Blues' on a Muddy Waters album. Out of that emerges decades of merchandising, puns and associations. In our case, when we became one of the underground's house bands, we were fortunate that the very abstraction of the combination Pink and Floyd had a suitable and vaguely psychedelic suggestiveness that a name along the lines of the Howlin' Crawlin' King Snakes might not have offered.

We would very occasionally head out of London for gigs that actually paid for us to perform. We played at one event in a large country house called High Pines at Esher in Surrey, and in October 1965 at a big party in Cambridge for the 21st birthday of Storm Thorgerson's girlfriend, Libby January and her twin sister Rosie. Among our co-performers that night were the Jokers Wild (featuring one David Gilmour) and a young folk-singer called Paul Simon. Storm remembers that this party represented the polarised split between the generations at the time. Libby's parents had organised the party and invited lots of their friends, who were there in lounge suits and cocktail dresses. Libby and her sister's friends, mainly students, were in loose, proto-hippy gear, and preferred their music loud. Some time shortly afterwards, Libby's father, disapproving of the young Thorgerson, in fact offered Storm a blank cheque to absent himself – permanently.

Although it wasn't obvious at the time, our next important break was landing a gig at the Marquee in March 1966. Prior to this our reputation had been based on the combination of Syd as our front man and our connection with the intriguing goings-on at the light and sound workshop at Hornsey College. We can't have had more than four or five original songs, most of which had been recorded when we'd made the demo at Broadhurst Gardens.

The only gig that might have brought us to wider attention had been at Essex University. At their rag ball, we shared the bill with the Swinging Blue Jeans, who did appear, and Marianne Faithfull who was billed as appearing – if she managed to return from Holland in time. It didn't sound hopeful. We were still called Tea Set at the time although we must have given the impression of being in transition to psychedelia, since in spite of having 'Long Tall Texan' in our repertoire, where we all sang to the accompaniment of acoustic guitars, somebody had arranged oil slides and a film projection. I imagine that someone who was there or subsequent word of mouth was responsible for leading us on to the Marquee…

We saw this booking at the Marquee as a great opportunity to break into the club circuit, although it transpired that the gig was a function called the Trip, a totally separate event for which the club had been booked privately. It took place on a Sunday afternoon and certainly no regular Marquee punter would have dreamt of attending.

I found the whole event pretty strange. We were used to playing R&B parties where the entry fee was a keg of bitter. Suddenly we were performing for a 'happening', and being encouraged to develop the extended solos that we'd only really put into the songs to pad them out during our Countdown Club residency. The organisers asked us to come back to the Marquee for some similar Sunday afternoon events, which subsequently became known as the Spontaneous Underground. This was fortuitous, since otherwise we would never have met Peter Jenner.

Peter had recently graduated from Cambridge, although he did not encounter any member of the Pink Floyd crowd during his time at the university (there was still a significant divide between town and gown). He was working at the Department of Social Administration at the London School of Economics, teaching social workers sociology and economics, and also involved in a record label called DNA. He was, in his own words, 'a music nut', into jazz and blues in particular and had set up DNA with John Hopkins, Felix Mendelssohn and Ron Atkins, to reflect their broad range of musical interest: 'We wanted DNA to be an avant-garde thing, avant-garde anything: jazz, folk, classical, pop.'

At the end of the academic year Peter was marking a pile of papers one Sunday, and had reached the point where he needed to get out for a breath of fresh air. He decided to head out from the LSE in Holborn across to the Marquee Club in Wardour Street, where he knew there was a private gig happening. He knew this through an acquaintance called Bernard Stollman, whose brother Stephen ran ESP, an arty American label, which included acts like the Fugs, and which had been an inspiration for the setting up of DNA.

Peter recalls, 'DNA had done some work with the free improvisation group AMM, recording an album in one day in Denmark Street. The deal was rotten: 2 per cent out of which the studio time, and probably the artists, had to be paid, and as an economist I came to the conclusion that 2 per cent of a £30 album was only 7d, and that it would take an awful lot of 7ds to earn £1,000, which was my idea of a fortune. I decided that if DNA was going to work we had to have a pop band. That's when I saw the Pink Floyd Sound at the Marquee Club that Sunday. I did think the "Sound" part of their name was pretty lame.

'I remember very clearly seeing the show. The band were basically playing R&B, things like "Louie Louie" and "Dust My Broom", things everybody played at the time. I couldn't make out the lyrics, but nobody could hear the lyrics in those days. But what intrigued me was that instead of wailing guitar solos in the middle, they made this weird noise. For a while I couldn't work out what it was. And it turned out to be Syd and Rick. Syd had his Binson Echorec and was doing weird things with feedback. Rick was also producing some strange, long, shifting chords. Nick was using mallets. That was the thing that got me. This was avant-garde! Sold!'

Peter wanted to get in touch with us, and was given a contact by Bernard Stollman. He came round to Stanhope Gardens to see us: 'Roger answered the door. Everybody else had gone off on holiday, as it was the end of the academic year. So we agreed, "See you in September!" The record label was a whim of mine, a hobby, so I had no problem waiting. Roger hadn't told me to fuck off. It was just "See you in September"…'

When Peter came round to Stanhope Gardens, I was away on a low-budget first trip to the States. My trip to America was seen as part of my continuing architectural education, a chance to go and see some of the great buildings in the USA, rather than a rootsy musical pilgrimage. Lindy was out in New York – training as a dancer with the Martha Graham Dance Company – which was another good reason to go, as she would have some time off in the summer recess (Juliette, Rick's girlfriend, was also out there at the same time, by chance).

I flew out on a PanAm 707 and spent a couple of weeks in New York. There was some cultural and architectural sightseeing – the Guggenheim, MOMA, the Lever Building – but I did also get to see some live music. I saw the Fugs, and went to see some jazz acts like Mose Allison and Thelonious Monk live at the Village Vanguard and the other Greenwich Village jazz clubs. I spent a certain amount of time going to record shops. A lot of music was unavailable on import, and the stiff American album sleeves, which looked very fancy in comparison to their rather flimsy British equivalents, were prized trophies.

For $99 Lindy and I then acquired a Greyhound bus ticket giving us unlimited travel for three months, and headed west on – for us – a gigantic journey of 3,000 miles coast to coast, non-stop apart from the occasional refuel and refreshment break. On the bus we got to know a newly married American couple – the groom was about to head off to Vietnam, which meant little to us in 1966; the full significance only hit me later on, and I still occasionally wonder if he survived.

San Francisco was not yet the 'Summer of Love' capital of the world. Haight-Ashbury was still simply a crossroads. The city was much more geared to sightseeing (trips to Alcatraz) and seafood. From there we took the Greyhound east to Lexington, Kentucky and met up with a Poly friend Don McGarry and his girlfriend Deirdre. Don had bought a late Fifties Cadillac, with unreliable brakes, which made the mountain passes rather exciting. We drove almost immediately – with the occasional architectural detour – to Mexico City, where we managed to muddle our way around, before spending some time in Acapulco, amazed at how cheap everything was out of season: rooms were a dollar a night. A further epic journey back to Lexington ensued, before I returned to New York and back across the Atlantic.

The Pink Floyd Sound had not penetrated my consciousness very much during this trip. I simply thought that, come September, I'd be back on the academic treadmill. However, in New York, I came across a copy of the *East Village Other* newspaper, with a report from London on up and coming bands, which mentioned the Pink Floyd Sound.

Finding this name check so far from home really gave me a new perception of the band. Displaying a touchingly naive trust in the fact that you can believe everything you read in the papers, it made me realise that the band had the potential to be more than simply a vehicle for our own amusement.

GOING UNDERGROUND 2

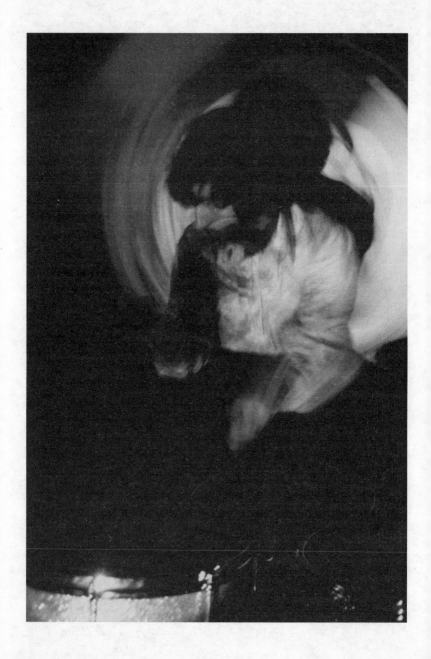

WHEN THE members of the Pink Floyd Sound reconvened in London after the summer break of 1966, Peter Jenner was still waiting. He came back to Stanhope Gardens and said, 'We'd love to have you on the label.' Roger told him that we didn't need a label, but we did need a manager.

This instantly rekindled our vague fantasies of success, daydreams that might have otherwise disappeared with the end of the summer. Slightly surprised by his persistence, but eager to seize any opportunity, we eventually agreed that Peter, and his partner Andrew King, should manage the band. On one occasion, when we had a discussion about management, Andrew remembers me saying, 'No one else wants to manage us, so you might as well…' We saw their involvement as a significant step for us, giving us the chance to acquire a number of items, all essential if we were ever going to make the transition from amateur to professional: regular, paid work, a level of credibility and some decent equipment.

Peter and Andrew had known each other since their schooldays at Westminster. Their fathers were both vicars: when Andrew was about to go into his final year, his parents had to move away from London and decided to find a good Christian home where their son could stay during term time. Consequently Andrew had lived with the Jenners in Southall, at the St George's vicarage. Peter was a year younger than Andrew, so they hadn't really known each other at school, but living in the same house led to shared interests. Sadly, I have no memory of the band receiving any spiritual guidance from the unholy alliance that resulted from their friendship. However, Andrew observes that pastoral care is a useful management tool in the music industry: 'In a vicarage you have to be ready to deal with anything and anybody coming through the door.'

In their year between the Oxbridge exams and going up in the autumn, Andrew and Peter went to the States, through another clerical connection (this time Episcopalian) and worked in a whiskey distillery in Peking, Illinois, for six months, a location that gave them easy access to Chicago at the weekends and a chance to absorb a rich mix of electric blues, jazz and gospel music.

The two had kept in touch during their time at university – Peter at Cambridge, Andrew at Oxford. When Peter decided to start managing us, he called his old friend Andrew for help, and more importantly, for cash. Andrew had a job with a company applying scientific principles to educational training via a machine that asked trainees to select answers to multiple-choice questions by pressing levers. After writing a program for the machine on thermodynamics (of which he only had the sketchiest knowledge), Andrew was loaned out to the BEA airline to help motivate their staff. Each company thought he was in the other's office, whereas Andrew was more likely in bed, or practising origami with some Rizla papers… Neither the airline staff nor Andrew himself seem to have been able to muster much motivation at all, and Peter's call seemed a much more attractive proposition.

Peter remembers, 'We were good mates and had been to see a lot of music together. We felt, "Why don't we manage this band. It could be interesting." Andrew had left his job and was not working, I thought it would continue to be a good hobby.' Together they set up Blackhill Enterprises, named after Blackhill Farm, a property in the Brecon Beacons that Andrew had bought with some inherited money. The rest of the legacy went on a straight split between wild living and some much needed equipment for the Pink Floyd Sound.

Previously, on the few occasions we had actually been paid for gigs, any cash had been spent on upgrading our own individual gear: Roger had picked up a Rickenbacker bass, and I'd moved on from my original makeshift kit to a Premier kit. After parting company with Chris Dennis and his PA, we'd either borrowed one or made do with whatever system a venue possessed, usually offering the kind of sound quality even a railway station announcer would have found unclear. Blackhill rectified the situation immediately, taking us on a trip to the Charing Cross Road and buying us a Selmer PA system, as well as new bass and guitar amps.

Initially, Peter had intended to continue running DNA as well as lecturing and managing us, while Andrew concentrated on Pink Floyd, but when it became clear that DNA was not a going concern, Peter focused on us. Of the two, Peter was the hustler – and the diplomat – who could talk his way into a deal. Peter describes himself as 'an A1 bullshitter – still am!' and had the added bonus of a link into the underground scene. Andrew was more relaxed, and a lot of fun to be around, but his taste for a good time sometimes led to moments of unreliability. However, he refutes the myth that our entire cash float for one Scandinavian tour disappeared after a particularly good night out. In fact, he says, he just pulled out some loose change from his pocket and a few krone rolled down a drain. It was unfortunate that Roger's eagle eye registered this moment.

Apart from the time they had spent in Illinois, which had allowed them to observe the Chicago music scene in action, the two really had virtually no experience of the music business. However, to our even less experienced eyes, they seemed to have sufficient connections to find more, and better, work and to open negotiations with record companies. It would have been lunacy for us to try and negotiate a record deal for ourselves as, dazzled by visions of Number One singles, we'd have signed for a pittance with the first company that made an offer. Peter and Andrew would at least have hesitated for a polite moment or so.

As well as the promise of more work, and the reality of new equipment, the Jenner–King team supplied us with a link into London's incipient underground movement through Peter's involvement with the London Free School, an alternative educational establishment. England in 1966 was going through some remarkable changes. The Labour government of Harold Wilson was in the middle of bringing in a raft of changes in the laws concerning obscenity, divorce, abortion and homosexuality. The Pill had become available. Female emancipation was developing into more than just a theory, allowing women like Germaine Greer and Caroline Coon (the founder of Release, the world's first phoneline for drugs and legal advice) to participate on equal terms.

It was also a period of cultural change. The Beatles had kicked off a phenomenon where suddenly English bands dominated the international music scene. In the wake of the Beatles, English bands had been adopted by the American music market. It was the original version of Tony Blair's 'Cool Britannia'. This was accompanied by a flourishing of English fashion, retail innovation, models, and photographers, bringing to prominence names like Mary Quant and Ozzie Clark, Carnaby Street and Biba, Twiggy, Jean Shrimpton, Bailey and Donovan. Even English football was in the ascendant after the World Cup victory of 1966.

This commercial explosion was paralleled by a similar burst of activity in the educational area. Much of this was down to the art schools, which were not only producing great designers and photographers but also a generation of talented rock musicians including Ray Davies, Keith Richards, John Lennon and Pete Townshend. An increase in the number of grants available had made further education not only a good career move, but also an excellent way of putting off the evil day of having to go out and earn a real living. Jobs were relatively plentiful and long-term careers easily available, which gave students a lot of choices, including simply opting to drop out (and back in) on an occasional basis. In fact, it's amazing to think we were actually worried about what we were going to do with all our leisure time once all the robots on *Tomorrow's World* did everything for us.

The only real downside to all of this was not to appear for another thirteen years. In the brave new, and very middle-class, alternative world, mainstream politics were rather neglected. By the time anyone realised, it was too late. The wallflowers, who had been left out of all the fun in the Sixties, got their own back during the 1980s by gaining control of the country and vandalising the health service, education, libraries and any other cultural institutions they could get their hands on.

In 1965, one of the significant moments marking the stirring of some kind of intellectual underground movement was a poetry reading organised at the Albert Hall in June – with a bill featuring Allen Ginsberg, Lawrence Ferlinghetti and Gregory Corso. The organisers expected a few hundred at most; 7,500 people turned up. This burgeoning intellectual underground began to coalesce around the Indica Bookshop. The money for Indica had been stumped up by Jane Asher's brother Peter, who was also an old school friend of Peter Jenner and Andrew King. Indica's other founders were Miles, the writer and journalist, and John Dunbar, a friend of Rick's who later married Marianne Faithfull. The bookshop originally incorporated an art gallery in Mason's Yard off St James's before moving to Southampton Row. It was a place where ideas and experimental literature could be promoted by importing the work of American poets, an area where the crossover with the States was well established. The name Indica was derived from the botanical name 'cannabis indica', although the coy version was that it was short for 'indications'. At another bookshop, Better Books, Andy Warhol came over from the States for one poetry reading, accompanied by an entourage including Kate Heliczer, the star of Warhol's film *Couch*, who had brought over the first Velvet Underground tapes heard in the UK.

Both of these shops opened up a route for the kind of avant-garde American rock music that otherwise most of us would never have heard, like the Fugs and the Mothers of Invention. Sometimes the names of these US bands, which sounded weird to us, suggested an alternative group, but their music would turn out to be quite conventional. When we did get to hear many of the Americans like Country Joe & The Fish or Big Brother & The Holding Company we were often surprised to find that their music was in fact inspired by American country or blues music, although the content of their lyrics was radical enough for them to be thought of as underground bands.

Some of the people involved in the Indica Bookshop also contributed to the London Free School. This had been set up by a group that included Peter Jenner as a way of bringing further education to Notting Hill. One of the prime movers in the underground, John Hopkins – known to everyone as Hoppy – had picked up the idea from New York's Free University, and this had in part sparked the whole venture. (Hoppy had been one of the first to deliberately 'drop out' of a set career path, leaving his job at the Harwell Atomic Research Establishment in the early 1960s to become a freelance photojournalist.)

Peter says, 'The London Free School was an idea for the alternative education of the masses. In hindsight it was an incredibly pretentious middle-class operation. We'd all come from privileged backgrounds and had all been well educated, but we were not happy with what we had learnt. We'd been educated in very blinkered ways.' The Free School was a response to the fact that people had become alienated from education, and that by teaching other people, the teacher could also learn from the pupils. It flared briefly for a year or so, and then disintegrated – all the principals were too busy with fingers in other pies from journalism to events management. The LFS, and the psychedelic movement, was in part inspired by the multiculturalism of Notting Hill. Peter makes the point that people do not remember the drabness of England post-war: 'It was grim to behold. Psychedelia was anti-drab.'

The London Free School would gather in an old house in Tavistock Crescent in Notting Hill (now torn down) which belonged to Rhaunnie Laslett, founder of the Notting Hill Carnival. The Free School needed money to survive, and the organisers also wanted to set up a news and information sheet to let everyone know about the new underground. Peter Jenner and Andrew King came up with the solution: like all good vicars' sons, they knew that if you wanted to raise money, you either held a whist drive or a dance. Whist seemed inappropriate, so the LFS hired the local church hall (also now torn down) at All Saints in Powis Gardens, Notting Hill, and put on the Pink Floyd Sound – we had decided to stick with Syd's name for the band during our stint at the Marquee Club – as part of a 'pop dance'.

We were probably not that overjoyed by the prospect: playing church halls wasn't what we had expected our new managers to be aiming for. But in fact it turned out to be one of the best venues we could have found, since London W11 rapidly established itself as the hub of the alternative movement. The whole district of Notting Hill was becoming the most interesting area in London, mixing cheap rents, multicultural residents, activities like the London Free School and a thriving trade in illegal drugs. To combat the latter, the local police had also developed creative skills, mainly to do with fabricating evidence. This was something new for the intellectual radicals: apart from the CND marches, the middle classes had rarely had to confront the darker side of the law.

The All Saints hall itself was unremarkable. With a high ceiling, wooden floorboards and a raised dais at one end, it was like countless similar church buildings throughout the land. But the event quickly took on a personality of its own. The audience was different from the R&B fanatics and *Top Of The Pops* viewers. As well as the local hip fraternity, there were students or college drop-outs, proud of being 'freaks', who would sit on the floor or just waft around waving their arms, a physical definition of what became known as 'looning about'. They arrived with few of the preconceptions or expectations of a normal audience, and were often in a chemically altered state sufficient to find drying paint not only interesting but deeply significant. The effect on us was terrific. They responded so well and so uncritically to the improvised sections in our set that we began to concentrate on extending those rather than simply running through a sequence of cover versions.

Light shows played an important role at the All Saints shows: the events were conceived as 'happenings' and people were encouraged to participate however they wanted. An American couple, Joel and Toni Brown, initially projected some slides when they were over on a visit. When they had to return to the States, the contribution of the light show had become important enough for Peter, his wife Sumi and Andrew to construct some replacements. With budget a priority and in the absence of any friends in theatre lighting, Andrew and Peter decided not to approach the professional lighting companies, but instead headed down to their local electrical store, and loaded up with domestic spotlights, ordinary switches, gels and drawing pins, probably getting a trade discount as jobbing builders. All this standard lighting equipment was mounted onto battens nailed on a few planks, the contraption was plugged into the mains, and the lights simply switched on and off by hand. This was makeshift equipment, but for the time it was revolutionary – no other band had this kind of stage illumination.

A *Melody Maker* report of 22nd October 1966 gives a flavour of a typical performance by us: 'The slides were excellent – colourful, frightening, grotesque, beautiful, but all fall a bit flat in the cold reality of All Saints Hall. Psychedelic versions of "Louie Louie" won't come off but if they can incorporate their electronic prowess with some melodic and lyrical songs – getting away from dated R&B things – they could well score in the near future.'

Our set was including fewer R&B standards and more of Syd's songs – many of which would form the basis of our first album. The R&B classics were mixed up with our longer workouts, so that 'Interstellar Overdrive', which we often used as an opener, might be followed immediately by a very straight cover of Bo Diddley's 'Can't Judge A Book' or Chuck Berry's 'Motivating', one of Syd's favourites.

Although this series of gigs was bringing us a regular audience, and we were becoming identified with what could already be defined as an 'underground', my impression is that none of the band members was particularly aware of the significance of the movement itself. We were sympathetic to its aims, but certainly not active participants. We enjoyed the mix of people involved, like Hoppy, Rhaunnie Laslett and the black activist Michael X, but our real interest lay in making it in the music business and buying our new PA system, not the ideals of a free newspaper.

The money from All Saints hall helped the Free School start their newspaper. *IT* (*International Times*) was created as a regular institution to give some cohesion to all the happenings and events going on in London. The model was New York's *Village Voice*, with its distinctive mixture of arts reviews, investigative journalism and a mouthpiece for liberal and radical views. To launch the first issue

– on sale, at all good alternative outlets, for one shilling, published by Lovebooks Ltd, and with a print run of 15,000 copies – *IT* organised a launch party at the Roundhouse in Chalk Farm, Camden on a cold October night.

The Roundhouse had been built in the 1840s as an inspection yard for steam engines, but the yard and its turntable became obsolete within fifteen years, as the size of the engines simply grew too large. Gilbeys, the distillers, had used it as a warehouse, but by the early 1960s the place was extremely run-down. It has been well documented that our road crew, who were in fact the management since we didn't have a road crew as such, backed the transit van into the giant jelly moulded by an artist for the launch party. This cataclysmic culinary disaster obviously didn't help reinforce any sense of order.

There was no stage, but there was an old cart that was used as a platform. Our entire combination of instruments, amps and light show was being run off one single 13-amp lead, which would barely have supported the power supply for the average kitchen. Consequently the illumination levels were extremely low, and torches and candles supplied most of the light. The power expired on an irregular basis signalling the end of – or breaks in – the sets.

Lighting effects at the Roundhouse were also minimal. They consisted of Andrew and Peter's hand-built rig and some underpowered Aldis 35mm projectors – the kind of machines families used to display their summer holiday snaps – containing slides filled with mixes of oil, water, inks and chemicals that were then heated with small butane blow lamps. Great skill was required not to overheat the contraption; otherwise the glass cracked, spilling the ink, creating the possibility of a small fire, and the certainty of an atrocious mess. Our lighting technicians could be instantly identified by the lurid stains on their fingers and the blisters on their hands.

The *IT* launch was a success. The Floyd's performance was described by *Town* magazine as 'shattering ear-drum and eye-ball', and by *IT* itself as doing 'weird things to the feel of the event with their scary feedback sounds'. This was like Powis Gardens with added glamour. The word was out, and the faces and the celebrities were starting to turn up. A couple of thousand people attended. The event brought together the beautiful people and the celebs, including Paul McCartney, Peter Brook, Michelangelo Antonioni and Monica Vitti, and awarded a politically incorrect prize for the 'shortest-barest', allegedly won by Marianne Faithfull. Soft Machine also performed, with the startling addition of a revved-up motorbike making a guest appearance at some point in their set. There were pop-art-painted American cars, a fortune-telling cubicle, an all-night alternative film show. And there was the largest audience we had ever faced.

We did spend quite a lot of time out in the audience sharing the experience, but this was one of the last times we did so; the time would come shortly when we began to retreat to the self-contained culture of the band dressing room. I do remember that most of us were wearing heavy make-up, and spent an inordinate amount of time curling or backcombing our hair into what we thought pop stars should look like. Our wardrobe was another drain on our budget. It was not until a few years later that a casual T-shirt approach became the norm, along with the attendant cash savings. For now we felt that satin shirts, velvet loon pants, scarves and high-heeled Gohill boots were mandatory.

At the end of October, we formalised our arrangement with Peter and Andrew by becoming partners in Blackhill Enterprises. The four of us with Peter and Andrew each owned one-sixth of the company, which meant we could all share in the Floyd's success and any other profits from Blackhill's ventures with other bands and the massive entertainment empire that Andrew and

Peter envisaged. The deal was very much of its time, 'organised in the appropriate hippie way' in Peter's phrase, 'a sweet idea', in Andrew's.

Blackhill set up shop, literally – there was a flat above and a shop front downstairs – at 32 Alexander Street in Bayswater, a property leased by Andrew's girlfriend Wendy, which much later became the original headquarters of Stiff Records. Andrew lived in the top flat, and Roger, Rick and Syd all lived there at various times, as did Joe Gannon, who was our original lighting man and who later became a successful US-based director, producer and lighting director, notably for Alice Cooper. The place was soon in chaos. Part band sitting room and storage, part office, it was only put in order through the arrival of June Child, our secretary, assistant road manager, chauffeur and personal assistant. She became an invaluable member of the team, providing the missing element of organisation to our working lives – and later married Marc Bolan, another of Blackhill's artists.

Robert Wyatt from Soft Machine remembers Blackhill as 'a lovely bunch of people. They were very nice, an honourable exception to the shady rule about managers, and really cared for the people they worked for. I think that most of us were less lucky than that.' Soft Machine were one of the few bands we got to know, as we frequently found ourselves working beyond the fringes of mainstream pop music. The happenings at Powis Gardens and the Roundhouse were not the traditional way of 'paying your dues'.

Considering their rather haphazard approach to management, Peter and Andrew proved to have terrific intuition when it came to discovering bands. Pink Floyd were not the only band they nurtured. Although they initially had to concentrate on our needs, they would in due course launch the careers of Edgar Broughton, Roy Harper, as well as Marc Bolan and Tyrannosaurus Rex, and work with bands like Slapp Happy and the Third Ear Band.

Their connection with the classical music promoter Christopher Hunt was an example of what made Blackhill such good news for us at this time. Instead of relying on the tried and tested circuit of existing clubs and venues, Peter and Andrew were constantly looking for alternative ways to promote their alternative band. Peter's wife Sumi was Christopher's secretary. He was able to organise a show for us in January 1967 at the Commonwealth Institute, a beautiful purpose-built auditorium in Kensington that was mainly used for the type of ethnic music recital by artists like Ravi Shankar that had recently come into vogue. We needed the clout of a classical promoter to open the door for us, since I am sure the authorities would otherwise have assumed that a riot was bound to take place; I imagine they still thought 'rock' was something to do with drainpipe trousers, Teddy boys and Bill Haley.

The Westminster connection also came in handy by supplying Jonathan Fenby, who wrote the first Pink Floyd press releases, and they were good, because he knew what the press would consider a good story – at the time he was a Reuters journalist, who later became editor of the *Observer* and the *South China Morning Post*, as well as a distinguished author. We gained some editorial coverage in the quality press through Jonathan – the first piece appeared in the *Financial Times*. Then Hunter Davies' column in the *Sunday Times* of 30th October 1966 ran a short piece on psychedelia with quotes from Andrew and Roger, who stated 'If you take LSD what you experience depends entirely on who you are. Our music may give you the screaming horrors or throw you into screaming ecstasy. Mostly it's the latter. We find our audiences stop dancing now. We tend to get them standing there totally grooved with their mouths open.' Hunter Davies made a one-word comment on all this: 'Hmm'. Hunter was the journalist who shortly afterwards made his name as an observer of the pop world with his biography *The Beatles* in 1968.

We continued with more one-off appearances. These were generally not so much actual gigs as private events announced by word of mouth, a few out of town in places like Bletchley and Canterbury, most in London, back at Hornsey College of Art, as well as more All Saints events – the last one there was on 29th November. There were also a couple of follow-ups at the Roundhouse including 'Psychodelphia vs Ian Smith', which announced 'All madness welcome! Bring your own happenings and ecstatogenic substances. Drag optional', but none of them quite captured the mood of the original *IT* launch.

Playing other venues was a steep management learning curve. When we played one gig at a Catholic youth club, the bloke in charge refused to pay up, claiming that what we were playing 'wasn't music'. Andrew and Peter went to the small claims court – and to their, and our, total disbelief, we lost, as disappointingly the magistrate completely agreed with the youth club manager's opinion…

An Oxfam benefit called 'You Must Be Joking?', held at the Albert Hall in December, was another useful showcase, although we were bottom of the bill. There were enough big names above us, including Peter Cook and Dudley Moore, Chris Farlowe, and the Alan Price Set, to guarantee an audience of five thousand. We also gained an insight into how the rest of the music business viewed us when Alan Price raised a laugh at our expense by banging the reverb on his Hammond organ and announcing that this was psychedelic music. At the time we were mortified, probably because all our mums were in the audience; any sense of resentment has nearly worn off.

We also returned to the Marquee Club in December, but had a fairly uncomfortable relationship with the club and its audiences. The manager, John Gee, came from a jazz background, and seemed unhappy with the music the club was now hosting. Irascible and understandably disapproving after exposure to an endless stream of noisy bands, he seemed to dislike both punters and bands with equal venom. With our weird music and funny lights as well as our particularly amateur brand of musicianship we must have been a total anathema to him.

Sadly the Marquee audience and our support groups had a rather similar view. The Marquee had opened in 1958 first as a jazz club, but with the times had emerged as the fulcrum of the British R&B movement. Even though initially the jazzers had looked down on R&B with disdain, if not outright hatred, particularly as some of the musicians who also made their living as session players could see their regular gigs and hence livelihoods disappearing fast, the club was really the heart of the British R&B movement rather than the underground, and although we did enjoy a short residency it was really much closer to a brief encounter.

The Marquee was an archetypal music club. The dressing room was tiny, scented with sweat and the great smell of cheap men's cologne – always so much simpler than attempting to shower in a sink – and on a successful night had the atmosphere of a student party held in a lift. Otherwise it was better to make for the bar at the back where fine ale was dispensed in plastic beakers just in case the patrons should take exception to the music or each other. You could work in the knowledge that you might get wet but at least you would avoid severe lacerations as long as you didn't leave the stage.

Fortunately, there was one club which could have been purpose-made for us – this was UFO, pronounced 'U-fo' and short for Underground Freak Out. If Indica was the underground's high street shop, the London Free School its education system, and *IT* its Fleet Street, then UFO was its playground, set up by Joe Boyd and John Hopkins (Hoppy). Joe was a Harvard graduate and music freak who had first been over to England in the spring of 1964 as tour manager for the Blues and Gospel Caravan. He met Hoppy when he came down to take photos of the Caravan.

When Joe returned later with a job as A&R man for Elektra Records, he was amazed to find that in his absence the whole underground movement had suddenly blossomed.

Within days of coming back to London in the autumn of 1965 he'd attended the first meeting of the London Free School, and a year later had become involved in the idea of setting up a nightclub. Hoppy and Joe found the venue: the Blarney Club in Tottenham Court Road, which was an Irish dancehall, with a decor featuring shamrocks, leprechauns and all things Hibernian. The club was just down from the police station and underneath two cinemas, which meant the show couldn't start until around 10 p.m. when the cinemas closed, because of the noise problems. The first night of UFO was on 23rd December 1966 – we played at the opening – and thereafter the club ran every Friday night through to eight in the morning.

UFO added another dimension to our career: even if it wasn't an established club, this was London's West End, and the place was crowded with people who wanted to see us and knew what to expect. We were familiar with a large number of the audience, and looked forward to playing there. It made a welcome change to the trepidation we felt whenever we played out of London. Knowing we had a partisan audience and the beginnings of a fan base, we would break away from the band room to wander around and watch the other acts: Soft Machine appeared regularly, and there were theatre groups, poetry readings and performance art events. There were also plaudits on offer, rather than the lack of understanding we tended to find outside the capital. UFO felt like a genuine base camp for those expeditions.

In June Child's words, 'it was the ambience that people went for. It was dark, you went downstairs… basically like an elongated cellar. There was a very limited stage and you had small speakers, probably AC30s, and the lighting rig which was like a little platform'. The lighting rig was set up on something like a painter and decorator's scaffolding tower.

Jenny Fabian, the author of the novel *Groupie* (which had a *succès de scandale* when it came out in 1969; we appeared thinly disguised as Satin Odyssey), remembers a typical night at UFO: 'The best thing was Friday night, when you could dress up like an old film star, drop acid, go down to UFO, see all the likewise people, get a stick of candy floss and float around until the Floyd came on. They were the first authentic sound of acid consciousness. I'd lie down on the floor and they'd be up on stage like supernatural gargoyles playing their spaced-out music, and the same colour that was exploding over them was exploding over us. It was like being taken over, mind, body and soul.'

UFO had various light shows as well as our own (we were still the only band who possessed one). Robert Wyatt recalls UFO's in-house lighting man Mark Boyle 'doing lights and burning himself to pieces to do these experiments with different coloured acids. You just saw him with these goggles, looking all burnt, high up on some rigging.' There was also a fifty-year-old called Jack Bracelin, who ran a nudist colony in Watford, and occasionally used one corner of UFO for a smaller light show, presumably whenever the weather in Hertfordshire turned inclement. While Robert remembers that the light show allowed him a certain amount of anonymity, so that his band could relax into 'the same swirly gloom' as the audience, we were still interested in using the light shows to illuminate rather than obscure us.

Town magazine ran a piece on the underground and captured the mood of UFO in particular: 'The Pink Floyd is the underground's house orchestra. Their music sounds more like Thelonious Monk than the Rolling Stones. Projected slides bathed the musicians and audience in hypnotic and frenzied patterns of liquid-coloured lights. Honeycombs, galaxies and throbbing cells whirl around the group with accelerating abandon as the music develops.'

We may have been adopted as the house orchestra, but we rarely got to share the psychedelic experience. We were out of it, not on acid, but out of the loop, stuck in the dressing room at UFO. We were busy being a band: rehearsing, travelling to gigs, packing up and driving home. Psychedelia was around us, but not within us. We might buy a book at Indica, but we certainly never had time to linger. We'd read *IT* but the primary reason was to check whether we'd had a review or not. Of the band, Syd was perhaps slightly more intrigued by the wider aspects of psychedelia, and drawn to some of the philosophical and mystical aspects that his particular group of friends was exploring. But although he was interested, I don't think – like the rest of us if we had wanted to – he had enough time to become fully immersed in the scene.

The rest of the world got its impression of psychedelia from the sort of ad that was placed in *Melody Maker* for 'Psychedelicamania' at the Roundhouse on New Year's Eve: 'WHAT IS A FREAK OUT? When a large number of individuals gather and express themselves creatively through music, dance, light patterns and electronic sound. The participants, already emancipated from our national slavery, dressed in their most inspired apparel, realise as a group whatever potential they possess for free expression. IT'S ALL HAPPENING MAN!'

Around this time, one turning point in my own personal musical development was the night Cream played at the Poly, where we still performed from time to time, although we were only paying punters for this particular gig. The moment when the curtain went back is crystal clear in my mind. Cream's road manager was on the stage – probably still trying to nail Ginger Baker's double bass drums to the floor. Ginger was famous for insisting on this, and there are ruined marble floors and carpets around the globe to prove it. From this moment on I had to have a double bass drum kit – and went straight out and bought one the next day.

Young Turks of psychedelia we might be, but we were as stunned by the display of hardware as we were by the band itself. I drooled over that champagne-sparkle Ludwig drum kit while the others lusted after the stacks of Marshall amplifiers as Eric Clapton, Jack Bruce and Ginger launched into the opening of 'NSU'. We were even impressed when the curtains closed again almost immediately as they decided to try and fix various technical problems. The fact that Jimi Hendrix later came on to guest on a couple of numbers – his first appearance in England – was the icing on the cake.

For me that night was the moment that I knew I wanted to do this properly. I loved the power of it all. No need to dress in Beatle jackets and tab-collar shirts, and no need to have a good-looking singer out front. No verse-chorus-verse-chorus-solo-chorus-end structure to the songs, and the drummer wasn't at the back on a horrid little platform… he was up at the front.

This simply reinforced what passed for our master plan: a desire to get more work, buy more equipment and land a record deal. At the end of 1966, a combination of timing and luck was starting to work for us, and with Syd's distinctive songwriting and our improvisational style, we did have a rather rough but definitely original musical approach to offer the record companies.

Events moved very quickly in this period. Our desultory contact with Peter Jenner either side of the summer vacation had snowballed through the autumn, and during the winter things, in Peter's phrase, 'took off like a rocket'. There was substantial interest in this new phenomenon from record companies, publishers and agents. *Melody Maker* ran a feature on what was happening, *Harper & Queen*'s antennae twitched. Peter recalls a moment when he realised that there was something afoot. He was on his way to UFO on Tottenham Court Road, and when he came into Oxford Street there were 'all these kids with bells round their necks. I thought, "Fucking hell, this is really starting to happen." Unbelievable.'

Lindy came back to England after finishing her dance training in the States and saw us at an event called 'Freak Out Ethel'. She can still remember her surprise at our swift transformation from student covers band to psychedelic frontiersmen. In Andrew's words, 'We didn't realise it, but the tide was coming up the beach, and the Pink Floyd were right on top of the wave.' In his view, what we actually played, and whether we could play, was much less important than being in the right place at the right time.

As well as running UFO, Joe Boyd was still involved in A&R and production, but his former boss at Elektra, Jac Holzman, only offered us a rather grudging one and seven-eighths percent. We would not go with this because at the time Elektra was known only as a small folk label – though they would go on to sign the Doors. We wanted a proper company. Joe was still desperate, as we were, to see us signed somewhere. Polydor were prepared to offer quite a good deal, which would allow Joe to act as an independent producer. As the deal looked like closing, Joe set up his own company, Witchseason Productions, to make it happen.

A recording session was arranged for us in January 1967 at Sound Techniques in Old Church Street off the Kings Road, with Joe producing and the studio owner John Wood engineering. All the recordings – including 'Arnold Layne', a song we'd been playing live for a while, and a version of 'Interstellar Overdrive' – were made on a four-track tape machine, for mono reproduction. We recorded bass and drums on one track, guitar and the trembly Farfisa Duo keyboard on two other tracks. Any effects such as the drum repeats on 'Arnold Layne' were added as these three tracks were bumped down onto a fourth track, and the vocals and any guitar solos were added as an overdub. A final mix of the song was then mastered onto a mono tape.

A professional recording studio always made you sound great. At the studios in West Hampstead, the first time we heard ourselves in playback, with some echo on the drums and vocals, and a decent mix, had sounded terrific. Sound Techniques was a step up again. The studios boasted the then state-of-the-art Tannoy Red speakers, the definitive speaker of the period. Clad in a veneered walnut finish, they stood about five feet tall, and compared to what we were used to, packed an incredible bass punch.

Listening back to 'Arnold Layne' now, and other songs from the same phase, I notice that I do not find myself cringing. I am definitely not embarrassed by our juvenilia. It all sounds pretty professional, even though it would have been recorded relatively quickly. With a limited number of tracks, you had to make decisions early on about which instrument would go on which track and then you mixed down. But the music genuinely doesn't seem to have suffered.

'Candy And A Currant Bun' was originally called 'Let's Roll Another One', including the lyric 'I'm high, don't try to spoil my fun'. Since this was deemed to be pushing our luck on a tape due to be taken into the still very conservative record industry, a complete alternative set of lyrics had to be cobbled together.

For some reason we were also convinced that we needed a promotional film for 'Arnold Layne'. Although TV programmes like *Top Of The Pops* rarely used film unless it was for some American act that couldn't possibly make it over to England, we already saw ourselves as a multimedia band. Derek Nice – an acquaintance of June Child, and the only film director anyone knew – was commissioned to make the film, and we set off to the Sussex coast to start work.

I think we chose Sussex because my parents lived nearby and

rather conveniently were away. This sorted out the accommodation, and provided the suitably bizarre setting of the English seaside in the middle of winter. Although crude by the video standards of today, and borrowing the feel of *A Hard Day's Night*, the black and white film is surprisingly undated and relatively humorous, featuring the four of us on the beach with a fifth band member who turns out to be a shop-window dummy. We shot the whole thing in one short grey day and in fact were leaving the car park of East Wittering as the police car drew up to put an end to the fun. Given the notoriety of another local resident, a Mr Keith Richards, and his pals, I think the law were hoping for another big bust. With our most innocent middle-class faces we maintained that we had seen nothing of a suspicious nature, but would of course inform them immediately should we note anything in the least untoward. It's lucky really that they didn't search the car. In it was the mannequin, nude save for a policeman's helmet.

Everything seemed set. We had an offer from Polydor, a producer, some recordings, even a promo. However, as frequently happens in the music business, someone had to be ejected from the lifeboat. And in this particular instance, it was Joe Boyd who lost out. The reason was that Bryan Morrison had intervened. Bryan, who ran his own booking agency, had hired us – although he had never heard or seen us perform – for a gig at the Architectural Association, having seen the coverage and the feedback we were getting. He wanted to see this hot new band for himself, and had turned up at one of our rehearsal sessions for 'Arnold Layne'. Joe remembers that his heart sank immediately, because Bryan started asking about the deal with Polydor and saying that we ought to be able to get a better one. Bryan, who had good contacts with EMI, funded the Sound Techniques recording, took a copy of the demo tape, and talked us up to the EMI executives, who didn't know much about us other than that we were the current buzz word. But Bryan had a way with words. They decided they wanted to sign us.

The insurmountable problem – certainly for Joe – was that EMI disliked using outside studios or producers. They owned Abbey Road after all. They wanted their own man, Norman Smith, who had recently been promoted from being the Beatles' engineer, to be our producer. That was the deal on offer, and we acquiesced – partly because the deal was better than Polydor's, and also because EMI were *the* big label, courtesy of the Beatles. There was no question about whether to go with EMI or not. They were the UK's dominant record company of the period, along with Decca – Polygram was not yet coming up on the rails. And Peter got on well with Beecher Stevens at EMI and his colleagues. They were offering a £5,000 advance, a serious deal – or in Andrew's words, 'a shit deal, but a thousand times better than the Beatles' [deal]' – and studio costs.

Peter Jenner was given the disagreeable task of breaking the news to Joe Boyd. Peter professes some guilt to this day about blowing Joe out, and behaving with a certain amount of insensitivity. Andrew says 'The alacrity with which Peter and I left Joe standing was shameless.' But in those days you did not sign with the company and then bring along your pet producer. So we were now EMI recording artists – and unlike most bands we came with a ready-made recording.

Shortly after signing we headed to a gig at the Queen's Hall in Leeds, formerly the garaging depot for the city's trams, and now the venue for 5,000 loon-panted Northern fans, seeing what all the fuss was about at a ten-hour rave headlined by Cream and Small Faces, and described by the *Daily Express* as 'the night Carnaby Street moved north'.

Our own progress north proved sluggish. We left London in the early afternoon since we didn't really know where Leeds was, the M1 stopped at Coventry – Britain's first stretch of motorway had only opened in 1959 – and we had Andrew King's old Renault as our unreliable transport. By the time we got back in the early hours of the morning I couldn't even make it into college just to sign the register. (At the Queen's Hall I decided to experiment with stage names. I thought Noke Mason would be a rather entertaining variant, and announced this to the local paper who duly printed it below our picture. This is not a ploy I have ever repeated.)

After that particular gig, I knew I couldn't continue combining course work and band life. I was still ostensibly studying architecture, but of course I was spending virtually all my time rehearsing, performing or on the road. Even with Jon Corpe doing all my class work for me, I was falling behind. Apparently degrees were not handed out on the basis of signatures in the register alone. Jon also remembers that I gave the impression of never being particularly interested in architecture. According to Jon, I always felt it was a job best left to architects. But help was at hand.

To my eternal gratitude my year tutor, Joe Mayo, suggested it would actually be a good idea for me to take a year's sabbatical from college. He assured me that he would let me back in the following year if I wanted. He didn't say it, but I think he recognised that I was shaping up to be a really mediocre architect. I'm sure he felt time spent living a different life would either provide me with a better career or at least make me a better designer. The head of school was less helpful, and wrote me a letter full of dire warnings about giving up a promising training, so I didn't bother to show that one to my mum and dad. I left college, expecting to return one day, but I haven't managed to make it back yet.

I was the last of the band to spot the writing on the wall. Roger was only too anxious to give up his job with Fitzroy Robinson and Partners designing vaults for the Bank of England. I believe he was required to sign the Official Secrets Act and promise not to reveal the specifications of the amount of concrete required to protect the money. It would be nice to feel that the designs he did were even now sheltering our ill-gotten gains. Rick had long decided to devote himself to music full-time, and Syd had stopped turning up at Camberwell College of Art.

EMI had one particular concern about this band they'd just signed, a concern that was to exercise their press department all year. They had acquired a band with a 'psychedelic tag', and although we could deny any knowledge of a drug connection, albeit in a rather shifty way, and maintain that the pretty lights were no more than all-round family entertainment, there was no doubt that the whole movement that had launched us could not be sworn to secrecy. Indeed some of them were filled with an evangelical zeal to turn on the world. This was a period where the idea of some crazed hippie putting LSD in the water supply was a popular nightmare – or dream, depending on your point of view.

We did various mealy-mouthed interviews denying we really even understood the meaning of the word 'psychedelic'. There clearly was a lot of confusion out in Top Rank land, because in one interview we felt it necessary to explain that a 'freak out' should be relaxed and spontaneous, rather than 'a mob of geezers throwing bottles', in Roger's words. A typical response of mine in a *Melody Maker* interview was, 'You have to be careful when you start on this psychedelic thing. We don't call ourselves a psychedelic group or say that we play psychedelic pop music. It's just that people associate us with this and we get employed all the time at the various freak-outs and happenings in London.' To which Roger added, 'I sometimes think that it's only because we have lots of equipment and lighting, and it saves the promoters from having to hire lighting for the group.'

We also had to fulfil one more EMI obligation by performing a 30-minute 'artist test' or audition. This was something every new act had to do, but was a futile exercise in our case, since we had already signed. Our next task was to provide the company with a single, and of course we just happened to have one we'd prepared earlier. On 11th March, 'Arnold Layne' (b/w 'Candy And A Currant Bun'), from the original pre-EMI Sound Techniques sessions produced by Joe Boyd (an attempt to re-record it had not improved on the original) was released. Just six months after our summer break, and the start of our involvement with Peter Jenner and Andrew King, we were professional recording artists.

A couple of months after we signed with EMI we had been treated to a full-scale record company shindig with a host of EMI luminaries, including Beecher Stevens who actually signed us (and shortly afterwards parted company with EMI – no connection I'm sure). A stage was erected at corporate headquarters in Manchester Square, our light show brought in, and we mimed 'Arnold Layne'. Everyone had canapés and champagne in quantity, and a few of the guests enjoyed a small side order of chemicals.

I clearly remember riding up in the lift with Sir Joseph Lockwood, the chairman who was only in his sixties, but seemed a nonagenarian to our eyes. He seemed unflappable at yet another quirk of the music industry. He did rather alarm Derek Nice, the director of our 'Arnold Layne' promo, when he suggested that they should install a backdrop of the Tower of London upstairs and then all the bands could simply come in and mime their hits to a camera before sending them out worldwide. Sir Joseph was years ahead of his time.

The requisite signature ceremony had been conducted with photographic evidence, apparently a requirement of the suspicious legal department in case any awkward musicians later claimed the signatures were a fake. We were genuinely excited and pretty full of ourselves. We had been propelled to a position that a few months before had been just a fantasy. So when asked to pose for photographs, our sense of euphoria meant that we gleefully fell into gambolling about in the most shameful way.

FREAK OUT
SCHMEAK OUT 5

FOLLOWING THE exuberant celebrations after signing with EMI it was time to get down to some serious work. Unlike many other bands, we had not paid our musical dues. In fact, we had barely put down a deposit. We had invested no serious time on the road, nor spent a year playing the clubs on the Reeperbahn. Our performances through the autumn of 1966 had taken place at a few favoured venues and within the comforting cocoon of a largely partisan audience. We had yet to confront the unknown civilisations that lurked beyond the confines of the psychedelic village.

Transportation was – and probably still is – a major problem for new bands. Borrowing a parent's car was an option with limited scope, especially with the almost immediate depreciation caused by cramming it full of drum kits and band members. Acquiring a van represented by far the biggest capital outlay – yet had none of the glamour of spending a student grant on a new guitar or bass drum. But though it was possible to muddle through a show with a mishmash of less than perfect or borrowed equipment, the band – and the ever-increasing pile of equipment – still had to get to the gig, and safely back home afterwards.

Before landing the record deal, travelling outside London had usually been restricted by the limitations of our Bedford van. We had become the proud owners of this vehicle back in the days of the Tea Set, when we bought it for twenty quid off a dealer's forecourt late one Saturday evening. The salesman couldn't believe his luck – the van was probably awaiting delivery to the scrapyard. In a fit of generosity he announced that he would sell it 'wiv new boots and blood', used-car parlance for a fresh set of tyres and road tax. The Bedford was unbelievably slow (my old Austin 'Chummy' could have overtaken it); its lack of speed was only surpassed by its unreliability.

We did encounter an additional obstacle when our equipment disappeared. Rick often used to earn an extra fiver by unloading our equipment at Blackhill's offices after gigs, but on one occasion he shirked his duties after a particularly late night, simply leaving the van overnight in Regent's Park. By the morning, all the expensive, portable gear, such as the PA amp (the one bought for us by Andrew King) and the guitars had been liberated. The management had no funds left, and no charitable institution stepped forward to bail us out, so it must be recorded for posterity that my mum, to her eternal credit, lent us the £200 we needed to replace the most important elements. Rick used to suffer an occasional, momentary twinge of guilt about the incident, although he never actually offered to make any reparation.

Shortly after the EMI deal, we acquired a Ford Transit, which was seen as a serious status symbol, the Rolls-Royce of band transportation. When the Transit was introduced by Ford in October 1965, it was in such demand that it was not unknown for thieves to unload a band's equipment and then steal the van. The Transit's specification included a three-litre engine, twin rear wheels and a modified cabin to take all the equipment in the rear compartment while roadie, lighting man and four band members travelled in considerable discomfort up in first class. By this time, running a decent van was imperative – because at last we were getting substantial amounts of work through our agent Bryan Morrison, who'd been so influential in setting up the EMI deal. Our first encounter with Bryan had taken place during a rehearsal session for 'Arnold Layne' at Studio Techniques. Peter and Andrew had warned us to expect a visit from a music industry heavyweight, and we awaited his arrival with some trepidation. The door to the studio swung open, revealing Bryan and his two henchmen. These three characters were clearly part of London's underworld rather than underground. No loon pants or kaftans here, but Italian suits and camel-hair coats with velvet collars. Hands in pockets, the trio fixed us with an impassive gaze – they looked singularly unimpressed at what they saw.

Andrew and Peter had talked to a number of agencies before deciding who to go with, including the well-established Noel Gay Agency in Denmark Street, where the bookers all wore morning suits. They, however, were asking for 15 per cent to represent us, while Bryan only wanted 10 per cent. Bryan got the job.

Although Bryan's sartorial appearance suggested an apprenticeship with a motor dealer, he had in fact attended the Central School of Art. His office opened as the management for the Pretty Things – whose members included Dick Taylor (who had been in the embryonic Rolling Stones) and Phil May, two other art school students – and then expanded into publishing and agency work. By the time we joined he had a substantial roster of artists, among them the Aynsley Dunbar Retaliation and Herbie Goins and the Night-timers, and later he added all the Blackhill acts, including Fairport Convention, the Incredible String Band, the Edgar Broughton Band, Tyrannosaurus Rex and Keith West and Tomorrow, a band which included Steve Howe, later of Yes.

Bryan had a proper music business office at 142 Charing Cross Road, the Tin Pan Alley district. Situated above an all-day drinking club (a device to circumvent England's then draconian licensing laws), I think it cost him all of £8 a week. The walls outside were covered with graffiti professing undying love for one or all of the Pretty Things and inside there was constant pandemonium. Bryan had dispensed with an intercom and just shouted at his secretary through the partition walls of his inner sanctum. In fact, everyone shouted, either down telephones or at each other. It was a far cry from the gentle, genteel world of Blackhill, which was decked out with kaftans and flavoured with the aroma of patchouli oil.

In addition to his management business, Bryan was the sole agent for some of the key London venues. When managing the Pretty Things, he had realised the additional advantage of not only managing them but also controlling their bookings. But sometimes, even Bryan, with all his experience, could be fazed. On one occasion, he had done a friend a favour and agreed to represent another agency, splitting the commission. At one particular club, he met two brothers who were the principals of the other agency. During the meeting one of the brothers made his excuses and left 'to sort out the exclusivity of the agency' upstairs with the club manager. The next thing Bryan heard was the sound of a body bumping down the stairs. The other brother also made his excuses, and went over to add a kick or three to the prostrate body of the luckless club manager. Bryan, who preferred to persuade his clients with a bottle of fine claret, quietly slipped away. Only later did he learn that the brothers' surname was Kray.

Andrew King also encountered the tougher end of the business, though nothing in the Kray league. One agency was alleged to have dangled the promoter (and later Polydor label boss) Robert Stigwood out of a window to help resolve a dispute, and had an associate dubbed Pinky, who was reputed to chop the fingers off guitarists who were backward in signing their contract. The closest Andrew got to that world was going to collect the money for a gig at the Royal College of Art from an agency in Soho. Andrew arrived, the door opened, and he saw a Christmas party in full flow, complete with big-haired gangster's molls, a party obviously funded by our gig money. He said he'd come to collect the fee for Pink Floyd. 'Oy, there's a kid here wants some of our money…' Everyone swung their attention to Andrew. There was a brief pause, then the whole room burst out laughing, and the guy at the door peeled the money off a huge wad of notes from his back pocket. As Andrew turned away, the partying resumed.

The two henchmen who had accompanied Bryan on his visit to Sound Techniques to check us out were his assistants Tony Howard and Steve O'Rourke. Tony, a Hackney lad, had started his working life as an office boy for the *New Musical Express*, as his original intention had been to make it as a music journalist. Briefly sidetracked into a career as a nightclub croupier and bingo hall caller, he had come across Phil May of the Pretty Things, who put Tony in touch with Bryan. Tony was persuaded to come and work for Bryan's agency.

Steve O'Rourke, after training as an accountant, had worked as a salesman for a pet food company. His employers eventually dismissed him when they discovered he was racing his company car at Brands Hatch every weekend and delegating his rounds to other salesmen so he could spend time running a club called El Toro in the Edgware Road. A subsequent three-month stint with another booking agency provided him with more than sufficient experience for Bryan to consider him fully qualified.

With Bryan as our agent we were finally getting the quantity of gigs we had always wanted. This was, however, something of a poisoned chalice, as the bookings represented a total mismatch of musicians and audience. This was particularly true of the Top Rank chain of ballrooms, where audiences only wanted to dance to a soul act or be dazzled by the stars they had seen on *Top Of The Pops*. Not only did we fail on both counts but the Top Rank also operated a dress code – to keep out undesirables – that required a jacket and tie, no long hair and *no jeans*. This not only meant we were prevented both from going to the bar for a drink and mingling with the natives, but also that our own small band of supporters would never have made it beyond the doorman.

For the Top Rank audience, watching Pink Floyd must have been a confusing experience. With no TV exposure until 'See Emily Play' was released, we were a totally unknown quantity to almost everybody there. The one Top Twenty hit we had had, 'Arnold Layne', was not at all representative of the rest of our set, and in any case had received limited radio play and no airing on TV. One promoter came up to us after the show and said, 'What a shame, boys, if only you could get some decent songs…'

Confronted with an hour of weird and frightening music, and a half-invisible, un-screamworthy band, their reactions ranged from the uninterested to the violent. This was our first exposure to punters who were not guaranteed to be supportive, and if we hadn't had an agent to insist on receiving the cheques in advance, we probably would never have got paid at all. Luckily there were enough new venues to keep us in work. The concept of rebooking was unknown, so we just kept moving one step ahead of the incomprehension we left in our wake. In 1967 we couldn't even rely on a sympathetic student audience. At the time there was no university circuit as such, partly because there were fewer provincial universities, and partly because organising gigs was apparently not deemed a suitable recreational activity for students. Consequently we were sentenced to working the rounds of clubs and ballrooms.

A glance at a list of the gigs we played in 1967 reveals a sudden increase from twenty gigs in the latter part of 1966 to well over two hundred the following year. This does not include our first tour in America, trips to Europe for TV promotions, or the time required to record three singles and an album. Not surprisingly all these gigs tend to merge into a featureless amalgam of dimly lit dressing rooms and A-roads leading to the home straight of the

M1 from Birmingham back to London. The Blue Boar services at Watford Gap were where all the bands stopped off, and crushed velvet trousers outnumbered truckers' overalls.

A few of the gigs, though, *were* memorable. Our Scottish tour of 1967 was fairly typical. It consisted of only five shows, the first two of which were at Elgin and Nairn up in the north of Scotland, where our Sassenach invasion was swiftly repelled. In the *Moray, Nairn and Banff Courant* we achieved equal billing with a local fruitcake contest, and a typical critique of our work by the audience was 'Do ye ken I could sing better in ma wee bath?'

Nearer home the reception was little better. At the California Ballroom in Dunstable the balcony above the stage was an ideal spot for the audience to express their disapproval by pouring their drinks directly onto the heads of the band members. As Roger philosophically remarked afterwards, 'They can't have disliked it that much, at least they held on to the glasses.' However, at the Feathers pub in Ealing, Roger took a direct hit to the forehead with a pre-decimal copper penny, a not insubstantial projectile. I particularly remember this because the rest of the gig was spent with Roger looking for the bloke who threw it. It was fortunate that Roger failed to find him, since without doubt the perpetrator would have had more and larger friends there than we did. As it is, we would probably have suffered more abuse had not one truly devoted fan unwisely and audibly revealed his appreciation of our talent. This gave the crowd someone easier to pick on, so they beat him up instead.

There was also an unforgettable performance on the Isle of Man during Scots Fortnight, the two weeks in July named in honour of all the Glaswegians who would head there for some serious holiday fun. The stage in this particular venue was high enough above the dance floor to prevent even the tallest Celt from grabbing a limb and dragging the performers into the mêlée. The promoter dolefully suggested that in his experience it was best to carry on playing whatever happened in the hall, to keep the house lights full up, and to forget about our own light show. We should have heeded his advice. His warnings were as nothing compared to the omens revealed as I took my seat behind the drums. I couldn't fail to note the pool of blood where the previous band's drummer had been sitting a few minutes earlier. He had clearly been found wanting and had taken a direct hit.

As we started to play, and dimmed the lights, the audience fell silent in astonishment. Initially we thought our music and light show had captured their attention, but an eerie rumbling soon indicated otherwise. In fact the darkness had given them the opportunity to fall on each other in a raging fury. Belatedly following the promoter's advice, we fulfilled our contract by providing a psychedelic musical accompaniment to the sound of the holiday Scots knocking merry hell out of each other. As our good friend Ron Geesin was fond of announcing, 'The next dance will be a fight.'

Strangely, these experiences did not dampen our enthusiasm. Like a platoon under fire, our band spirit was strengthened by the sheer horror of some of the gigs, and the bombardment of abuse. As part of some strange cathartic therapy, we even managed to laugh about them on the way home, convincing ourselves that the next gig would be better.

We frequently came up against one particular technical problem in these ballrooms, which, under the influence of *Saturday Night At The Palladium*, had decided that revolving stages were a sophisticated way of changing the acts during the evening. But as our sound equipment and light rig increased in quantity, the scene when the stage began to rotate was one of complete chaos. As the speaker leads were stretched to breaking point, quivering towers of equipment would plummet to the floor.

Amid this remake of the *Last Days Of Pompeii*, as speaker units tumbled around us, the road crew scrambled frantically to replug the electrics. The final lurch as the stage shuddered to a halt made the band, standing gamely in position throughout all of this, look like the crew from *Star Trek* taking a direct hit from a Klingon warship.

By now we did have the semblance of a road crew, although we tended to get other bands' cast-offs when it came to the roadies who lugged our gear around. In one instance we rather naively thought that anyone arriving from a career as Cream's roadie must be terrific. What we hadn't done was ask for any sort of reference. The reason this particular roadie had left Cream's employment was his complete failure even to set off for one gig, due to a hangover. He and his accomplice simply crept around to the manager's house, posted the keys to the van through his letter box and skulked off into the night. In our case, he managed to arrive at the gigs, but some extraordinary discrepancies between the milometer readings and the fuel bills he was claiming – clearly indicating a diversion between London and Brighton involving a trip to the Balkans – meant his stay with us was eventually brought to an abrupt end.

A subsequent roadie was scarcely more successful. He eventually had to go when we found out why we'd been having endless problems with our WEM speakers. We had set up a sponsorship deal with Watkins Electronic Music ('Wham!! It's WEM'), but neither we nor Charlie Watkins could understand why the damage to our speakers was so extensive and so frequent. We discovered that our less-than-loyal retainer had been carefully substituting the new replacement cones with the old blown ones, and then heading off down to the West End to sell the new speakers to the electrical shops in Lisle Street. Small wonder we had a unique sound.

Given the unpredictable quality of the crew, it was a requirement for everybody involved with Blackhill – band, management and support staff – to muck in and put in long hours. In one night the crew, however makeshift, might have to set up for a doubleheader in the early evening out in Norfolk, and then cart everything down to London for a UFO appearance at two in the morning. Eventually the road crew did become more organised, particularly after the arrival of Peter Wynne Willson.

Peter was an experienced theatre lighting man. He had been expelled from Oundle school for taking part in an Aldermaston march, and moved into local, then provincial, and finally West End theatre work. He had a flat in Earlham Street in Covent Garden, with his girlfriend Susie Gawler-Wright (known as 'the psychedelic debutante'), which Syd came to live in – Susie had spent some time in Cambridge and knew a lot of the same circle of friends.

At the time of our All Saints Church gigs, Peter had sporadically come to see us. Joe Gannon was looking after our lighting at the time, so when Peter joined our crew he took on the responsibilities of road manager. However, he had one particular handicap for this role – no driving licence. So Rick would drive the van while Peter manhandled the equipment. Peter then took over the sound (not, by his own admission, one of his strengths), before – following Joe's departure – running the lighting, assisted by Susie.

Peter inherited Andrew King and Peter Jenner's cobbled-together lighting rig, which, although to Peter's professional mind 'extremely dodgy', functioned surprisingly well until one art college gig, where the weird wiring linked two phases, sending a sudden surge of 440 volts coursing through the lighting system and destroying it in a blaze of glory. Peter concentrated on building a more advanced system based around three 1000W Rank Aldis projectors, and began experimenting with different ways of treating the light, by putting it through polarisers and stretched membranes made of latex. The colours created were 'spectacular, but very dim'. Peter found that the best polarised stress patterns were produced by using condoms. This led to the occasion when the van and our road crew were pulled over by the police one night. The officers of the law were intrigued to find one of the crew, John Marsh, cutting up a pile of condoms on the front seat of the van. 'Don't worry about him,' said Peter calmly. 'That's our roadie – he's mad.'

Another way of treating the light was to set a mirror at an angle of 45 degrees in front of the end of a long lens. This mirror was then vibrated to make Lissajou patterns. Inserting chopper and colour wheels into the gate and playing with the speed of the wheels created what he describes as 'worms of colour'.

One of Peter's other creations used a movie light, pushed beyond the recommended limits to achieve maximum brightness. In front of this was mounted a coloured glass wheel spun at extremely high speed by a motor. This apparatus was mounted in a box about two by three feet in size, and angled up at the band on some large rubber feet Peter had sourced. As there were no specialist suppliers, Peter raided the government surplus shops on the Edgware and Tottenham Court Roads for military-quality equipment, cables and connectors – which were particularly robust and able to be driven round the UK in an era before flight cases.

The effect of Peter's device was spectacular. With two wheels the possibilities were not just doubled but squared. By adjusting the speed of both wheels colours were produced that could only be sensed – 'silvery purple metallic colours. Nick's arm would trail rainbows on the back projection screen in a delightful way.' But the uneven temperatures, the shaking and banging, and the wildly spinning colour wheels, meant the glass had an alarming tendency to run out of control and shatter noisily, sending vicious shards of glass flying into the band at very close quarters. We had to carry round rafts of spare glass – we should really have had a paramedic's first aid kit too. Roger and I dubbed these machines 'the Daleks' in tribute to their robotic nature and their obvious hostility to humanoids. The lights were now an integral part of our show, and in one *Melody Maker* interview of the time, I solemnly intoned 'the lighting man literally has to be one of the group', although clearly not intending this to extend to a share of any royalties.

On the road economies were made wherever possible. We would buy any alcohol in advance at a roadside off-licence to avoid inflated bar prices. Hotels were ignored in favour of a long drive home, which precluded all the wild living every other band was apparently enjoying. Thanks to the knack the Bryan Morrison Agency had of booking gigs that required a constant criss-crossing of the country, it felt as though we were permanently in the van. To add to the excitement, we lived in constant fear of running out of petrol since the roadies would only go to garages that offered a minimum of quadruple Green Shield stamps – the original customer loyalty system.

Money was generally tight: despite the increased work, we were still in a spiral of debt, since we were constantly upgrading our equipment. We were in theory paying ourselves a salary of £30 a week, but in fact only managing to extract £7 10s, and consequently, to supplement this income, moneymaking schemes were always popular. Much later, on some ferry crossing to the Continent, John Marsh offered to crawl from one end of the boat to the other barking like a dog if Roger would give him £20, a deal Roger found irresistible, and the other passengers troubling. John completed his side of the bargain and, enthused with the success of this profit-making scheme, offered to jump off the side of the ferry mid-Channel and swim back to England in exchange for

Roger's house. Roger, a gambling man, was seriously tempted. He knew the odds were that John would not make it. But since this would also mean we wouldn't have had a light show for the rest of the trip, reason finally won the day.

In between the endless journeys, we occasionally had a home fixture at UFO, although only once a month or so after January 1967. However, two major dates in the spring helped keep us in touch with our original audience. The '14-Hour Technicolour Dream' on 29th April was an all-night event at Alexandra Palace, with acts including Alex Harvey, Soft Machine and Arthur Brown, the whole thing organised by Hoppy and the *IT* crowd to raise more funds for the magazine following a police raid. 'Chaos, but it worked,' Andrew King recalls. For many people this lingers in their memory as a seminal psychedelic event, the pinnacle of that whole phase, with bands and acts playing through till daybreak. Peter Jenner, for example, says, 'The "Technicolour Dream" symbolised everything. It was the pinnacle of pure amateur psychedelia, the crowning ceremony, the last big event of the gang. By the time the Pink Floyd came on in this somewhat dilapidated hall, it was dawn, the light was streaming through all the old stained glass windows, and people were climbing up the scaffolding around the Ally Pally organ. Virtually everybody was tripping, apart from the band, though Syd might have been. A great gig – though God knows what it actually sounded like.'

But others found the whole thing just too commercial, the musical end of the underground movement dominating because it was the most profitable element – the 'Technicolour Dream' was really just a big rock concert. Miles recalls the band the Flies, who'd earlier urinated on the audience to establish their proto-punk credentials, standing at the side of the stage while we were playing yelling abuse and shouting 'Sell-outs!' I don't remember this, but if they did, they might have had a point: the whole event was a sell-out. And our loyal UFO audience, used to enjoying shared experiences, found themselves faced with security notices, a ten-foot stage, and a role as exhibits in a freak show.

From our point of view the 'Technicolour Dream' was more of a logistical nightmare. That night we had been playing at a gig in Holland in the early evening, finished the show, packed up, been driven through the night at high speed by over-excited Dutchmen to catch the last flight out, and rushed madly over to North London to make our appearance. Given this itinerary, the chances of enjoying any benefits of a psychedelic love-in were remote. Syd was completely distanced from everything going on, whether simply tripping or suffering from a more organic neural disturbance I still have no idea.

In comparison, I think 'Games For May' a fortnight later was one of the most significant shows we have ever performed, since the concert contained elements that became part of our performances for the following thirty years. Peter and Andrew had set up the event at the Queen Elizabeth Hall in the arts complex on London's South Bank through Christopher Hunt, the promoter who had arranged for us to play at the Commonwealth Institute. Once again Christopher's classical music credentials proved invaluable, as he was one of the few people who could engineer an entrée into this prestigious venue.

Although we had little time for preparation or rehearsal to fill our two-hour slot, we did manage to conceive the evening as a Pink Floyd multimedia event. Unlike our regular gigs, there were no support acts, so we were able to control the environment and create a particular mood. The audience at the Queen Elizabeth Hall were seated, so the intention was clearly that, uniquely for a rock concert, they should listen and watch, rather than dance. A large part of this show was improvised. We had our usual repertoire of songs, and premiered 'See Emily Play' ('You'll lose

82

your mind and play free games for May…'), but most were chosen as vehicles, like 'Interstellar Overdrive', to act as a framework for constantly changing ideas. Everyone remembers Syd for his songwriting, but he probably deserves equal credit for his radical concept of improvised rock music.

We had some extra lights and a bubble machine, as well as the domestic slide projectors, which had to be installed right in the middle of the stalls to get any sort of light throw. This required some technical and legal improvisation, since at the time lighting and sound mixing was controlled from the side of the stage. It was some years before it became standard practice to have the sound and lighting desks in the middle of the auditorium.

IT reported that the event was 'really good thinking… a genuine twentieth-century chamber music concert. The cleanness of presentation of the hall itself was perfect for the very loose mixed media.' It's just a shame we couldn't capitalise on this reception and avoid the next year of drudgery fulfilling endless routine gigs.

The Azimuth Co-ordinator, which had its first outing at 'Games For May', was a device operated by Rick, which we had commissioned from Bernard Speight, a technical engineer at Abbey Road. There were two channels, each with a joystick, one for his Farfisa organ, the other for sound effects. If a joystick was upright the sound was centred, but moving it diagonally would dispatch the sound to the speaker in the equivalent corner of the hall. Rick could send his keyboard sounds swirling round the auditorium, or make footsteps – supplied from a Revox tape recorder – apparently march across from one side to the other. Nobody remembers who came up with the name of the device, but the Oxford English Dictionary defines an azimuth as 'the arc of the heavens extending from the zenith to the horizon, which cuts it at right angles'. It seemed rather well put, I thought.

We were also banned from ever performing again at the Queen

Elizabeth Hall, not because of over-excited fans ripping up the seats but because one of the road crew, dressed as a full admiral of the fleet, tossed flower petals into the aisles. The hall authorities deemed this a potential safety hazard for the less sure-footed of the audience…

This was typical of the disrespect, and often downright hostility, that existed between rock bands and venue management. On matters of safety and lighting, they would impose innumerable petty rules, some justified, many purely to indicate their disapproval. One that particularly annoyed us was when venues would demand higher levels of auditorium lighting for rock bands than for other forms of entertainment, especially damaging for us, as the impact of our light show would be severely diminished. An air rifle was occasionally employed to make sure the house lighting was modified to our liking. It was in fact de rigueur to be banned from all major venues, and as Andrew King says, you always told everyone you were banned even if you hadn't been. I think like virtually every other group we were banned from the Albert Hall 'for life' for a short while…

'Arnold Layne' had also received a ban, from the pirate radio stations Radio London and Radio Caroline, as well as the BBC, which really did make it difficult to promote since there was only a handful of radio stations broadcasting at the time. The ban was due to vague references in the lyrics that could be construed, if you tried really hard, as a celebration of 'sexual perversion'. Of course, not long afterwards, the BBC completely – and with a charming naivety – failed to notice anything sexual in the lyrics of Lou Reed's 'Walk On The Wild Side'. It seems absurd now – and wonderfully old-fashioned given the ultra-explicit nature of lyrics in the twenty-first century – but at the time there was still great sensitivity to censorship. The Lord Chamberlain had retained power over the London theatres until 1967, and even as late as

1974 we were still expected to get clearances for the films accompanying our live concerts from the British Board of Film Censors (including, bizarrely, getting a special dispensation not to have to show the censor's licence on screen before the films, which would rather have spoilt the effect).

In any case, getting played on the radio was difficult, as available airtime was still very limited. The Musicians Union had negotiated a deal with the BBC that restricted the amount of records that could be broadcast on the radio to forty hours a week. This left hours of music to be performed by the jobbing musicians who made up the radio orchestras. This was fine when the songs were a nice bit of crooning with a trumpet solo, but when they tried to recreate 'Purple Haze' it was the aural equivalent of a one-armed paper hanger.

Faced with these obstacles one option open to us – and any other band hoping to enjoy Top Twenty success – was to hype the record. In an age before electronic point of sale data, the system was very simple: it was fairly well known which shops supplied their returns to indicate record sales, and various persons would be sent in to the relevant outlets to buy the chosen single incessantly. Apparently you had to be very careful in one hyper's office. An inadvertently opened cupboard could cause serious injury as a cascade of unplayed records came spilling out. One particular specialist, in return for £100, would load up his sports car with flowers and chocolates and set off around the record shops to convince the girls behind the counter to adjust the sales figures, which they were delighted to do.

'Arnold Layne', released in March 1967, had reached Number Twenty in the UK charts. For the follow-up, 'See Emily Play' was chosen, and we tried recording it at Abbey Road. However, we just could not reproduce the sound of 'Arnold Layne', and so we all trailed back to Sound Techniques to recreate the magic formula, which gave Joe Boyd a certain wry pleasure.

By the time 'Emily' came out, we had gained some additional benefits from the banning of 'Arnold Layne'. I think the stations were a little shamefaced, and it looked as though their street cred might take a turn for the worse if they were not seen to be accommodating the new bright young things. All the radio stations played the record and we reached Number Seventeen after two weeks. This Top Twenty chart position entitled us to an appearance on *Top Of The Pops*. This marked an important new rung in the upward ladder, and gave us real exposure. Being seen by a national television audience would directly affect our drawing power and thus our earning capacity as a live band. 'AS SEEN ON TV!' was worth at least another hundred quid a night.

Most of the day was spent with run-throughs, make-up, pressing of fancy clothes, hair washing and trimming, all at the BBC's well-equipped facility at Lime Grove. What the road crew quickly found out was that since the hair and make-up departments did not know who any of the new bands were, they could also go in, chat up the girls, and get their hair washed, trimmed and blow-dried. Rarely have I seen such deliciously gleaming road crew as those roaming the corridors of the BBC that night.

However, I felt the show itself was pretty much of an anti-climax. Miming feels pretty daft at the best of times, and this was not even the best of times. It was always a chore to mime, especially for a drummer. To keep the sound level down you had to avoid hitting the drum skins completely or just use the drum sides. Both methods looked very awkward. In later years the whole ghastly exercise included using plastic cymbals and pads. In addition, you had all the adrenalin of performance with no physical activity or real audience response to absorb it. Compared to the show, though, the complete lack of excitement afterwards was soul-destroying. I suppose I expected the world to change after being on the telly. Surely we were now real pop stars? But it seemed not. The world carried on as before, and off we went to yet another dreadful venue where the audience still hated us, but I suppose at least they hated us 'AS SEEN ON TV!'

The following week the record was up to Number Five so we went and did it all over again. A third appearance was planned, but Syd threw a spanner in the works, refusing to do the show, and giving an indication of the trouble that lay ahead. He articulated the reason as 'If John Lennon doesn't have to do *Top Of The Pops*, why should I?'

Any chance of the record reaching Number One was out of the question. Procol Harum had 'A Whiter Shade Of Pale' out at exactly the same time, and it would not budge from the top spot. Each week we looked despairingly at the chart assuring ourselves that everyone must have bought a copy of 'Whiter Shade' by now – but clearly even if they had they suffered from poor short-term memories or wanted two copies. (Procol's Gary Brooker was reviewing singles for *Melody Maker*: he spotted 'Emily' straight away. 'The Pink Floyd. I can tell by the horrible organ sound…')

Commercial success was appealing to all of us, apart from Syd. Norman Smith – who was now our official EMI producer – remembers that when there was talk about picking a follow-up to 'Arnold Layne', and that maybe 'See Emily Play' should be the single, Syd reacted as if the word 'single' was a nasty concept. Although he was happy to chip in with catchy musical ideas, he hated the idea of anything being 'commercial'.

Norman Smith had been dispatched by EMI to oversee the recording of 'See Emily Play' at Sound Techniques, and to produce the recording sessions for our first album, *The Piper At The Gates Of Dawn*, which were held at Abbey Road, starting in March 1967. After trying, in his words, 'to become a famous jazz musician', Norman had applied for a job at EMI after seeing an ad in *The Times* for apprentice engineers. The age cut-off was twenty-eight, and Norman was in his mid-thirties, so he pruned six years off his age, and, to his surprise, was asked back for an interview, along with over a hundred other applicants. Asked by one of the interviewers what he thought of Cliff Richard, who was just emerging at the time, Norman was far from complimentary about Cliff. The interviewers, again to his surprise, tended to agree. And Norman was appointed as one of three new apprentices.

From then on he was set to sweeping floors, being told to nip out and get a pack of cigarettes or make some tea, and occasionally pushing a button on the orders of an engineer. Then one day 'these four lads with funny haircuts came along'. The Beatles had arrived at Abbey Road, and, by pure serendipity, Norman was assigned to record their test – after which he thought to himself, 'That's the last we'll see of you boys, because they weren't terribly good, to put it mildly.' The Beatles had other ideas, and Norman recorded them up to the end of *Rubber Soul*.

Norman had always had aspirations to be a producer, and after George Martin left EMI to set up AIR studios, he was asked to take over the Parlophone label. In response to his initial flurry of letters of introduction, he had got a call back from Bryan Morrison asking him to take a look at a band called Pink Floyd. Norman and Beecher Stevens – who had just joined EMI as head of A&R – did not see eye to eye, and were both trying to carve out their own territory. The fact that they both wanted to sign us to EMI probably played into our hands as they independently hustled hard for us to join the label. Norman remembers that the hierarchy took a while to be convinced about this unknown group, and the £5,000 advance was a tremendous amount at the time. When they finally agreed, they told Norman – possibly in jest – that he could sign us but his job was on the line.

I think Norman saw us as his opportunity to do a George Martin. He was interested, like us, in using studio facilities to the full, was very good-natured and a capable musician in his own right. Most important of all for us, he was happy to teach us rather than protect his position by investing the production process with any mystique.

For our recordings, Norman was assisted by Peter Bown, an experienced EMI house engineer, and again a man who had been at the studios for years, seen it all, and done most of it himself. At one early session, urged on by Peter and Andrew, we ran through our repertoire to select a number to start recording and to impress our new comrades. Regrettably they had all been on late sessions the day before. After thirty minutes Peter Bown had fallen asleep across the console, and Norman remembers that he followed suit a short while later.

Given our lack of experience in the studio, we were extremely lucky to have someone like Norman. It was still rare for musicians to be allowed anywhere near the mixing desk, and not unknown for session players to be brought in to save on studio time: the Beatles had begun changing this, as their success convinced record companies to interfere less and less. Virtually every subsequent band owes a huge debt of gratitude to the Beatles for creating an attitude where popular music was made by the artists, and not constructed for them.

From our first day, Norman encouraged us to get involved in the whole production process. He was aware of our interest in the science and technology of recording when, in his words, 'most bands at the time were just trying to be part of the Mersey Sound bandwagon'.

At the time the Abbey Road Studios (officially the EMI Studios) were an odd mixture of conservatism and radicalism. The company also had a huge engineering department where they built many of their own recording machines, mixing desks and outboard gear. Recording took place on four-track machines, which was then mixed down onto $^1/_4''$ mono or stereo tape. All editing was carried out by trainees using little brass scissors, in order to prevent any magnetism affecting the sound. The whole building was painted throughout in a shade of green that I can only imagine was inspired by the KGB headquarters in the Lubyanka.

Very much like the BBC, this type of organisation produced a wealth of good engineers. They had become well versed in the techniques required to record every sort of instrument and ensemble, and were unfazed by recording rock music one day and Herbert von Karajan with an eighty-piece orchestra the next. There was, though, a sharp divide between classical and pop in the upper echelons; although the pop releases were subsidising the classical recordings, the staff who created them were treated like other ranks by the top brass. The chairman, Sir Joseph Lockwood, must take a lot of credit for bringing down this antiquated hierarchy. To put things in context, two years before he joined EMI, the board had decided there was 'no future' in the long-playing record.

One of the features of such a well-equipped studio as Abbey Road was that since electronic effect machines had still to be invented, the empire owned vast quantities of instruments that were scattered around the studios. Bell pianos, Hammond organs, clavinets, tympani, gongs, triangles, Chinese blocks, temple bells and wind machines were there to be used (and can be heard throughout *Piper* and *A Saucerful Of Secrets*, as well as, I believe, numerous Beatles records). An extensive sound-effect library was also available, as well as purpose-built, tile-lined echo chambers that we especially favoured for recording footsteps.

Although my memory is that the recording for *Piper* went pretty smoothly, that there was general enthusiasm from everybody and that Syd seemed to be more relaxed and the atmosphere more focused, Norman Smith disagrees. 'It was never easy on my part. I always felt I was treading on this ice the whole time, and I had to watch exactly what I said to Syd. He was always terribly fragile. He would perhaps have laid down a vocal track and I would go up to him and say, "OK, Syd, that was basically good, but what about blah, blah, blah?" I never got any response, just "Hum, hum". We would run the tape again, and he would sing it exactly the same way. We could have done a hundred takes of the vocal track and it would always have been the same. There was a certain stubbornness in the man's make-up.'

We were finishing songs in one or two days in the studio, where sessions were firmly regimented – three-hour blocks, morning, afternoon and evening, with lunch and tea breaks strictly adhered to – and then heading off to do some gigs during the rest of the week. The ease of recording was in part due to the fact that we were effectively recording our live set, and listening to *Piper* now gives a rough indication of the set list we'd been playing at UFO and the Roundhouse, although the studio versions – to fulfil the demands of the three-minute track – were inevitably shorter, with more concisely constructed solos.

However, some of the more whimsical songs on the album may have been advisedly dropped from the set when we faced the menacing crowds at places like the California Ballroom: God knows what they would have made of the gnome called Grimble Gromble. Finding replacement songs was not a problem, though. Andrew recalls, 'Syd was writing at a rate of knots. Songs were pouring out of him, as often happens; there's a point where the writing suddenly erupts. Some people can sustain it, others cannot.'

'Interstellar Overdrive' is an example of a piece that on vinyl (as was) is a cut-down version of the way it was played at gigs. 'Interstellar' had formed a central plank of our live shows ever since Powis Gardens. Based around Syd's riff, the piece would generally be played with different elements structured in the same order each time. On the album it runs to less than ten minutes; live it could have lasted as long as twenty minutes. The trick was to construct these songs again so that they worked within the limitations of what was then a traditional song length. An added problem was that within a live performance there would inevitably be good and bad moments each time the song was played, particularly with the improvisational sections. A recording, on the other hand, has to be able to bear repeated listening. The two versions are of necessity very different beasts.

On the other, more structured songs, Norman was able to bring his production skills to bear, adding arrangements and harmonies and making use of the effects that could be engineered through the mixing desk and outboard equipment. He also helped to reveal all the possibilities contained in Abbey Road's collection of instruments and sound effects. Once we realised their potential we quickly started introducing all kinds of extraneous elements, from the radio voice cutting into 'Astronomy Domine' to the clocks on the outro of 'Bike'. This flirtation with '*musique concrète*' was by no means unique – George 'Shadow' Morton had already used a motorbike on the Shangri-Las' 'The Leader Of The Pack' – but it was a relative novelty at the time, and from then on became a regular element in our creative process.

Since Norman had worked with the Beatles it was predictable that at some stage of the recording we would get an audience with their eminences. Apart from anything else, we were between us taking up unprecedented amounts of Abbey Road's studio resources, and consequently it had become almost a residency for both bands. When we realised that we wanted to spend more time in the studio, we renegotiated our deal with EMI, taking a cut in our percentage from 8 per cent to 5 per cent in exchange for unlimited studio time.

We were ushered into Studio 2, where the Fab Four were busy recording 'Lovely Rita'. The music sounded wonderful, and incredibly professional, but, in the same way we survived the worst of our gigs, we were enthused rather than completely broken by the experience. It is hard to explain just how oddly confident we managed to remain, considering our inexperience and lack of technical proficiency. There was little if any banter with the Beatles. We sat humbly, and humbled, at the back of the control room while they worked on the mix, and after a suitable (and embarrassing) period of time had elapsed, we were ushered out again. Whenever the Beatles took over Abbey Road, there was definitely a sense of occasion, as their entourage cocooned them in an exotic micro-climate within the confines of the studio.

Piper was released in August 1967. Peter Jenner was impressed by Norman Smith's contribution: 'Norman was great. He managed to make a fantastic, very commercial record, condensing what Pink Floyd was doing into three minutes, without destroying the weird musicality, or the quirky nature of Syd's writing.' However, Peter still does not know what the album sold. 'I was only interested in singles, no idea how the album did – a sign of my naivety.' By the time the album came out, though, the underground movement, which had helped us on our way, was starting to totter under the onslaught of commercial pressures.

The business community had latched on to the new craze for psychedelia and every pop show, dance and sing-song was now being advertised as a freak-out. The alternative spellings alone were something to behold. By mid-April Peter, Andrew and ourselves had felt obliged to run a spoof ad entitled 'Freak Out-Schmeak Out' to poke fun at them, but even so promoters who were jumping on the bandwagon, or just plain dumb, failed to get the joke, and their ads were still blithely using the line 'Turn up, shell out, get lost' – a variation on the LSD guru Timothy Leary's

'Turn on, tune in, drop out'. The original concept of everyone making their own entertainment had already gone to the wall in favour of a commodity that could be sold.

The instigators of the underground were also under attack. In a heavy-handed show of force by the establishment, *IT* had been taken to court on charges of obscenity. Hoppy was jailed for possession of marijuana and sent down to Wormwood Scrubs for six months, the severity of his sentence causing a considerable outcry. The crowd at UFO had changed: although Joe Boyd – ever the sharp promoter – had the Move and the Floyd drawing huge crowds on consecutive weekends in June, the audiences the gigs were attracting were now turning up to observe the phenomenon rather than participate.

An unexpected development was that the tabloid press had got hold of the notion of a dangerous counter-culture and put the boot in. Earlier in the year a story ran in the *News Of The World* about the sordid goings-on at UFO – as a result of which the club ran into considerable difficulties – and mentioning those dangerous subversives the Pink Floyd. Suddenly this was sex and drugs and rock and roll. What made it particularly galling was that I hadn't experienced any of this good stuff they were talking about. In fact, the article had failed to uncover anything of importance and had mistakenly reported that we had referred to ourselves as 'social deviants'. The word 'deviant' has frequently been a trigger for tabloid journalists; in this particular case the reporter had got over-excited at seeing the phrase 'social deviants' on one of our posters. What he had failed to realise was that this was not a description of ourselves, but the name of our support band, a group led by Mick Farren. Lawyers were instructed, and eventually a meeting was held. We were subjected to the Mr Nice and Mr Nasty routine and agreed meekly to the standard apology in type *this big* on the back page.

The press had missed the real story: that our front man, guitarist and songwriter was beginning to unravel in a serious way. We weren't oblivious to the fact, but from our point of view Syd was having good days and bad days, and the bad days seemed to be increasing in number. Blinkered by our desire to be a successful band, we were determined to convince ourselves that he'd grow out of this phase. Other people around us had a clearer view. June Child was matter of fact about it: 'Syd took a lot of acid. Lots of people can take some acid and cope with it in their lives, but if you take three or four trips a day, and you do that every day...'

Syd was living in a flat on the Cromwell Road, which Peter Jenner remembers as 'the catastrophic flat where Syd got acided out'. We never ventured inside – just picking Syd up for rehearsals or gigs, and not coming into contact with the other inhabitants. The rumour was that you should never accept a drink there, not even a glass of water, unless you poured it yourself, because everything was spiked. It was not a world the rest of us frequented. At that point, Roger, Rick and I were still loyal to the student culture of beer and occasional spirits. We were much more aware of the effects Syd's lifestyle was having on our performances.

At the '14-Hour Technicolour Dream', Syd had been as tired as the rest of us, but his symptoms were much more severe. June Child had looked after him: 'First of all we couldn't find Syd, then I found him in the dressing room and he was so... gone. Roger Waters and I got him on his feet, we got him out to the stage. He had a white guitar and we put it round his neck; he walked on stage and of course the audience went spare because they loved him. The band started to play and Syd just stood there. He had his guitar round his neck and his arms just hanging down.'

Shortly afterwards, we were due to perform at the Windsor Jazz Festival. We were forced to cancel. Syd was suffering from 'nervous exhaustion', was the message sent out to the music press. When we had to pull out they sent poor Paul Jones on instead. Paul had recently split from Manfred Mann and was enjoying a successful solo career singing R&B. He mounted the stage to the cry of 'Do you like soul music?' A roar of 'NO!!!' came back from the assembled flower children, along with a hail of love beads and beer cans. Meanwhile, the rest of us reacted to these cancellations with embarrassment and fury, while the management tried to formulate a plan.

After lots of talk and not much action, mainly because there was hardly any information around on how to deal with drug problems, Peter arranged an appointment for Syd with the eminent psychiatrist R.D. Laing. I think Roger drove Syd up to North London for the consultation, but Syd refused to go through with it, so Laing didn't have much to go on. But he did make one challenging observation: yes, Syd might be disturbed, or even mad. But maybe it was the rest of us who were causing the problem, by pursuing our desire to succeed, and forcing Syd to go along with our ambitions. Maybe Syd was actually surrounded by mad people.

Roger also called Syd's brother, saying we were extremely worried about him – he came down to London and went to see Syd, emerging to say he thought everything would be all right. This was a recurring reaction. There would be a lot of talk about Syd's condition, but then he would have a good, focused period and we would think, great, he was back to normal.

Eventually it was decided to send Syd off to Formentera, a small island just off Ibiza, along with the recently qualified Doctor Sam Hutt, who was going there on holiday to consider his own future. Sam was the underground's very own house doctor, sympathetic to drug users and musicians: as Boeing Duveen And The Beautiful Soup and later Hank Wangford, Sam was able to introduce a performer's perspective. 'I was a very hip doctor. The gear I wore in hospital in the summer of love – instead of the white coat, the

The Hotrods – left to right: Michael Kriesky (bass), Tim Mack (lead guitar), me, William Gammell (rhythm guitar) and John Gregory (sax). There are, as yet, no plans for a comeback tour.

My first car, a 1930 750cc Austin 'Chummy', parked outside the family home in Hampstead Garden Suburb.

My grandfather Walter Kershaw's banjo band. My mother helpfully told me her father was 'the one with the moustache'… He is, in fact, second from left in the front row.

The Sigma 6 rehearse at the Regent Street Poly – left to right: Clive Metcalf, Sheila Noble, Keith Noble, Roger, me and a guitarist previously unidentified but who I can now happily reveal as Vernon Thompson.

With Roger in our first year at the Regent Street Polytechnic.

Roger assisting Mike Leonard (inset) with one of his light machines.

At Stanhope Gardens –
CLOCKWISE FROM TOP LEFT:
Bob Klose, Syd, Roger and Rick.

A winter's day on Wittering beach, where we later shot a promo film for 'Arnold Layne' – Roger, me and Syd, with Rick behind.

The Tea Set and (un)trusty Bedford van outside Roger's mother's house in Cambridge. Left to right: Bob Klose, Rick, Roger, Chris Dennis on the roof, and me.

Peter and Sumi Jenner on their wedding day in August 1966.

Andrew King, clearly not yet a consummate photographer.

At the Marquee Club, appearing as the Pink Floyd Sound, with Premier kit and Carnaby Street trousers.

A good example of the kind of light effects we were using at All Saints –
and throughout the Autumn of 1966.

A typical night at UFO, with the audience sitting on the floor.

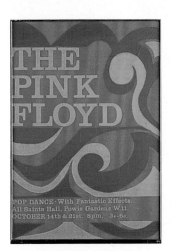

One of the first Pink Floyd posters, designed and printed by Andrew King's girlfriend, and later wife, Wendy Gair.

John Hopkins, 'Hoppy', at UFO, surveying his fiefdom.

The UFO posters were created by Michael English and Nigel Waymouth, whose company traded under the name Hapshash & The Coloured Coat.

Portrait of Syd at UFO, by Andrew Whittuck.

A Dezo Hoffman shot for EMI publicity – note the complete lack of mikes and leads of any sort.

Flyer for our first single, March 1967.

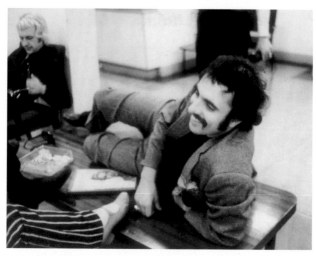

Bryan Morrison at the Abbey Road studios, during the *Piper At The Gates Of Dawn* recording sessions in Spring 1967.

Some of our first publicity shots, taken in London's Ruskin Park by Colin Prime.

The Azimuth Co-ordinator featured in 'Games For May' at the Queen Elizabeth Hall in May 1967. The poster for the event included an illustration by Barry Zaid that captures the whimsy and weirdness of the period.

GAMES FOR MAY
THE PINK FLOYD

On Friday, 12th May, 1967 at 7:45 p.m. in the Queen Elizabeth Hall, South Bank, S.E.1, Christopher Hunt and Blackhill Enterprises present GAMES FOR MAY – space-age relaxation for the climax of Spring. Electronic compositions, colour and image projections, girls, and THE PINK FLOYD. Tickets: 21/-, 15/-, 10/- from the box office, Royal Festival Hall, S.E.1 (WAT 3191) and agents.

QUEEN ELIZABETH HALL/MAY 12

Syd and Roger on board a ferry taking us to a gig at Copenhagen's Star Club in 1967.

Appearing on *Top Of The Pops* in July 1967, with my double bass drums on prominent display.

A flyer produced by irony-free promoters, which recycled verbatim the spoof wording we had used in a *Melody Maker* ad.

Norman Smith (left) and Andrew King at the Abbey Road studios.

Just outside Studio 3 at Abbey Road – left to right: June Child, Rick, Syd and Peter Jenner.

Out-take from a group portrait session from 1967.

sleeveless, coat-length jacketeen in pink Indian silk with what looked like sperms on it in purple with a gold moiré silk lining. And the William Morris flares.'

We frantically cancelled the planned gigs for August and shuffled them along a month. Syd set off for Formentera accompanied by his girlfriend Lindsay Corner, Rick and Juliette, Sam Hutt, his wife and their new baby. Roger and Judy were staying in Ibiza, a short ferry ride away. It was not a success: Syd showed no signs of improvement, but did display odd bouts of violence. On one night, when a powerful electric storm was raging, the turbulence outside reflected Syd's inner torment – Juliette's memory is of Syd literally trying to climb the walls.

Meanwhile back in England, we were still planning a future for the band. Roger was telling *Melody Maker*, 'We're being frustrated at the moment by the fact that to stay alive we have to play lots and lots of places and venues that are not really suitable. We all like our music. That's the only driving force behind us. We can't go on doing clubs and ballrooms. We want a brand new environment and we've hit on the idea of using a big top.' There was a vision of a way forward, but there seemed to be no way we could achieve it.

When Syd returned from his stay on Formentera, in no better shape, we blindly plunged back into work. We managed – with some difficulty – a few dates in September in the UK and Holland, and went to De Lane Lea Studios to record Syd's latest, and slightly unhinged, songs. On top of all that, we hastily prepared for our first tour of the US. We were due to open at Bill Graham's Fillmore in San Francisco on 26th October, but the trip did not run smoothly. Beforehand, Andrew King says he had been worrying about everything to do with this tour. His apprehension was well placed.

When Andrew set out in advance to see the agent in New York and get the contracts for the tour, the agent nonchalantly reached into a drawer and handed Andrew a gun for his personal use during the tour. Andrew, unfamiliar with firearms, questioned whether it was required. 'You don't have to have it, kid. If you don't wanna use it, I'll put it back in the drawer.' Even the toughest end of English tour promotion never went that far.

Andrew then headed across to the West Coast. Our work permits had not arrived, which meant we would miss our opening dates. Andrew remembers sitting in the offices of the legendarily short-fused impresario Bill Graham, listening to Bill lambaste some hapless record company executive on behalf of Jefferson Airplane who he was managing. Hanging up the phone he then turned his attention to this callow Brit whose band was not going to be able to turn up. 'Bands always show for Bill Graham,' he roared.

Back in London, for us the situation meant waiting on a daily basis to hear if the paperwork had been completed, and whether or not we could catch the flight out that evening. We spent endless hours waiting at the US embassy in London for the correct visas to come through. There is a massive amount of paperwork on current tours, but even then, there was as much bureaucracy, combined with slower and more difficult communications. There were problems with the documents as well as the arrangement for setting up an exchange with the American musicians Sam The Sham and the Pharaohs – union rules still required an equal interchange of British and American acts.

Bill Graham's solution was to ring the American ambassador to London in the middle of the ambassador's night, and he managed to force through the paperwork. To replace us, he hired in Ike and Tina Turner, who were playing in the Bay area, becoming the first black act at the Fillmore. Eventually, the visas finally arrived and off we went in time to make our dates at Bill's other San Francisco venue, the Winterland. The omens were not good. Syd was told by an anxious stewardess to extinguish his cigarette prior to take-off, and before her horrified gaze he carelessly stubbed it out on the airplane carpet instead of the ashtray. No wonder the PanAm service on that particular flight left something to be desired. We arrived in San Francisco very late at night and totally exhausted, to be greeted not by the screams of our American fan club but by Bill Graham, still furious at having been kept hanging around.

We were also reunited with Andrew King, who was still worried. He had walked into the Winterland, a 5,000–6,000 seater, seen the size of the place with its huge stage, and examined the powerful 35mm film projectors against which our basic 1kw Aldis equipment would pale. The venue's regular light shows were run as independent specialist set-ups, and were both on a completely different scale and geared to the size of the auditorium. Andrew generously, and wisely, said we'd 'combine resources', realising that we had bitten off more than we could hope to chew. In fact we'd bitten off enough to eat for several weeks.

The next day was spent desperately trying to assemble some equipment: we'd only taken the guitars, nothing else. I had assumed a drum kit would be there. All promises of support had mysteriously evaporated. The record company proved no help at all. A keyboard was found for Rick and a drum kit assembled. The Premier Company was English and worked through a network of affiliated agents in the States. The local dealer was probably shattered to be asked to release his stock to a virtually unknown British band representing Premier whose best-known endorsee Keith Moon was renowned for his appetite for destruction when it came to tame drum kits. Consequently, I suspect he gave me all the mismatched drums, cymbals and fittings he had lying around in the back of the storeroom – every element of the kit was a different colour.

Finally we made it to the Winterland, and the first pleasant surprise of the tour. The organisation at the venue was very professional and the other musicians on the bill were refreshingly welcoming and enthusiastic about what we were playing, and lacked the competitive 'blow everyone else off stage' attitude we were familiar with in the UK. However, though we were billed as 'The Light Kings of England', the light show was, in Andrew's words, 'laughable. I did feel an arse, quite frankly'.

We were supporting Big Brother & The Holding Company (the early and excellent Janis Joplin band), Richie Havens for one weekend, and H.P. Lovecraft the weekend after. Janis was wearing the legendary fur coat presented to her by the Southern Comfort company in recognition of services rendered. I'm not sure if that was for her personal level of consumption or for carrying a bottle of Southern Comfort on stage in an early example of product endorsement. Roger had brought along his own bottle, and offered Janis a swig. By the end of the show she returned it, emptied.

The audiences were closer to our UFO following than the Top Rank crowd. California, and San Francisco in particular, was the whole centre of the hippy ideal. Unfortunately we were unable to be quite so laid-back; jet-lagged on arrival, we were swept into a chaotic series of dates, under-financed, under-equipped and overwhelmed. And to top it all, Syd's approach to this important show was to detune his guitar during 'Interstellar Overdrive' until the strings fell off.

However, all was not lost, and a few of the dates, like the Cheetah Club at Venice in Los Angeles, were more successful. Whereas in the larger auditoria we were not the headline act – and the other acts on the bills were tight, well rehearsed, and were using their own equipment – in a club, as the main act, our lights would have some real impact, and we could control the overall ambience and mood, just as we could at UFO.

The Cheetah Club show was the occasion that Syd decided his permed hair was too curly and had to be straightened before he could go on. He sent someone out for a tub of hair gel, which he then applied in copious amounts to correct the problem. Clad in an extraordinary pair of green boots tied up with rubber bands, he hit the stage and once again detuned his guitar throughout the first number. In a frenzy of anger, Roger gashed his hand in a furious attack on his bass guitar. He had been lent a pear-shaped Vox bass that lacked a cover for the strings, and so he kept catching his hand on the bare ends. At the end of the show he smashed the guitar to pieces. Its owner, apparently thrilled, calmly took the pieces away in a bag. Despite this, it was a great gig. The audience loved us, as did the unusual support act, Lothar And The Hand People. Apparently there was no one actually called Lothar – this was in fact the name of the group's theremin, a remarkable Russian invention which produced *Dr Who*-like sounds when hands were waved in front of its antenna, and had been used by Brian Wilson on 'Good Vibrations'. In addition, the group also contained several very nubile young women. I seem to remember they had no instruments, but simply writhed around to the music as the mood took them, in a rather avant-garde way.

Part of the promotion for the band revolved around television. Years before MTV, the system was for a band to appear on one of the celebrity shows then current. The presenter, usually a popular singer of a certain age anxious to extend his career, would sing a couple of numbers, and then bring guests on to chat, with musical interludes from the likes of us. With Syd approaching a catatonic state, you might think this was not a recipe for success, and you'd be right. Syd was being difficult, if not bloody-minded. After miming the song perfectly for the run-through, he would then stand there listlessly for the actual take, while the director vainly said, 'OK, this is the take.' So while Roger and Rick were forced to undertake the vocal duties, Syd would stand staring vacantly and gloomily into the middle distance. After miming 'Emily' in an ecstasy of embarrassment we were led forward for a little chat. If other guests were within microphone range they ruthlessly used the opportunity to grasp valuable camera time, butting in with stories, jokes or inane comments.

On another show, hosted by Pat Boone, he kindly kept his other guests at bay in order to enjoy a casual chat with us. Despite some desperate and deft footwork by the rest of us, he picked the by now very unstable Syd to converse with. The world held its breath as he asked Syd what he liked. We trembled in anticipation while our minds flooded with endless unsuitable responses. 'America,' Syd said brightly. Pat smiled, the audience whooped and hollered and the rest of us broke into a sweat as we carted him off.

Away from the television studios Syd was little better. Coming out of a meeting with Capitol Records, we stood on the corner of Hollywood and Vine. 'It's nice here in Las Vegas,' observed Syd. Later, at the Hollywood Hawaiian, a typical LA motel, with floodlit cactuses and garish decor, Roger found Syd asleep in a chair with a cigarette burning through his fingers.

After this we'd had enough. Andrew reached Peter in London by phone and said 'Get us out of here'. We completed our West Coast commitments, but cancelled the East Coast leg, and flew back direct to a gig in Holland. If proof was needed that we were in denial about Syd's state of mind, this was it. Why we thought a transatlantic flight immediately followed by yet more dates would help is beyond belief.

Back in England Bryan Morrison had negotiated us a slot on a Jimi Hendrix tour. This was a great opportunity to watch Jimi Hendrix perform and actually spend time with some musicians we admired. At last we found we had some common ground with other bands, particularly the Nice, who seemed to have similar musical leanings, but astonishing technical proficiency, and in the case of their keyboard player Keith Emerson, later the 'E' of ELP, true virtuosity.

This package tour was run to a very tight schedule, the principal aim, as far as the promoter was concerned, being to make sure that Jimi's fans got good value for money, and that whatever else happened his slot would be on time. To check we didn't overrun our eight minutes, there was somebody standing with a stopwatch in the wing. Andrew remembers if we overran by even thirty seconds, there was a stern warning, if it happened again we would be off the tour. So our longer numbers like 'Interstellar Overdrive' must have been extremely pruned back. Peter Wynne Willson remembers that when the package tour had the house lights up our lights were virtually redundant. He tried to persuade the management to insist on a rider in any contract that the house lights should be down, and a screen and projection site provided, but that would not happen for some years.

Syd was still a loose (and hallucinating) cannon. On one occasion he failed even to get to the theatre. We realised early on that he wasn't going to show and managed to co-opt Dave O'List from the Nice to play. We had very little light on Dave and we certainly played 'Interstellar Overdrive'. I know it felt perfectly passable as a performance, and I don't think many people spotted the substitution.

The tour was really our first exposure to the world of rock'n' roll as we had always imagined it. Pop stars with tight trousers and loose morals accompanied by screaming girls with tight dresses and even looser morals. This was one of the rare – I can't tell you how rare – occasions that we were chased down the street by over-excited girls. I have ever since had great sympathy for the plight of the fox, as the thunder of hooves (or teenage girls' shoes) stampeding behind you is bloody frightening. In this particular field sport – perhaps more balanced than usual – the role of hunter and hunted was not always clear, as the various musicians and entourage on the package tour were also in full mating cry...

The girls were probably only just out of school, but you could see them in the hotel lobbies looking extremely cool as they spotted who they might snare next.

There was a tour coach that everyone boarded, like a crazy school outing with all the musicians in the coach, except for the headliners. Our recent modes of transport had become unpredictable. Some months earlier we had seen fit to purchase a Bentley under some misconception that this would be practical transport and enhance our image to boot. Yet another car salesman had triumphed and we experienced some exciting motoring since no garage ever really got the brakes to work properly. Roger still dreams about this particular vehicle, and clearly remembers leaving one particular gig and being forced to negotiate a roundabout by driving straight over the top of it. We had also rented one car from Godfrey Davis, which Andrew King had signed for, since they would not hire cars to musicians. After we embarrassedly dropped the car off weeks late, with 17,000 miles on the clock and rubbish piled knee-high in the back, apparently the rental company changed their rules so that not even a company director's signature was sufficient guarantee if the company had anything to do with the music business.

To coincide with the Hendrix tour, we released a single called 'Apples And Oranges', another attempt to create a hit. This was another of Syd's whimsical compositions, and would have made a great album track, but it was probably not really suitable for the job. However, under pressure, we tried to turn it into a hit, with Norman Smith's help, adding overdubbed choruses and echoes. I don't remember playing it live much, if at all. It is possible that there was a certain amount of US pressure to release it to tie in with our tour, but we had no time to do any real promotion out there. This was a case of trusting the advice we were given, and learning that sometimes, if not always, it was best to stick with our own instincts, and make our own decisions.

The tour finished and we played a show at Olympia in December 1967, an event called 'Christmas On Earth Continued'. Syd was completely out of it yet again, and the rest of us were finally reaching breaking point. It was time to come out of denial. We had tried to ignore the problems, and willed them to go away, but even our lust to succeed could no longer obscure the fact that we could not continue with Syd in this state, coupled to which it just was not fun any more – and doubtless no fun for Syd either. We did not want to lose Syd. He was our songwriter, singer, guitarist, and – although you might not have known from our less than sympathetic treatment of him – he was our friend.

Our initial idea was to follow the Beach Boys' lead. This was a solution suggested by the stories we had heard about Brian Wilson: apparently incapable of live performance, he was effectively a home-based writer. We thought we could augment the band with an extra guitarist to take the pressure off Syd. Jeff Beck's name was mentioned, which would have been an interesting (and spectacular) experiment. I don't think any of us would have had the courage to make the phone call at the time. Roger eventually managed it twenty-five years later.

But we knew someone we could call: Roger and Syd's old friend from Cambridge, David Gilmour.

Evening with

PINK
FLOY

THE SUM OF
THE PARTS 4

TICKETS: 30|- 25|-

OUR FIRST discreet overture to David Gilmour had come about when I spotted him in the audience at a Royal College of Art gig at the end of 1967. The RCA, next to the Albert Hall, was at the time the closest thing we had to a home venue following the demise of UFO. We had friends in a number of the departments at the college, which led to a certain amount of cross-pollination between poster design, sleeves, photography and music, as well as the continual use of RCA facilities for extra-mural activities.

As David was not a student, I assumed he was there to check us out. During a break I sidled up to David and muttered something about the possibility of him joining us as an additional guitarist. This was not a unilateral recruiting drive on my part, just the first chance any of us had had to broach the subject with him. David was certainly interested, mainly, I imagine, because although he thought of us – correctly – as less experienced than his previous band, Jokers Wild, we had acquired all the trappings that they had never been able to: an agent, a record deal and a couple of hit records.

Jokers Wild had been one of the most highly rated bands in the Cambridge area. They were all seen as accomplished musicians. Willie Wilson, who replaced the original drummer Clive Welham, resurfaced with Tim Renwick in Sutherland Brothers and Quiver, and later formed part of the shadow band we used on the live shows of *The Wall*.

I now can't recall the first time I met David. We had certainly both played at the same venues, including at Libby January and her sister's party, and we had clearly encountered each other in some social settings, since I was able to pick him out in the crowd at the RCA.

As a native of Cambridge – his early musical encounters with Syd had been at the Cambridge Tech – David had found plenty of work around for Jokers Wild either locally, playing to US airmen awaiting World War III, or on the occasional foray to London. However, David had ventured further afield following a busking holiday in the south of France with Syd and some friends in August 1965. He decided to return to the Continent with Jokers Wild, and they had stuck it out for a year or so including the 'Summer of Love', pragmatically re-christening themselves the Flowers. That band had finally broken up and at the time I saw him at the Royal College of Art David was at something of a loose end, driving a van for the designers Ossie Clarke and Alice Pollock, who ran the Quorum boutique in Chelsea.

We approached him formally just before Christmas 1967, when we proposed that he join as the fifth member of Pink Floyd. Syd had been talked into agreeing that David joining was a good idea. We went through the formalities of a highly reasonable band meeting, but it must have been made clear to Syd that disagreement was not an option. David accepted our offer, and we promised him a salary of £30 a week, omitting to tell him the real take-home pay was a quarter of that. Steve O'Rourke, who by now had become our primary point of contact within the Bryan Morrison Agency, provided a room in his house, which was equipped with a Revox tape recorder and some free sandwiches, where David mastered our entire repertoire in a matter of days.

A far more taxing problem for David was establishing himself within the existing band. Officially he was the second guitarist and additional vocalist. But Syd saw David as an interloper, while the rest of the band saw him as a potential replacement for Syd.

However, we took yet another opportunity to avoid articulating this to David, happy to avoid the harsh truth. With these unclear signals, David had to make the best of an awkward situation.

Events thereafter moved quite quickly. There was a handful of gigs in early 1968 where we tried playing as a five-piece. What Syd was experiencing at these shows we can only guess at: he was probably completely confused, and angry that his influence was being steadily eroded. On stage, he put the minimum of effort into his performance, seemingly just going through the motions. This lack of contribution was probably his refusal to take part in the whole charade. As he withdrew further and further, this merely convinced us that we were taking the right decision.

The clearest example of Syd's attitude was a rehearsal session in a school hall in West London, where Syd spent a couple of hours teaching us a new song he'd titled 'Have You Got It Yet?' He constantly changed the arrangement so that each time we played the song, the vocal chorus of 'No, no, no' was guaranteed to be wrong... It was one final, inspired demonstration of all his anger and frustration.

Things came to a head in February on the day we were due to play a gig in Southampton. In the car on the way to collect Syd, someone said 'Shall we pick up Syd?' and the response was 'No, fuck it, let's not bother'. To recount it as baldly as this sounds hardhearted to the point of being cruel – it's true. The decision was, and we were, completely callous. In the blinkered sense of what we were doing, I thought Syd was simply being bloody-minded and was so exasperated with him that I could only see the short-term impact he was having on our desire to be a successful band.

Considering we had never previously rehearsed together as a four-piece, the performance worked well musically, with David covering all the vocal and guitar parts. It was an indication of how little Syd had been contributing to the recent gigs, but even so, it is astonishing how blithely confident we must have been to take this step. Most importantly, the audience didn't ask for their money back: it was clear that the absence of Syd was not a critical drawback. We simply didn't pick him up again.

Although we had conveniently forgotten to inform the management of our modified line-up and new travel arrangements, Peter and Andrew – and Syd, naturally – rapidly realised what was going on. The matter would have to be resolved. Since what we had at the time was a six-way partnership, Roger, Rick and I didn't even have a majority to claim the band name, and with Syd's added importance as the main songwriter, his claim was probably stronger.

Surprisingly, perhaps, this was never an issue. Just as the partnership had been set up as an eminently equitable arrangement, so too dismantling it was conducted in a civilised manner. A meeting was held with everybody, including Syd, at Peter's house in early March. Peter says, 'We fought to keep Syd in. I didn't really know David, although I knew he was a talented guitarist and a very good mimic. He could play Syd guitar better than Syd.' However, Peter and Andrew conceded, and after only the odd outbreak of recriminations, the partnership was dissolved. Syd's suggestion for resolving any problems, by the way, was to add two girl saxophone players to the line-up.

We agreed to Blackhill's entitlement in perpetuity to all our past activities. The three of us continued as Pink Floyd and Syd left the band. Peter and Andrew clearly felt that Syd was the creative centre of the band, a reasonable point of view given our track record up until that point. Consequently, they decided to represent him rather than us. 'Peter and I deserved to lose Pink Floyd,' says Andrew. 'We hadn't done a good job, especially in the US. We hadn't been aggressive enough with the record companies.'

Andrew thinks that none of us – David apart – came out of this phase with flying colours. And he makes the point that the decision to part company was definitely a shock to Syd, because he had never considered the rest of us (as others might have) to be effectively his backing band – 'he was devoted to the band.'

'It was a natural parting of the ways,' says Peter. 'We wanted to develop Blackhill, so we couldn't have Pink Floyd as partners if we were concentrating on other acts. Pink Floyd questioned whether we could look after them without Syd. And Andrew and I might always have been harking back to the Syd days.' His view was that if Syd was taken away from the pressures of being in the band and given more space and time, he would become more stable. Peter says, 'I wish I knew what happened. I wish I had not let it happen. We all wanted to help, we all tried and we could not find the solution. If Syd is unhappy about what happened, I feel bad about my share of the fault. If Syd is not unhappy, then he achieved a state of reclusive peace and tranquility. I would love to know the answer.'

Following the break-up of our partnership with Blackhill, and lacking the obligatory management, it seemed logical to ask Bryan Morrison to take us on. We went to see him, and he agreed to supply Steve O'Rourke's services to manage us. Bryan would continue to develop his publishing empire, while Tony Howard would handle the bookings. Steve remained our manager for the rest of his life.

Both Andrew and Peter think that Bryan and Steve were able to see the possibilities of exploiting the situation we had created together. Bryan remembers lecturing Steve on the benefits of sticking with us rather than attempting to discover new talents. Andrew recalls sitting with Steve in the Speakeasy Club (the influential music business club off Upper Regent Street) long before the split, and Steve telling him, 'Do you realise how important and influential Pink Floyd will be on millions of kids?', and also observes that Steve always took the job of managing us very seriously. He was never flippant about it, as Bryan could sometimes be.

Steve came from a very different background to the band. His father Tommy was a fisherman on the Aran Islands, off the west coast of Ireland; when the great American documentary maker Robert Flaherty made his film *Man of Aran* about life on the islands in the 1930s, Steve's father was one of the featured characters. Tommy was then persuaded to come to England to seek his fortune in films, and although the outbreak of war and conscription put paid to his chances of screen glory, he settled in London, where Steve was born.

With his previous background in sales, and techniques honed at the Bryan Morrison finishing school, Steve brought a harder edge to our management. He exuded a sense of confidence, was a tough negotiator, and attired in his dark blue suit he looked like he meant business. It remained his preferred style of management, only the quantity of suits multiplied. We learnt that as a pet food salesman he would whip out a tin of the product, dip in a spoon and eat it. We found this commitment to his clients both admirable and seriously alarming, and Steve probably regretted going into such detail about his sales technique, since Roger was prone to dredge it up in conversation in later years.

After the final details had been sorted out, a formal announcement about Syd's departure and David's arrival was made in early April. It still surprises me that any trepidation we should have felt at losing our creative mainspring was eclipsed by feelings of relief.

Fortuitously, we had managed to avoid Syd becoming a dominant figurehead, despite his stage presence and looks. Our official publicity shots always featured the whole band, not just

Syd, which may have helped. It may also be that the strength of a group without an acknowledged leader provides greater input from all the members – it was a time when So-and-so and the Whatsits had been superseded by The Whatsit.

This should have been a difficult time for us, since we were a band who'd not had a single in the charts for nearly a year, the follow-ups to 'Arnold Layne' and 'See Emily Play' having not fulfilled any early promise. By rights we should have been forced to start over again, but somehow we had clung onto our particular rung within the music industry. We were about to enter a period I remember as particularly happy. We were now once more committed to the same goals and musical ideas, and to playing together in a more structured way. There was again that sense of being a complete band.

Without doubt David had the toughest task. He had the unenviable job of continuing to be Syd. Clearly he could add his own interpretation to any live performance, but our recent recordings included an awful lot of Syd pieces that would take a year or so to replace. Apart from anything else David was required to mime Syd's singing on all sorts of European TV shows. Looking back at some of those early shows I realise that what probably made it bearable for him was that even if the rest of us had actually played on the records, when it came to remembering the parts, David was much better at miming.

David brought new strengths to the band. Already an able guitarist – though never to my knowledge 'A Able Accordionist' – his singing voice was strong and distinctive. He was as interested as the rest of us in experimenting with new sounds and effects, but alongside his inventiveness he also added a more thoughtful, structured approach, with the patience to develop a musical idea to its full potential. He also looked good, and had managed to leapfrog the phase when a hair perm was considered the height of tonsorial fashion. Meanwhile, Rick was supplying texture and melody, and Roger drive, discipline and musical forethought. As drummers are a law unto themselves, I fortunately have never had to justify my existence in quite the same way.

Although he had initially felt uncomfortable with the five-piece, David certainly was never perceived as 'the new boy'. People who perform as a lead guitarist and singer are rarely shy and retiring. Norman Smith remembers that on first meeting David as part of the band, he thought 'This guy's going to take over the group'. (Norman had obviously failed to register the rather tall bass player standing at the back.)

If David lacked anything, it was an inheritance to pay off our debts, which were then running at the substantial amount of around £17,000. One of the side effects of our deal with Blackhill to acquire the rights to the name Pink Floyd was that we had to take on sole responsibility for the hire purchase loans on the van, our lighting equipment and sound system.

Before David's arrival, Syd had effectively been the musical director because he was the main songwriter. Norman Smith remembers being extremely concerned when he heard the news about Syd, because he had no knowledge of the rest of us writing songs. However, Roger and Rick started writing new material, and Roger in particular – who had written 'Take Up Thy Stethoscope And Walk' on *Piper* – attacked the task resolutely, but it was a slow process, and for the foreseeable future we would be playing essentially the same sets we had done with Syd in the band.

Gradually a new collection of initially improvised, and then more structured pieces, was developing. 'Careful With That Axe, Eugene' is a good example. In its original version it was a B-side instrumental, for 'Point Me At The Sky', which had been constructed and executed in a single three-hour session at Abbey Road with the final track lasting about two-and-a-half minutes. In time it extended into a lengthy piece of up to ten minutes with a more complex dynamic form. That complexity may only have been 'quiet, loud, quiet, loud again', but at a time when most rock bands only had two volume settings – painfully loud and really, really painfully loud – this was groundbreaking stuff.

We were still doing a considerable amount of touring, but there were important differences between the kind of gigs we'd been taking on the previous year and what we were doing now. The original underground scene was fragmenting and we'd exhausted the Top Rank circuit. Under Tony Howard's guidance we landed unexpectedly in a purpose-built environment: the university circuit. New universities were mushrooming in the major provincial cities, and student unions quickly discovered that gigs were an excellent way of raising money, and even turning a profit. Most of these places had sufficient funds to attract name bands, a captive audience, suitable venues and frequently a social secretary with a manic desire to prove himself as a businessman – many went on to be the promoters of the Seventies and beyond: Harvey Goldsmith is a classic example, and Richard Branson emerged from the same kind of environment.

We did not, however, completely abandon the London scene, although when Syd left the band we did lose some of our credibility with 'the underground' (there was, and still is, a school of thought that Syd's departure marked the end of the 'real' Pink Floyd, a point of view I can understand, even if I don't concede it). Things were changing in any case as new clubs cashed in on the original idealistic intentions of UFO.

Middle Earth, for example, which had started as an outgrowth of UFO in 1967, was a more commercial music venue rather than a forum for mixed-media artistic experiences, a sort of psychedelic Marquee Club featuring bands that could loosely be described as underground. Loosely, because most of them were R&B bands who had cheerfully swapped their Cecil Gee suits for loon pants, acquired crops of permed hair and adopted a flower power name, but still carried on playing the same old Chuck Berry riffs.

Playing at Middle Earth allowed us to maintain our own reputation as an underground band, at least enough to get us invited to play at parties like the one Vanessa Redgrave threw to celebrate the end of shooting for her film *Isadora*. This was definitely an entrée to a world we were happy to rub shoulders with, but it was something of a rarity at the time. None of the band seems to have retained any memories of this Bohemian soirée, but some did retain a number of rather elegant silk cushions as souvenirs.

We were acquiring a more professional attitude, and now even had a proper crew. Peter Watts was our first genuinely experienced road manager. He had joined us, through an introduction by Tony Howard, after working for the Pretty Things. Any disagreements among that particular group had been sorted out by a demand for the car to be stopped at the side of the road. The doors were then opened, the passengers disembarked from the car and a fight took place before the journey recommenced. Peter said he was happy to take care of our equipment but that following his Pretty Things experience, he didn't want anything to do with the band.

Peter later reconsidered his decision. This was fortunate, since we only had the one vehicle. Starting with a WEM four-channel mixer at the side of the stage, Peter oversaw an explosion of tour technology. Within three years we were using multi-channel mixer boards positioned in the centre of the auditorium, requiring multi-core cables, connectors and a proliferation of microphones on stage. With the responsibility for handling the sound, carrying all the equipment in and out, repairing it on the hoof, and driving us around, the road manager's job demanded a combination of skills: electrical engineer, weightlifter and long-distance lorry driver.

Occasionally even these skills were insufficient. Peter was the advance party for one visit to Dunoon west of Glasgow in Scotland. He had driven the equipment all the way there, but due to delays on a flight up, the band had to rent a fishing boat and corkscrew across a loch in pitch darkness during a force eight gale. We landed on the beach and staggered queasily up to the hotel where a restive audience was considering taking the place, and our equipment, apart. At the end of the gig the grateful promoter announced that as we had arrived late he would, with regret, be unable to pay us. After a brief argument where it was made clear that he was within his rights as exercised by his six-foot frame and even larger Highland friends, and with no flights till the next day, we climbed aboard the van for the endless journey south.

Or it would have been endless if the by now exhausted Peter had spotted the sign saying 'Road Works' before we hit them. The van was damaged beyond immediate repair and we spent the rest of the night in the police cells of the local village, which were kindly made available to us until we could catch an early morning ferry. Our fellow passengers, a hardy bunch of local farmers, marvelled at our exotic snakeskin boots, Afghan jackets and beads: we looked more like itinerant goatherds than the natives. Eventually we made it to Glasgow airport and the comparative safety of London.

This was not touring, but gigging. There was no attempt to construct rational and logistically sensible journey cycles. We simply took any available paying job. And if that meant a gig near London followed by a one-off performance at the other end of Britain, before heading back to appear in, say, Hull the following night, that was the way it was.

In due course, Peter Watts acquired an assistant, Alan Styles, an ex-army physical training instructor with very long hair and a flamboyant wardrobe featuring seriously tight trousers: after his appearance on stage to do the mike checks, our own arrival was often something of an anticlimax. Alan was yet another native of Cambridge, where he had enjoyed minor celebrity as the man who looked after the punts for rent on the Cam, as well as playing the saxophone in his own inimitable manner (he carried a flute on the road). He was not generally a violent man, but if pushed sufficiently by the 'Is it a boy or a girl?' brigade, could respond accordingly. One favourite incident was the time Alan had tried to get past some yobs on a stairway shouldering some heavy PA columns. After some banter Alan sighed, and then in slapstick fashion, neatly swung around with the columns, sending his antagonists flying.

Both Peter and Alan accompanied us on a growing number of trips to the Continent – we were certainly paying our dues now – which was proving to be surprisingly receptive to our music. This may have been because we hadn't damaged our reputation by playing at our most crazed, or with Syd at maximum altitude in the ozone layer. Whatever the reason, these tours had one important side effect: they gave us space away from the UK to develop ourselves as a band, which helped immensely. Europe had not figured strongly in our 1967 schedules, but in 1968 we spent time in France, the Netherlands and Belgium – and we loved it.

The Dutch and Belgian venues were regular destinations at the time, France less so, although it later became one of our strongest markets. There were plenty of towns geographically close together, which made the logistics of playing four towns in four days much easier. And there was already an existing rock culture that embraced us all the more readily. A couple of well-known clubs – the Paradiso and Fantasia in Amsterdam– were modelled on the Fillmore, small ornately decorated theatres now dedicated to music entirely, which was still quite rare in Europe at the time.

Throughout it all wafted the aroma of patchouli oil and Indonesian chicken wings.

Playing further south in Europe was more of a problem. A festival in May at the Palazzo dello Sport in Rome was a remarkable introduction to working in Italy. At Leonardo da Vinci airport the Italian customs confiscated an axe belonging to the Move, who were also on the bill; it was an essential stage prop that they used to destroy a TV set. The customs officers were able to identify the hatchet as an offensive weapon, but perhaps the language barrier prevented them spotting the danger contained in boxes marked 'Explosive: fireworks'. The show rapidly moved from art to violence. As the pyro was let off, the police responded with the only contribution they could make – tear gas. Over the years, the forces of law and order have frequently joined in, battling outside the stadium with the people who, for reasons political or financial, have come along for a good scrap. To this day, preparations for the Italian leg of any tour include the provision of buckets of eyewash at the side of the stage to alleviate the effects of gas wafting across the stage.

Leuven in Belgium was one of the – thankfully – rare times that we were forced off stage. It was at a university where the two rival factions of young academics – Flemish and Walloon – preferred to express their dislike for each other physically. The Flemish had clearly booked the band for the evening, whereas the Walloons had bought the beer and wanted to sing drinking songs. About ten minutes into the set I saw what I took to be an ancient student tradition: the fountain of glass. A few seconds later I realised this was not the case. It was the students hurling glasses at each other, and we looked like being the next natural target. With indecent and craven haste we finished and were off the stage, escaping to the waiting Transit with only superficial damage to the equipment and a few battle scars. We cheered ourselves up with the knowledge that since we had been paid in advance, it was by far the most we had ever earned per minute played.

Our promoter in the Netherlands was Cyril van den Hemel. His tours took place with the bare minimum of crew and where possible three gigs a day. 'We got the money, we go now,' was Cyril's line hissed from the side of the stage: we would finish the song we were playing, say goodnight and split for the next show. On one bank holiday, we told the management we were taking a two-day holiday, but actually extended the tour by two days and divvied up the extra cash between us. This was particularly welcome as band account cheques at the time were a little on the rubbery side. The cash may have alleviated the lack of comfort on tour. Some *frites* from a roadside vendor and a claustrophobic bunk on the ferry out of Dunkirk was our usual taste of Continental nightlife.

Generally overseas touring went smoothly. The band and crew got on well together, we didn't miss gigs and our equipment was still relatively manageable and easily transportable: a stack of 4x4 speaker cabinets for David, Roger and Rick, with a four-channel mixer at the side of the stage feeding a couple of PA columns, but no mikes for the drum kit. Rick had a Hammond organ by this time, and we might have started carrying a gong around with us for Roger to beat, but there were few extras. The Azimuth Co-ordinator stayed at home.

Our light show continued to rely on the slide projectors, backed up by a rack of mounted spotlights, and the whirling Daleks. Under their glow, and since most of the venues were small, we would get extremely hot and sweaty, but our stage performance was earnest rather than flashy. After briefly experimenting with a Keith Moon-like barrage of energy, I had settled for a less flamboyant style. Rick never subscribed to the Little Richard school of performing arts, preferring the traditional use of hands rather than feet. David would generally concentrate on what he was playing.

However, Roger was given to roaming round the stage from time to time, and occasionally attacked the gong with gusto. I still have a strong visual memory of him bending backwards, teeth bared, head thrown back and the neck of his bass vertical, extracting the most from a typically long and descending run. He frequently gave the impression he was trying to wring its neck. Both he and Rick smoked on stage, and while Rick's cigarette burned holes in the edge of his Farfisa, the glowing end of Roger's cigarette, jammed in the top of the strings, was a useful point of reference whenever the lights were down.

Meanwhile, when we were off the road, we were working in the studios on a new album, once again fitting the recording sessions around our touring schedule. EMI had obviously been rather taken by surprise when we announced that Syd was leaving the band: we had not wanted to unsettle them by communicating this to them with undue haste. They may have considered that since Syd was under contract to them they had all the bases covered. To their credit, they had the good manners not to intervene... and in fact only formally wrote a letter to confirm his departure four years later.

The bulk of the follow-up to *Piper*, *A Saucerful Of Secrets*, was recorded at Abbey Road, and the album represents most of the forces at work during that period. It contains the final guttering flame of Syd's contributions: even the lyrics of 'Jugband Blues' seem to be a requiem ('I'm most obliged to you for making it clear that I'm not here'). For the recording of this – which we'd done in December the year before – Syd had suggested a brass band overdub. Norman asked him if he had any ideas for figures or counter-melodies: 'Syd just said, "No, let's use the Salvation Army." I got a dozen Salvation Army bods in, and of course I hadn't written anything down. We were all there except Syd. I talked to the musicians and said, "Look, fellows, Syd Barrett has a certain talent – there's no doubt about that – but I think you might find him a rather odd character, so don't be surprised when he arrives." We waited half an hour or so and Syd finally turned up. I asked him what they should do, and he said "Just let them do what they like, just anything". I pointed out that we couldn't really do that because nobody would know where they were, but that's how it had to happen.'

We did have a number of other songs of Syd's in reserve, including 'Old Woman With A Casket' and 'Vegetable Man'. They were initially intended to be potential singles, but were never satisfactorily finished. Both of these had vocals from me included in the mix, which may have some bearing on the matter. Neither track has ever officially been released, but they did find their way to the marketplace courtesy of Peter Jenner.

Peter remembers that Syd wrote 'Vegetable Man' straight off at his house in the space of a few minutes: 'It was just a description of himself at the time. "I am a vegetable man." Terrifying to read the lyrics. I let those songs out. I felt that if you wanted to understand Syd, these were important, fantastic songs, although terribly upsetting. People needed to hear them.'

We returned to Abbey Road to work on the new album once David was on board. Rick contributed 'Remember A Day' and 'See-Saw'. 'Remember A Day' had a different drum feel to our usual pounding style, and I eventually relinquished the playing to Norman. I really didn't like giving up my drum stool – and never have – but in this particular instance I would have struggled to provide a similar feel. Re-listening to this it feels more like a Norman Smith track than anyone else's. Apart from the rather un-Floyd-like arrangement, Norman's voice is also prominent within the backing vocals.

Roger supplied three songs, 'Corporal Clegg', 'Let There Be More Light' and 'Set The Controls For The Heart Of The Sun'. Within months Roger had been galvanised from the awkwardness of 'Take Up Thy Stethoscope And Walk' to a lyric style that was much more flowing. 'Light' and 'Clegg' had considerable production input from Norman, and the latter some verbal input too. 'Corporal Clegg' has Norman muttering 'Git yore hair cut' on the fade-out, an in-joke, and lyrically the subject matter can be seen as a humorous forerunner of 'The Gunner's Dream'. 'Let There Be More Light' was engendered by references to Pip Carter, one of the odder characters of the Cambridge mafia, now deceased. Out of the Fens, and with some gipsy blood, Pip worked for us at odd times as one of the world's most spectacularly inept roadies – a hotly contested title – and had a distressing tendency to remove his shoes within the confines of the van.

'Set The Controls' is perhaps the most interesting song in relation to what we were doing at the time since it had been constructed to make the most of what we had learnt. The song – with a great, catchy riff – was designed to sit within Roger's vocal range. Lyrically it is suitably Sixties (based, according to Roger, on late Tang period poetry) and rhythmically it gave me a chance to emulate one of my favourite pieces, 'Blue Sands', the track by the jazz drummer Chico Hamilton in the film *Jazz On A Summer's Day*. 'Set The Controls' is a song that has lasted incredibly well. The song was fun to play live – and we had played it over a number of months, allowing it to evolve and ironing out any wrinkles – but in the studio we could enhance it with echo and reverb, adding a whispery quality to the vocals.

And the title track, 'A Saucerful Of Secrets', is in my view one of the most coherent pieces we have ever produced. Instead of the standard song structure made up of verses, choruses, middle eight and bridge, and in contrast to the evolution of the more improvised pieces, it was carefully constructed. Roger and I mapped it out in advance, following the classical music convention of three movements. This was not unique to us, but it was unusual. With no knowledge of scoring, we designed the whole thing on a piece of paper, inventing our own hieroglyphics.

One starting point was a sound that Roger had discovered by placing a mike close to the edge of a cymbal and capturing all the tones that are normally lost when it is struck hard. This gave us a first section to work from, and with four individuals contributing freely, the piece developed quickly. The middle section – or 'Rats In The Piano' as it was sometimes more familiarly labelled by the band – was a development of sounds that we used in improvised sequences in earlier shows, probably lifted from a John Cage piece, while the rhythm was supplied by a double-tracked drum loop.

The end sequence was an anthem that built throughout and in performance gave us an opportunity to use ever-increasingly large house organs, culminating in the one at the Albert Hall – an instrument with such power that it was rumoured certain stops should never be used as they might either damage the building's foundations or cause an attack of mass nausea amongst the audience members.

We also used a Mellotron, with its weird fluxing tape loops of string sounds, which the Musician's Union were up in arms about, as they thought it would mark the end of live string players. The instrument now seems so quaint it feels as though it should be in a museum alongside the serpent and crumhorn, but its sound is so distinctive it is now digitally re-created in soundboxes with all its imperfections part of the continuing charm.

I remember the general atmosphere in the studio working on *A Saucerful of Secrets* as being industrious and constructive. All of us wanted to be involved all the time, so creating a percussion sound would find Roger holding the cymbal, David moving the microphone closer, Rick adjusting the height, and me delivering the *coup de grâce*.

We were learning the technology and some studio technique, and the work was getting done, even if it wasn't entirely to Norman's taste. Perhaps when Syd left, Norman may have thought we would return to more conservative song making. There is certainly a story that during the recording of *Saucer* he was heard to remark that the boys would have to settle down and do some proper work once they had got this piece out of their system.

Eventually we parted company with Norman, although Norman retained an executive producer credit on the next two albums. In the early Seventies he went on to have a couple of hit records of his own as 'Hurricane' Smith ('Don't Let It Die' and 'Oh Babe, What Would You Say?') and, to the delight of the audience and himself, was literally wheeled onstage aboard a mobile podium to conduct the orchestra for 'A Saucerful of Secrets' when we performed it live at the Royal Albert Hall in June 1969.

Steve O'Rourke's notable contribution to the recording sessions for *Saucer* was the continuation in Studio 3 of his wedding on 1st April 1968. Steve arrived with his new bride Linda, and some of their tired and emotional guests decided to explore the studio complex and try their hand at some of the unusual and intriguing musical instruments they came across. Roger says they later found the bride fast asleep in the grand piano. A short while later Sir Joseph Lockwood issued an edict banning alcohol from the studios.

The cover design of *Saucer* marked the arrival of Storm Thorgerson and Aubrey Powell (who was known as Po long before the Teletubbies were ever dreamt of) as collaborators rather than observers. The cover contains all the politically correct ingredients of the period, and is a testament not only to the stream of ideas that flowed from their company Hipgnosis, and which still flows for our benefit from Storm well over three decades further on, but also to the facilities of the Royal College of Art, where they had both been at the film school. Since many of their friends were current or ex-students they relied on the RCA for technical support, as there was no budget for the professional labs.

On the day of the album's release – 29th June 1968 – we played at the first free Hyde Park concert, along with Roy Harper and Jethro Tull. This was a marvellous event: the weather was fine, the atmosphere mellow and relaxed. Perhaps most tellingly, it had not occurred to anyone to construct a VIP area, and everyone seemed to be in the same good mood. Plus it gave us the chance to renew acquaintance with our original fan base, albeit in front of a much wider public, and with Blackhill, who were responsible for the whole event. This was our first opportunity to work with Peter and Andrew after the split and that there seemed to be no hard feelings was a bonus. Peter Jenner says, 'Hyde Park was a great pleasure. The fact that the Floyd played there proves there was no lingering hostility. Both parties had been gentlemanly. There was mutual respect.'

I think almost everybody who was there has happy memories of the concert, particularly those clever enough to rent the rowing boats on the Serpentine Lake. They didn't see much of the show, but it was daylight so the lighting effects were non-existent. Other fans were obviously less attuned to the mood, though, since *Melody Maker* reportedly fielded a number of calls from anxious fans who wanted to know exactly how much it would cost to get into the free concert.

In August, we returned to the States, ten months after our first disastrous sortie. Before we left, Bryan approached us and explained that as a formality he needed us to sign another agency agreement in order to smooth the path of the tour. Roger smelt a rat, and only signed on the basis that it was a six-week contract.

He was right to be suspicious. Two days later we learned through the press that the agency and management side of Bryan's business had been sold for £40,000 to NEMS Enterprises, Brian Epstein's old music company, now owned and run by Vic Lewis.

Vic was very much old-school music business – complete with pencil moustache and Brylcreemed hair – and we were ushered in to meet the great man at his grand offices in Mayfair. Horror-struck we listened as he told us proudly of the album he had recorded of Beatles songs arranged his way with strings. He suggested the possibility of Pink Floyd getting the same treatment. Was this a threat, a promise or a joke? Unable to tell, we glanced at each other nervously.

Although we had signed the agency contract, Bryan had overlooked the management aspect and neglected to get us to sign the relevant contract. This gave us enough leverage to extract some cash from NEMS – a great assuager of artistic pain, I find – and to insist that Steve, who was due to join NEMS, be released to become our personal manager.

Bryan now maintains that one of the primary reasons he sold the agency to NEMS was that his doctor had told him to cut his lifestyle and workload back, as he was suffering from ulcers. But, to his credit, Bryan did understand the importance of getting us back to America for a second tour, and was instrumental in making it happen.

It was, and probably still is, fantastically important to achieve success in the US, both in terms of record sales to such a huge market, and live performance… However, a strike by American air traffic controllers in 1968 ensured that a relatively small-scale tour became a full-scale drama. Because our work visas had been delayed yet again, we were forced to arrive as holidaymakers, and then to make a quick jaunt to Canada (it had to be a round trip because we couldn't afford an overnight stay) to get the correct paperwork in the middle of a residency at Steve Paul's Scene Club in New York. This basement club on 47th and 6th was an established New York showcase and, although tiny, was an ideal launch pad for us. As an added draw, Fleetwood Mac was booked as support for a number of nights, although I have no memory of how we dealt with equipment changes between sets. A free bar for the bands compensated for low pay. With New York summer temperatures and a low ceiling height, the atmosphere was intense. Carried along on a wave of percussive creativity, and perhaps also by the bar arrangements, Roger sustained some nasty cuts to his hands throwing glasses at the gong during 'Set The Controls'. After his run-in with the Vox bass at the Cheetah Club on our first tour he seemed to be making a habit of spilling blood in America.

This audience was not a laid-back UFO crowd, but a much more pepped up New York audience. Among the crowd were other musicians and performers from the local Broadway shows. I do remember staggering back to our hotel after the show accompanied by one of the girls then appearing in *Hair*, which had recently opened on Broadway. Enormously proud of my conquest, it was many years later that I discovered that her reputation as a singer was somewhat eclipsed by her super-groupie status…

In New York, we stayed for a while at the Chelsea Hotel. For such a legendary hotel it really was remarkably run-down. Famous for featuring in songs by inhabitants such as Bob Dylan and Leonard Cohen as well as for its rock'n'roll and bohemian clientele, it enjoyed a collection of permanent residents, an understanding credit control, who would let an artist hand over a painting in lieu of rent, and a menagerie on the top floor with a selection of wild animals. We had two rooms for all the band, crew and any visitors or friends we might make en route. Such squalor had not been seen since our flat in Stanhope Gardens. On this particular tour, Roger travelled with just one carry-on bag. Dirty laundry went into the lower compartment and was then recycled into the top section when that was empty. The system proved to be fairly hygienic since a bottle of scotch had got broken in the bag on the flight out.

Clubs like the Scene formed a solid backbone for the tour, but everything was still being run on a shoestring. At one point, we were stuck in the Camlin Hotel in Seattle, living on room service, until some cash arrived from our American agency and we could settle up and move on.

This was our first major tour, and was enlivened by spending time with two other British bands that were on the road with us during the same period, the Soft Machine and the Who. The Soft Machine was a group we had always felt considerable affinity towards. They had initially experienced trouble gaining greater public acceptance because of their more esoteric jazz-inspired music. The Who embodied most of the qualities that we aspired to as a working band – heading the bill, playing 5,000-seater venues and displaying a convincingly professional attitude. We played with them at a show designated 'The English Invasion' in Philadelphia (the bill also featured the Troggs and Herman's Hermits) and we got lucky when a sudden rainstorm broke during our set. This meant that the Who couldn't go on next and eclipse our performance. We gained points for appearing at all, as well as topping the bill by default, and then headed off with Keith Moon and various courtiers to do some live radio.

This was in the days when FM radio in the States was very freeform indeed, but that night things got freer than ever. We all had plenty of adrenalin still flowing around our systems, and the DJ and most of his guests were chemically relaxed. Rick, not normally a wild man, picked up the stylus while one record was playing on air, announced that he didn't care for the song, and demanded something else. Keith Moon kept up a barrage of comment throughout the broadcast to enliven the occasion further. Now, over twenty-five years later, when we go back to Philadelphia, people still talk of that night's radio show in hushed tones.

In a nearby bar, later that night, Pete Townshend impressed me with the firm way he dealt with a drunk who approached us to discuss loud music and pansy clothes. When he started being aggressive, Pete, rather than continue the discussion, calmly asked the barman to throw him out. This, Pete pointed out, proved two matters. First the power of money (we were spending more and therefore we controlled the bar) and secondly that drunks, particularly in the States, enjoy discussion for a short while but as soon as they start losing an argument, have a tendency to resort to physical violence or draw a gun – yet another useful rule for the book of touring hints and tips.

As on the first tour, we had almost no equipment, once again victims of empty promises from agents and record companies. It was Jimi Hendrix who saved us. Hearing of our problems (his managers also handled the Soft Machine) he sent us down to Electric Lady, his recording studio and storage facility on West 8th Street, and told us to help ourselves to what we needed. There are some real rock'n'roll heroes.

Contact with the local record company was erratic, and sometimes nigh on impossible. Steve O'Rourke, desperate to have a meeting with some marketing executive who was not returning any of his calls, tracked down this individual's favourite shoeshine stall and sat waiting patiently – his shoes so beautifully buffed a regimental sergeant-major would have been impressed – until the elusive gentleman showed up.

Around this time the British Customs and Excise took

exception to bands that were on tour in America returning with large quantities of very cheap musical instruments. They were particularly concerned about drum kits and classic electric guitars that could be bought new from Manny's in New York for less than half the price back home or picked up in the pawn shops for a snip. Eventually a mammoth raid was carried out in which it seemed every working band was visited. There was some fining and general ticking off, rather than executions, but for months afterwards a Mr Snuggs from the Excise would call up guitar players to say he'd seen them on *Top Of The Pops* and could they explain exactly how they had come by that rather nice 1953 sunburst Gibson Les Paul.

On our return to the UK we settled back into the routine of touring, working extensively on the university circuit and in Europe, including an outdoor show in Germany where some students, inspired by a year that had seen the Paris *évènements* and radical activity throughout Europe and the US, decided entry should be free to all and that it would be appropriate to gatecrash the event. Using VW camper vans, they substituted the Californian surf ethic with a battering ram strapped to the roof.

Just before Christmas 1968 we had one last crack at the singles market: 'Point Me At The Sky' was our third attempt since 'Emily' and our third consecutive failure. The light dawned, we decided to treat the single-buying public with disdain, and duly ordained ourselves an 'albums only' band for the following eleven years.

Our next album was a score for the film *More*, directed by Barbet Schroeder. We had appeared in Peter Whitehead's 1967 documentary *Tonite! Let's All Make Love In London*, and in 1968 we had provided a score for a film called *The Committee* by Peter Sykes with Paul Jones in the lead role, although our contribution had been more of a collection of sound effects than music.

This film, however, promised to be a more serious project.

Barbet, a protégé of Jean-Luc Godard, approached us with the film virtually complete and edited. Despite these constraints and a fairly desperate deadline, Barbet was an easy man to work with – we were paid £600 each, a substantial amount in 1968, for eight days' work around Christmas – and there was little pressure to provide Oscar-winning songs or a Hollywood-style soundtrack. In fact, complementing the various mood sequences, Roger came up with a number of songs for the film that became part of our live shows for some time after.

A lot of the moods in the film – a slow-moving, fairly frank and moralistic tale of a German student who travels to Ibiza and finds himself on a fatal descent into hard drugs – were ideally suited to some of the rumblings, squeaks and sound textures we produced on a regular basis night after night. There was no budget for a dubbing studio with a frame-count facility, so we sat in a viewing theatre, timed the sequences carefully (it's amazing how accurate a stopwatch can be), and then went into Pye Studios in Marble Arch, where we worked with the experienced in-house engineer Brian Humphries.

A major tour of the UK in spring 1969 ended at the Royal Festival Hall in July, at an event we called 'More Furious Madness From The Massed Gadgets of Auximenes'. This was another landmark show – and one of my personal favourites in the same way that 'Games For May' remains. It is possibly less so for David who, courtesy of some bad earthing, received a bolt of electricity sufficient to hurl him across the stage and leave him vibrating mildly for the rest of the show. We decided to enhance this event with some performance art from an old Hornsey College of Art friend and one-time Stanhope Gardens inhabitant called Peter Dockley. He had created a monster costume involving a gas mask and some enormous genitalia rigged up with a reservoir to enable him to urinate on the front row of the audience. This proved very effective indeed as during 'The Labyrinth', a gloomy, rather eerie piece of music, Peter crept around the audience while we used dripping sound effects in the quad system. One unfortunate girl, possibly under chemical influences, turned to find this horrific creature sitting next to her. She screamed and rushed from the auditorium never to be heard from again, not even via her lawyer.

Part of the show also involved a piece called 'Work' using percussive noises as we built a table. We manufactured this piece of furniture on stage, using wood, a saw, hammer and nails, timed to segue into the next section by the sound of the whistling kettle on the portable stove (smoking was strictly prohibited on stage, but a stove seemed perfectly acceptable). Much of this was subsequently reused in the studio either on 'Alan's Psychedelic Breakfast' or in the abandoned *Household Objects* album. There was a plan to link with John Peel's radio show as we relaxed with the tea, although I can't recall how successful this was. The idea later resurfaced on *Wish You Were Here*, where the sound of a radio playing a song is eventually cross-faded with the recorded music. Perhaps this underlines the fact that tenacity has always been a group quality – if we like an idea we rarely give it up and then only if it has been declared clinically dead.

Over the summer we worked on *Ummagumma*, a double album. The first two sides captured our live sound at the time with a set – 'Astronomy', 'Careful With That Axe', 'Set The Controls' and 'Saucer' – recorded in June at Mother's in Birmingham (a kind of Midlands version of Middle Earth, and a club we were very fond of) and Manchester College of Commerce. On our later live albums, we would record up to twenty separate nights. For *Ummagumma* the choice was limited to the better of the two versions, and there was very little repair or overdub work. The second album on *Ummagumma* was made up of half a side from each of us. On its release in October 1969, the record got generally enthusiastic reviews, although I don't think we were that taken with it. It was fun to make, however, and a useful exercise, the individual sections proving, to my mind, that the parts were not as great as the sum.

To create my section, 'The Grand Vizier's Garden Party', I drew on available resources, recruiting my wife Lindy, an accomplished flute player, to add some woodwind. For my own part, I attempted to do a variation on the obligatory drum solo – I have never been a fan of gymnastic workouts at the kit, by myself or anyone else. Norman Smith was particularly helpful on the flute arrangements, the studio manager less so by reprimanding me for editing my own tapes.

Rick was perhaps the most enthusiastic of all for the format of the record, embracing the concept of a more classical approach to his part, while both David's and Roger's sections included songs that ended up as band repertoire. I think that both 'The Narrow Way' and 'Grantchester Meadows' were played in the 'Massed Gadgets' show while Roger's 'Several Species…' indicated the influence of his budding friendship with Ron Geesin, whose arranging skills we later called on to assist us in completing 'Atom Heart Mother'.

Roger and David had also been working with Syd, helping him put together his first solo album, *The Madcap Laughs* with input from Robert Wyatt and other members of the Soft Machine. There was still a belief that Syd's creative flow could be restimulated, but it proved extremely difficult to marshal his songs into any kind of order, or to realise their potential. Syd released a second solo album, *Barrett*, later the same year. This proved to be his last recording, despite further attempts to encourage him back into the studio. From then on, Syd became increasingly reclusive, eventually returning to Cambridge and rarely venturing out. There is something particularly sad about such a gifted songwriter producing so much good work and then being unable or unwilling to continue.

We rounded off 1969 with a bizarre experience in December working for the Italian director Michelangelo Antonioni on his film *Zabriskie Point*. After our happy encounter with Barbet Schroeder we liked the idea of working with film – it fitted with our desire to work outside the normal round of records and gigs. Antonioni's project – a movie mixing together student radicals, West Coast psychedelia and the destruction of society as we then knew it – was part of the death throes of MGM studios, who in a final desperate bid to survive had offered Antonioni a hefty budget, hoping that the success of his film *Blow Up* heralded a new era of European cinema.

Suddenly we were in Rome, staying at the palatial Hotel Massimo D'Azeglio. What we took a short time to adjust to was that the studio was paying a fixed daily rate for accommodation and food. If you didn't use it you lost it. Due to the short notice of the project, and Michelangelo's work schedule, we could only get time in the studio between midnight and nine in the morning. This meant a routine of trying to sleep during the day, cocktails from seven to nine, and dinner until eleven – relying on the help of the sommelier to use up the $40 per head allowance – before we rolled down the Via Cavour, exchanging banter with the hookers on the street corners, to the studios where we would do battle with the director and his film.

The problem was that Michelangelo wanted total control, and since he couldn't make the music himself he exercised control by selection. Consequently each piece had to be finished rather than roughed out, then redone, rejected and resubmitted – Roger would go over to Cinecittà to play him the tapes in the afternoon. Antonioni would never take a first effort, and frequently complained that the music was too strong and overpowered the visual image. One device we tried was a mood tape. We sub-mixed various versions and overdubs in such a way that he could sit at the mixer and literally add a more lyrical, romantic or despairing feel by sliding the mixer fader up or down. It still didn't work. Antonioni ended up using an assortment of pieces from other musicians like Jerry Garcia and John Fahey, and despite a dramatic and explosive finale, the film bombed critically and commercially.

Continuing our policy of recycling anything remotely useful, we quietly gathered up all our out-takes. There was sure to be some opportunity to use them in the future.

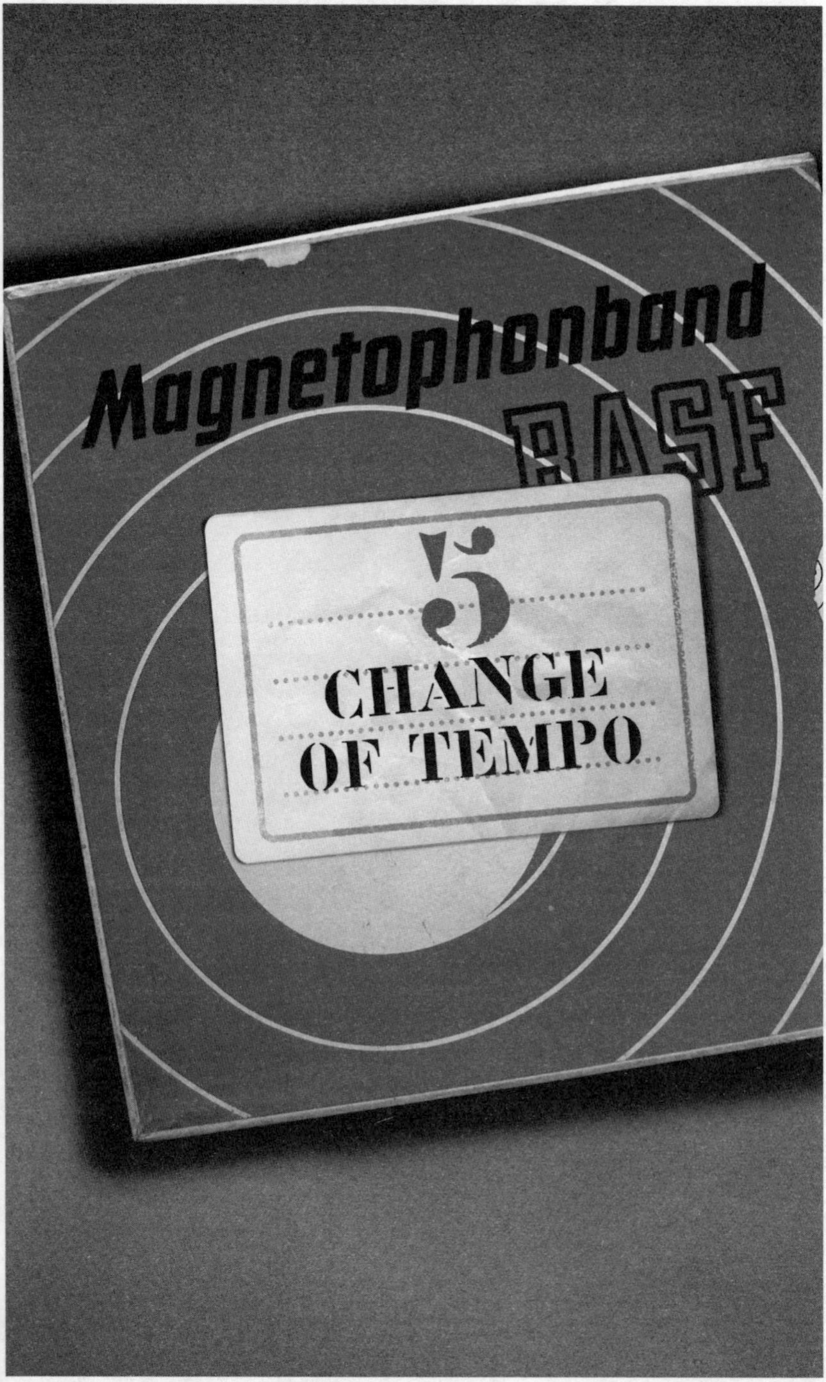
Magnetophonband
BASF
5
CHANGE
OF TEMPO

THE BATH & WEST Showground in Shepton Mallet, a small town in Somerset, was the site of the Bath Festival of Blues & Progressive Music in June 1970. We had chosen this event, in the depths of the English countryside, as an opportunity to perform 'Atom Heart Mother', an ambitious piece we had recently recorded complete with French horns, tuba, trumpets, trombones, a solo cello and a twenty-strong choir – the kitchen sink must have been unavailable for session work.

The festival, a two-day extravaganza, in an attempt to emulate the scale of Woodstock the year before, had imported an array of groups from both sides of the Atlantic. There was a hefty quota of headline acts from the States, including Jefferson Airplane, Santana, the Byrds and Steppenwolf, alongside the British bands: as well as ourselves, the bill featured Fairport Convention and Led Zeppelin. In an attempt to keep up with the John Paul Joneses, it seemed entirely appropriate that we should make the grandiose, but logistically challenging, gesture of herding the entire complement of backing musicians out to the wilds of the West Country.

Rock festivals by nature tend to start off with good intentions and then slide gently into chaos as the crowds increase and technical problems multiply, particularly if Mother Nature takes a hand – although on this occasion the weather was idyllic. This volatility has since become one of the things people seem most to look forward to: much of the anticipation for attending Glastonbury seems to be the prospect of continuing the great Woodstock tradition of some decent mud bathing.

The police would be warned to expect an attendance of approximately half the expected number, since if they knew the true total in advance each event would have been banned for failing every conceivable health and safety provision. At this particular festival I think Freddy Bannister, the promoter, finally had the requisite nervous breakdown as the full horror of what he had taken on revealed itself.

In order to get past the traffic clogging up every major and side road on the way, we had enjoyed a desperate drive up the wrong side of the road. The coach carrying our backing musicians had a driver with a far less cavalier approach. He took the safer, surer, but eight-and-a-half-hour option. Even the brass players, noted as a breed for their resilience, were showing signs of wear and tear by the time they were finally decanted. After all their tribulations, they found they had in fact arrived far too early since the festival was running well behind schedule: the programme note 'All times subject to change' was frequently a euphemism for 'Everything will be running about half a day late'.

Sensing the way things were going we tried to negotiate an earlier slot by changing places with one wild-eyed guitar hero. Anxious but unable to help, he apologised explaining that having just loaded up on the pharmaceuticals he thought necessary to give his best performance, he lacked sufficient supplies to reach those heights again, and so would be obliged to stick to the running order.

Our original slot had been 10.15 p.m. By the time we were finally able to lead our merry band of musicians on stage – most of whom had never encountered anything quite so chaotically magnificent even in their long and varied careers – dawn was breaking. As a result events conspired to give us a dramatic backdrop that really lifted the impact of our arrival on stage. The choir's conductor, John Aldiss, did a magnificent job of controlling the choir and orchestra, and we managed to stagger through the show, even though the tuba player found that some bucolic reveller had poured a pint of beer down the horn of his instrument.

One might have thought that after such an event a short rest would have been in order. However, it was festival time, so we found ourselves leaving the stage and on another demon drive through the early morning mist straight back to London to catch a flight to Holland to play another, but less extravagant, festival the following night. With no time to recover, we were plunged back into exactly the same kind of scenario, although at least this time we were minus the orchestra, a merciful release for both parties.

'Atom Heart Mother' had been assembled during a number of rehearsals after we returned from our stay in Rome courtesy of Michelangelo Antonioni. Once we had settled on the nucleus of the piece (a theme supplied I think by David), everyone else had contributed, not only musically, but also in devising the overall dynamics. I can't remember now if we had decided to create a longer piece or whether it just snowballed, but it was a way of operating we were starting to feel comfortable with.

After some lengthy sessions in early 1970, we had created a very long, rather majestic, but quite unfocused and still unfinished piece. One way to develop such a piece was to play it live, so we played shortened versions, sometimes dubbed 'The Amazing Pudding', at a number of gigs. Gradually we added, subtracted and multiplied the elements, but still seemed to lack an essential something. I think we had always intended to record the track, but the songwriters must have all felt they had hit a specific block, as in the early summer we decided to hand over the music as it existed to Ron Geesin and asked him if he could add some orchestral colour and choral parts.

I had been introduced to Ron through Sam Jonas Cutler. Sam

had given up a career as a special needs teacher to become a tour manager. His earlier skills no doubt helped him greatly in his involvement with the world of rock'n' roll: he had worked with the Rolling Stones on their 1969 tour of the US, including the ill-fated free concert at Altamont, and later with the Grateful Dead.

Ron Geesin is a talented musician and arranger, as well as a virtuoso performer on banjo and harmonium, when his style might best be described as ragtime poetry on speed. He had also built for himself what was effectively one of the first electronic home studios. Ron, who was not much older than us, but appeared significantly wiser with his demeanour of a wild-bearded professor, had a basement in Elgin Crescent in Notting Hill where he pursued his craft, surrounded by a collection of recording machines, spools, miles of tape, and a number of bespoke and proprietary musical devices.

Although this might sound chaotic, one of Ron's great strengths was that he was very well organised. Working with recorded music on tape has one inherent and major problem: all tape looks exactly the same, which is a logistical nightmare. Unless you keep very close tabs on which bit of tape has been transferred from one spool to another and immediately keep a record of the changeover, it can take you days to find the piece of tape you need again. Due to his meticulous organisational skills, Ron never seemed to have a problem laying his hands on the correct piece.

Ron had been working on his own for quite some time, so his idiosyncratic techniques and modus operandi were entirely his own. He had interested both Roger and me in home production and his influence can clearly be detected in one element of Roger's contribution to *Ummagumma*, namely 'Several Species'. Roger and Ron also worked together on the music for an unusual medical documentary called *The Body* – based on the book by Anthony

Outside the Palm House at Kew, 1968. Storm, who took the photograph, assures me that the proffered piece of jewellery was in fact 'the Ring of Agamotto'. What an extraordinary piece of luck that he was able to find such a rare gem on sale in Portobello Market.

The Hendrix tour, December 1967. Jimi Hendrix with Pink Floyd, Mitch Mitchell and Noel Redding from the Hendrix Experience, and assorted members of Amen Corner, the Move, Eire Apparent and the Outer Limits.

David Gilmour with Jokers Wild – from left: 'Sunshine' Geoff Whittaker, David, Johnny Gordon, Clive Welham and Tony Sainty.

One of the few photographs in existence showing Pink Floyd as a five-man outfit in January 1968 – Syd's position hovering at the rear may have been a fluke or more deliberate.

David recording *Saucerful Of Secrets* at EMI, 1968.

Capt Mason, R.N. during a break on the Norfolk Broads with (from left, above) Lindy, Roger and Judy.

At the Scene Club in New York, July 1968.

Roger attacks his percussive duties with customary determination. I'm glad I'm not a cymbal.

Next to the Tiger Moth used in the promo film for 'Point Me At The Sky', shot at Biggin Hill airfield.

All our equipment laid out for inspection on the back cover of the sleeve for *Ummagumma*.

Syd in his London flat in 1970, by Mick Rock.

Ron Geesin, and (below) Rick and David, during the recording sessions for 'Atom Heart Mother'.

On the beach at St Tropez, summer 1970. Back row, left to right – Miv Watts holding Naomi Watts, Peter Watts, Linda O'Rourke, Lindy Mason, Steve O'Rourke, Judy Waters holding Gaia Wright, Alan Styles, Juliette Wright. Front row, left to right: Ben Watts, David, me, Roger, Rick holding Jamie Wright.

Alan Styles, Peter Watts and Roger on the road.

David and Roger during filming for *Live At Pompeii* in 1971, recreating the outdoor amphitheatre feel for continuity purposes.

I had a brief flirtation with a perspex drum kit made by the American company Fibes. I was captivated by the idea of an 'invisible' kit, but in fact they were very difficult to record successfully.

Peter Dockley's huge inflatable octopus makes a tentacular entrance as it gatecrashes the Crystal Palace Garden party in May 1971.

Discussion backstage at the Brighton Dome, January 1972.

The might of the Pink Floyd Football Club First XI, and cheerleaders, ready to take on, and draw 3-3 with, a team from the band Family in January 1972.

Rick and (left) Tony Howard in Japan, playing with newly acquired cameras.

Steve O'Rourke, sheltering from the elements at Hakone Festival, Kanagawa, Japan in August 1971.

Group portraits from the *Dark Side* era.

Smith – which was released in 1970 and on one track of which, 'Give Birth To A Smile', Rick, David and I also played.

Ron passed on a variety of tricks with Revox tape recorders hooked up in tandem that went well beyond the bounds of standard use as recommended in the manufacturer's manual. He did all his own wiring and instructed me in the rudiments of soldering. With stereotypical Scottish parsimony he would collect discarded tape from professional studios. After erasing the tape for reuse, he would then splice together any half reels to make up a full one, or painstakingly re-make any of the studio's edits that failed to come up to his own high standards. Apart from anything else Ron taught me to splice tape beautifully.

One pleasant spin-off of this relationship was that Ron wrote the music for the soundtrack of one of my father's documentaries – *The History Of Motoring* – and I like to think they both enjoyed the experience. My father in particular was delighted by the fact that Ron always turned up not only with the music but also with some new home-made gadget or cable that he had purpose-built to simplify the transfer of the music from Ron's machine to the film.

Ron seemed an ideal choice to create the arrangements on 'Atom Heart Mother'. He understood the technicalities of composition and arranging, and his ideas were radical enough to steer us away from the increasingly fashionable but extremely ponderous rock orchestral works of the era. At the time arrangements of such epics tended to involve fairly conservative thinking; classical music graduates had been indoctrinated with a lack of sympathy for rock and 'crossing over' was still seen as something of a betrayal of their years of discipline and training. The good news was that with Ron at the helm, it was unlikely that we'd end up with 'The London Symphonic Philharmonia Plays Pink Floyd'.

Ron set to work on our piece, and with little further input from us, he arrived at Abbey Road armed with a sheaf of scores ready to record. He immediately ran up against a major hurdle. The session players balked at being directed by Ron, who they perceived as belonging to the world of rock music. Revenge could only be exacted in the confines of the studio, and my God how the blood could flow! In the case of Ron, an actual human sacrifice in the studio itself was being offered up.

As Ron waved his baton hopefully, they made as much trouble as they could. Ron had not only written some technically demanding parts, but the phrasing he wanted was unusual. The musicians hated this even more. With microphones open they knew every comment would be noted and their discreet laughter, clock-watching, and constant interruptions of 'Please sir, what does this mean?' meant that recording was at a standstill, while the chances of Ron being had up on a manslaughter charge increased logarithmically by the second.

This was not his only problem. At the time the piece was recorded EMI had just taken delivery of the latest in recording technology, the new eight-track Studer recorders. These utilised one-inch-wide tape, and with admirable caution EMI issued a directive that no edits were to be done on this, as they were worried about the quality of any splicing.

Unfortunately 'Atom Heart Mother' is twenty-four minutes long. Roger and I embarked on what can only be described as an Odyssean voyage to record the backing track. In order to keep tracks free for the overdubs we had bass and drums on two tracks, and the whole recording had to be done in one pass. Playing the piece without any other instruments meant that getting through it without mistakes demanded the full range of our limited musicianship; matters such as tempo had to be left in abeyance. The delights of quantizing – using computers to digitally adjust tempos without affecting pitch – were still some twenty years in the future.

Sure enough the finished piece lacked the metronomic timekeeping that would have made life easier for everyone. Instead the rhythm track accelerated and then lurched back to the correct tempo in a volatile fashion that Ron now had to take into account. The day was saved by John Aldiss, the choirmaster. John was a former King's College, Cambridge choral scholar who had formed the John Aldiss Choir, noted for performing works by contemporary classical composers. At the time, he was also Choral Professor at the Guildhall School of Music in London. His disciplined classical choir had (it must be noted) a far more positive attitude and plenty of experience of dealing with orchestras. With their unruffled help, the recording was completed. However, there was another problem we were unaware of at the time. We had been forced to supply relatively high levels of backing track to the orchestra on monitor speakers, some of which had been picked up by their microphones. This unerasable spill forever ensured that 'Atom Heart Mother' lacked the sonic clarity we have always strived for.

My report card comments for the 'Atom Heart Mother' track would be: good idea, could try harder. 'Alan's Psychedelic Breakfast' on the second side is a similar example. This was a sound picture of an English breakfast, starting with the flare of a match lighting a gas ring, followed by the sound of the bacon sizzling away, along with dripping taps and other old favourites from the sound library. Why we used our crew member Alan Styles as the protagonist, I have no idea. Roger, Rick and David each managed to produce a song to complete the second side – including a favourite in David's 'Fat Old Sun'. It would appear that the threat of being incarcerated in Abbey Road for life, with no chance of parole, was sufficient to galvanise even the most reticent songwriters to perform.

The title of *Atom Heart Mother* was a last-minute affair. Under pressure to come up with a name we scanned the evening papers for an idea, and saw an article about a woman who had given birth after being fitted with a pacemaker. The headline provided the title. The cow cover was an inspired piece of work, conceived by Storm and John Blake, which we linked to the album by giving the individual sections of the 'Atom Heart Mother' track names like 'Funky Dung' and 'Breast Milky'. Storm remembers that when he showed the cover to EMI, one of the executives screamed at him, 'Are you mad? Do you want to destroy this record company?…'

Having committed 'Atom Heart' to vinyl, and after the pastoral adventures at Shepton Mallet, the next orchestral rendition of the piece was at Blackhill's second free concert in London. 'Lose Your Head At Hyde Park' on 18th July 1970 promised to present ourselves, Edgar Broughton, Kevin Ayers and the Whole World, the Third Ear Band, 'and thousands of beautiful people'. This event had a much less spontaneous feel than the original free concert: more restrictions, a larger backstage area and a VIP section as hierarchical as anything organised by the court of the Sun King. The experience had lost a certain amount of its charm, or maybe we had become more jaundiced.

We also took the show to Europe that month. By now we were becoming more adept at working with an orchestra. There were still plenty of opportunities for crises, though – there was one gig in Aachen where we arrived, set everything up and then discovered that all the sheet music had been left behind. Tony Howard was phoned in London and given the mission of flying them over on the next plane. Determined not to have to face the humiliation of admitting our mistake, we stalled for time by doing an endless sound check. At the very least we must have impressed the brass section with our commitment to perfection.

We interrupted the protracted recording work on *Atom Heart*

Mother to do a short French tour, and used the opportunity to meet Roland Petit, the director of the Ballet de Marseille. Sometime earlier, Roland had contacted Steve asking us to write a new piece of music for his company – and we arranged to have a brief meeting with him in Paris during the summer of 1970, en route to a combined holiday/mini-tour of the south of France. We still hadn't learnt that work and pleasure is a combination to be avoided if possible.

In four second-hand E-types and one Lotus Elan – yet another car dealer had spotted us all coming – we hammered down the long, straight French roads, leaving ominous trails of blue oil smoke in our wake. We had a particularly successful time with Roland, not least because on a French public holiday he managed at short notice to find Roger, myself and our respective wives a terrific hotel, and a sensational restaurant to eat in for the evening.

We then sped on down to the Côte d'Azur to rendezvous with Rick and David, who had not lingered in Paris. Initially we stayed in a hotel on the front at Cannes. This was pure vacation: we learnt to waterski under the tuition of an extraordinarily strong Frenchman, who was able to hold up his pupils bodily while they learnt to ski. His great experience on skis was only undermined by his tenuous grasp of English. It was only later on we discovered that his insistent command of 'No pushing' should actually have been 'No pulling'.

We were on the Riviera for a package of Festival appearances, playing at lovely locations surrounded by pine trees and with a view of the Mediterranean. After performing at the Antibes Jazz Festival, we rented a huge villa near St Tropez where the base crew, band and management, plus families, could stay while we did further gigs at Fréjus and other resorts along the Côte d'Azur. These were still quite low-budget days, and the house we rented was not on a promontory jutting into the ocean, but inland in the middle of some scrubland.

The atmosphere was not always a scene of domesticity despite the presence of wives and assorted children. On one occasion I met a couple of strange women acting suspiciously in the villa. Challenging them to explain themselves I suddenly recognised them as being Steve O'Rourke and Peter Watts getting ready for a night out at a St Tropez club, both in full drag. Thankfully I was suffering from a combination of food poisoning and sunstroke and so was unable to join them. As an experiment in communal living it was not a huge success. Although when there were just four of us travelling in close proximity on tour it could occasionally get quite tense, with so many more people, there were endless opportunities for friction.

My relationship with Roger was in any case going through a temporary *froideur*. The trouble stemmed from an earlier incident when Roger and I and our respective wives had somehow got onto the subject of Roger's infidelity on the road. Roger had found some difficulty in tolerating my joining in with the girls' censorious tutting at his behaviour, mainly because I had been no better, I'd simply left out the confession part. On this occasion I would have to concede that the meter was well into the duplicity rather than diplomacy zone, and it took Roger some time to forgive this particular episode.

Judy Waters remembers the pang of jealousy she felt when Lindy and I contrived to come up with an excuse to leave St Tropez early. Waving gaily we put another few litres of oil in the increasingly smoky Lotus and headed for Yugoslavia…

The chance for rest and recuperation was short. The American tour that followed almost immediately coincided with the release of *Atom Heart Mother*, and so we felt obliged to repeat the orchestral experience. David and Steve flew to New York to book the musicians, putting together separate brass sections and choirs for the East and West Coast legs of the tour – announced in Los

Angeles by a forty-foot billboard of Storm's cow over Sunset Strip. The American session players, under the baton of Peter Phillips, were both very able and relaxed about playing different kinds of music – and I am happy to report the total absence of any recalcitrance, jobsworthiness or beer-drenched tubas.

By now American touring was becoming more routine as the novelty wore off: this was our second tour in 1970 – we'd already been over in May for several weeks. In addition, a communal fear of flying often led us to undertake eight-hour car trips in the mistaken belief we would find this less stressful. In fact, of course, these mammoth journeys simply induced terminal boredom. In the Hilton in Scottsdale, we fell back on any opportunity for a wager – I recall David riding a motorbike through our hotel restaurant for one particular bet. The diners either thought that this was normal, or that he was packing a gun, because they completely ignored him.

On the first tour of 1970 the most significant show had to be playing the Fillmore East in New York. Bill Graham was not sure we could fill a 3,000-seat theatre, especially as our last date in the city had only been a 200-seater club, so instead of promoting the show himself he rented the theatre out to us for $3,000. We sold out. It was the most money we had made, and contributed to an ongoing dissatisfaction with the Tower label, which was then EMI's American operation. We were building good audiences, but this was not being reflected in our record sales. Someone or something was at fault and, confident as always that the blame was not ours, we made a note to do something about it as soon as possible.

Fillmore East was also notable for two other reasons. We had a scruffy-looking bunch of blokes ejected from our dressing room only to discover later that they were members of the Band, Bob Dylan's backing group – which included Robbie Robertson and

Levon Helm – and of course recording artists in their own right. This was particularly embarrassing for us since *Music From Big Pink* was a favoured album in all our record collections. And we also met Arthur Max, the lighting designer who was working for Bill at the theatre. Arthur added his own lighting to our show that night, and his innovative skills were noted and filed away for future reference.

That May 1970 tour of America had come to an abrupt end when all our equipment, parked in a rental truck outside the Royal Orleans Hotel in the centre of New Orleans, was stolen during the night. Thankfully this was by far the most luxurious hotel of the tour so if we were to be marooned, better it should be there than anywhere else. The other advantage was that the luxurious pool on the first-floor terrace was staffed by attractive girls who diluted our grief with a complimentary bar service.

More practically one of them had a boyfriend in the FBI and he came down to see if he could help. He indicated as tactfully as he could that it was not impossible that the local police might be able to be more helpful if we offered a reward. We left it up to Steve to resolve the problem. To our astonishment the equipment reappeared a day later (short of a couple of guitars). There was obviously an imaginative community policing initiative in place whereby officers could offer an all-in, one-stop service of removal and recovery… The only real puzzle now was what the reward should be to the police who returned it. Their suggestion of 'Let your conscience be your guide' was not much help since our conscience thought they deserved nothing. However, pragmatically we decided we might want to return to New Orleans one day. Although we had the equipment back we decided not to reinstate the gigs we had cancelled, and returned home forthwith.

After the *Atom Heart* tour of the States that autumn, we were on an English tour all the way through to the end of the year.

Although we wanted the workload, we were probably unaware how exhausting it all was. But at the start of 1971, we turned our attention and any energies we did have to our next album, which we started at EMI in January.

With no new songs, we devised innumerable exercises to try and speed up the process of creating musical ideas. This included playing on separate tracks with no reference to what the rest of us were doing – we may have agreed a basic chord structure, but the tempo was random. We simply suggested moods such as 'first two minutes romantic, next two up tempo'. These sound notes were called 'Nothings 1–24' and the choice of name was apt. After some weeks not much of value had emerged, and certainly no complete songs. There were few even worth considering as working ideas. After 'Nothings' we went on to produce 'Son Of Nothings', followed by 'Return Of The Son Of Nothings', which eventually became the working title for the new album.

The most useful piece was simply a sound, a single note struck on the piano and played through a Leslie speaker. This curious device, normally used with a Hammond organ, employs a rotating horn that amplifies the given sound. The horn, revolving at a variable speed, creates a Doppler effect, just as a car passing the listener at constant speed appears to change its note as it goes by. By putting the piano through the Leslie, this wonder note of Rick's had an element of the sound of Asdic, the submarine hunter, about it. We could never re-create the feeling of this note in the studio, especially the particular resonance between the piano and the Leslie, and so the demo version was used for the album, cross-fading into the rest of the track.

Combined with a wistful guitar phrase from David, we had enough inspiration to devise a complete piece, which evolved into 'Echoes'; its final, slightly meandering shape had a rather pleasant sense of slow pacing and elongated construction. This felt like a real development of the techniques we had hinted at in *A Saucerful Of Secrets* and *Atom Heart Mother*. And it certainly felt much more controlled than having to do the damned thing in one take as we'd had to on 'Atom Heart Mother', since we could assemble the music using cross-fades on the mixing desk.

The guitar sound in the middle section of 'Echoes' was created inadvertently by David plugging in a wah-wah pedal back to front. Sometimes great effects are the results of this kind of pure serendipity, and we were always prepared to see if something might work on a track. The grounding we'd received from Ron Geesin in going beyond the manual had left its mark.

This experimentation could be seen as either a brave radicalism or an enormous waste of expensive studio time. Either way it allowed us to teach ourselves techniques which might at first be clearly nonsensical but eventually lead to something usable. One still unused experiment from this time was an exploration of backward vocals. A phrase written out backwards letter for letter and then read out will not sound correct when reversed, but a spoken phrase recorded and played backwards can be learnt and recited. This gives a very odd effect when it is in turn played backwards. 'Neeagadelouff' was one I remember: it should come out as 'fooled again'.

The final version of 'Echoes', running at twenty-two minutes, took up one entire side of the album. Unlike CD technology, vinyl imposed a certain set of restrictions, since loud passages actually took up more of the surface, and in any case even playing *pianissimo* throughout it would be difficult to record more than half an hour on any one side. We now had to find the rest of the record. It seems a little strange in hindsight that we ran 'Echoes' as the second side. It may be that we were still thinking, perhaps under record company influence, that we should have something suitable for radio play to open an album.

'One Of These Days' was built round a bass guitar sound that Roger created by feeding the output through a Binson Echorec unit. The Binson had been a mainstay of our sound for many years, starting in the Syd Barrett era – noticeably on 'Interstellar Overdrive', 'Astronomy Domine' and 'Pow R. Toc H.' – and it was really only digital technology that superseded it. The Binson used a rotating steel drum surrounded by tape heads. By selecting different heads it gave a range of repeat patterns to any signal fed into it. The sound quality was horribly degraded, but if you describe hiss as white noise it makes the effect more palatable.

There were various alternative echo units around which were similar in technology but lacked the same sound quality. The Italian-made Binson, though, was highly fragile and not suited to the rigours of a life on the road. Like a highly trained rifleman, Peter Watts could often strip them down and reassemble them at speed during a gig to perform running repairs in order to get at least one moved back up to the front line.

The bass line on 'One Of These Days' was played in unison by Roger and David. One of the basses needed new strings and we dispatched one of the road crew to the West End to replenish our stocks. He went AWOL for three hours, during which the recording was completed, using the old strings. When he eventually returned, we suspected he had been visiting his girlfriend who ran a boutique. His protestations of innocence were rather undermined by the smart new pair of trousers he reappeared in. The song included, unusually, a bass solo as well as one of my rare vocal performances, and an example of one experiment that did make it out of the lab. The line was recorded at double-tape speed using a falsetto voice; the tape was then replayed at slow speed. There are times when it really does seem necessary to do things in the most complicated way possible.

The titles of the other songs on that side related very much to our lives of the period. 'San Tropez', a song Roger brought in complete and ready to record, was inspired by the Floyd expedition to the south of France the previous summer and the house we had rented there. Roger, Judy, Lindy and myself used to play the Chinese tile game mah-jong on a fairly regular basis and this craze provided the inspiration for the title 'A Pillow Of Winds', the name of one of the scoring combinations.

'Fearless' was an overused expression – a soccer-inspired equivalent of 'awesome' – that had come from Tony Gorvitch, the manager of Family and a good friend of Steve and Tony Howard's. The football theme was continued in the fade-out with Liverpool's Kop choir singing 'You'll Never Walk Alone' – it was odd that Roger was so keen to do this, considering that he was a committed Arsenal fan. Tony Gorvitch had also supplied us with the expressions 'elbow' – as in 'being given the…' – and 'Who's Norman?' The latter was a band room phrase we used to indicate somebody we didn't know and whom we might wish to have removed – maybe the technique we had used on the Band at the Fillmore.

Finally there was 'Seamus'. In a rather embarrassed way I can only describe this as a novelty track. Dave was looking after a dog, the Seamus in question, for Steve Marriott of the Small Faces. Steve had trained Seamus to howl whenever music was played. It was extraordinary, so we set up a couple of guitars and recorded the piece in an afternoon. Curiously we did it all over again when we made the *Live At Pompeii* film, this time using another dog, called Mademoiselle Nobs. On the positive side, even when hard pressed, at least we resisted the temptation to construct an entire album of barking dogs, and to audition a clutch of session dogs desperate to make it in the music business.

Overall, the whole album was immensely satisfying to make. As *Atom Heart Mother* had been a bit of a sidetrack, and

Ummagumma a live album combined with solo pieces, *Meddle* was the first album we had worked on together as a band in the studio since *A Saucerful Of Secrets* three years earlier. It is relaxed, and quite loose, and 'Echoes' has, I think, lasted well. Certainly, compared to its predecessor, *Atom Heart Mother*, *Meddle* seems refreshingly straightforward. David certainly has a great deal of affection for this album, which for him contains a clear indication of a way forward.

The principal *Meddle* recordings were split between EMI and AIR London with a small amount of work carried out at Morgan Studios in West Hampstead. This was because EMI, in another display of their innate conservatism, would not commit to the new sixteen-track tape machines. In a fit of high dudgeon, we insisted we had to have access to one and marched off to AIR, where we did the bulk of the work.

AIR was George Martin's studio perched high above Oxford Street in London's West End. After many years, George had moved on from EMI and set up his own dream studio, taking with him Ken Townsend, the studio manager at Abbey Road, to ensure the highest standards. His studios, which were absolutely state of the art, had a very different atmosphere to Abbey Road, which was now actually in dire need of an overhaul and upgrade. Commercial studios were being designed for rock bands rather than as all-encompassing facilities, since rock music was where the new clients were coming from.

The recording of *Meddle* was spread over a considerable amount of time, not because we were locked in the studios but because once again we were on the road so much during 1971: when I look back at the calendar, I find we were in Germany in February, various European countries in March, the UK in May, Europe in June and July, the Far East and Australia in August, Europe in September, and the States yet again in October and November.

To fill the gap while *Meddle* was in the works, we fell back on that age-old music industry solution: the compilation album of singles and other offcuts. *Relics* – 'a bizarre collection of antiques & curios' – featured just one original song, Roger's 'Biding My Time', in which Rick finally inflicted his trombone playing on us. *Relics* came out in May, just before we played at the Crystal Palace Garden Party. This was our first major concert in London for some time and one of the outdoor events that the British can be very good at – one-day events lack the marathon aspects of the three-day festivals, and have more of a feel of the nation's penchant for bandstands. A curious mix of bands was on this particular bill, including Leslie West and Mountain, ourselves, the Faces and Quiver, the latter including Willie Wilson.

It was an afternoon concert, and our light show was non-existent, but with the help of our art college chum Peter Dockley and friends, we submerged a huge inflatable octopus in the lake in front of the stage. As a climax to the show the octopus was inflated and came rearing out from the lake. The moment would have been improved if a number of over-enthusiastic and mind-altered fans had not stripped off and taken to the water; in scenes reminiscent of *Twenty Thousand Leagues Under The Sea*, these lunatics got tangled with the air pipes and threatened to spoil the performance by thoughtlessly drowning. The event was promoted by Tony Smith, who went on to manage Genesis. Tony remembers that in the aftermath of the show he and his team spent a lot of time clearing up not the usual festival detritus but a shoal of dead fish from the lake who had expired from shock and/or awe.

Of all the overseas tours, our first visit to Japan in August 1971 was a particular success. The record company organised a press conference (something which we generally hate) and presented us with our first gold records. Although these were completely bogus, as they had not been earned through sales, we nonetheless appreciated the gesture.

The real reason for the success of this tour was an outdoor show at Hakone. Not only was this a beautiful venue set in countryside a couple of hours outside Tokyo, but a festival audience in Japan was a lot less inhibited than one at an indoor show. For many years these indoor audiences were rather restrained by rock industry standards. Notable for being light on applause, whoopin', hollerin' and standing ovations, Japanese concerts generally start at six in the evening. The reason for this, we're told, is that public transport stops early, people live outside the city and it is too difficult for them to make two journeys. However good the reasons, this did give gigs there the atmosphere of a '*thé dansant*' and a suggestion that rock should not occupy the minds of people over thirteen. While we were in Japan we managed a trip on the bullet train, visits to temples and stone gardens and an introduction to sushi. For us, and many other bands, sushi became the sophisticated version of egg, sausage and chips on tour. A popular way of improving morale during a tour was to have the local sushi man in, armed with his knives, to bolster flagging spirits (by preparing raw fish, rather than threatening the depressives, that is).

After Japan we continued to Australia for a short tour, also our first visit, which got off to a challenging start with an outdoor show at Randwick Stadium, the racecourse in Sydney. Still not attuned to the inversion of seasons down under, we were surprised to arrive in August and find ourselves in the depths of an Australian winter, so cold I needed gloves to stop the sticks dropping from my nerveless fingers. The audience, in a testament to true Aussie grit, didn't seem to notice. We were grateful the rest of the tour was indoors.

A highlight of this trip was that we got to meet the film director George Greenough. He showed us some footage from a film he was making called *Crystal Voyager*, a documentary celebration of surfing. Using a camera strapped onto a surfer's body, he had been able to shoot film within the tubes formed by breaking waves, further enhanced by sunrises and sunsets. It was stunning. We gave George permission to use our music for his film and in return have enjoyed a reciprocal arrangement where we have used his film – updated from time to time – at virtually all our subsequent shows. For the 1994 *Division Bell* tour he supplied some new footage of even better quality to project during 'Great Gig In The Sky'.

On a stop over at Hong Kong airport heading home we phoned the Hipgnosis studio to brief Storm on the cover design for *Meddle*. The title had been hastily concocted and, maybe inspired by some Zen-like image of water gardens, we told Storm we wanted 'an ear under water'. Time differences meant that neither party was on top form for the telephone discussion, but even across the intervening miles, we could hear the sound of Storm's eyes rolling.

On the flight back to the UK, a truly alarming thunderstorm somewhere over the Himalayas terrified even the cabin crew. As the plane lurched into one deep air pocket, either Roger or David was jerked awake by the clutching hand of a terrified stewardess. This severely set back any chances of us recovering from our fear of flying. We all suffered from this, thanks to various incidents over the years. One time Steve O'Rourke had chartered an elderly DC3 to fly us and some other bands to a festival in Europe. As we sat on the tarmac a baggage cart tore a chunk out of the wing. 'Don't worry,' we were told, 'we'll have it repaired in a jiffy.' Pulling rank, we left the plane immediately and jumped on the next BEA Trident, leaving the luckless support bands to take the terror flight home. Sometime later we had been involved in a near miss with another plane on the approach to Bordeaux airport. On occasions like this, the fact that the four of us would grip our armrests in unison, beads of sweat forming, probably helped contribute to some good group bonding.

Group dinners were the focal point for all band fights, policy decisions and general jockeying for position. I now feel deeply sorry for some of the unfortunate promoters and record company people who took us out. We frequently behaved appallingly. Our table manners were generally not a problem, but our small talk let us down. We would seize the middle of the table and banish anyone we didn't know or care to know to the far ends to talk amongst themselves. Fuelled with as expensive a wine as possible, our discussion would become heated, frequently combusting into a full-scale argument. To the outsider it must have looked as if we were on the verge of splitting up. The record executive hosting the meal not only saw his expenses being disallowed, but also the prospect of being held solely responsible for the break-up of the band.

The members of the band inevitably know each other better than anyone else and therefore how to tease, hurt or indeed cheer each other up. We still treasure in group lore the night Steve O'Rourke sat down to dinner with us and announced that he was in such a good mood that nothing could upset him. Within seven minutes he had left in a fury to have dinner on his own in his room. Roger, aided and abetted by the rest of us, had with very little difficulty found the trigger that would infuriate and finally drive Steve to distraction, simply by suggesting we should discuss a reduction in Steve's commission. On another occasion, at a breakfast in the City Squire in New York, Roger announced that it was possible to tell truly creative people because their heads were always tilted slightly to the right. Conversely, the non-creative tilted to the left. Peter Barnes, who handles our publishing, remembers looking round the table. Everyone's heads, he noticed, were leaning to the right, all – that is – except Steve's.

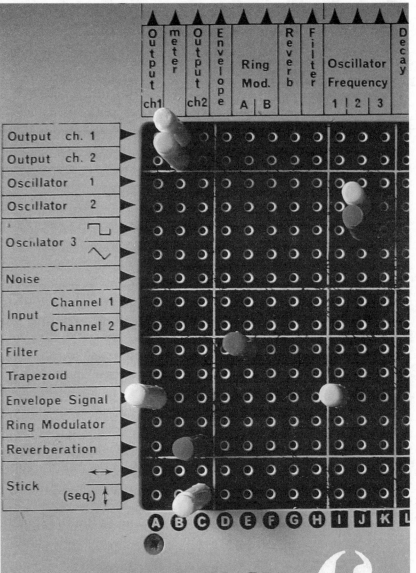

THERE IS NO
DARK SIDE 6

BY THE end of 1971, it seemed as if some of the lethargy I'd been feeling had been shaken off. Roger, talking to *Melody Maker*, was still relaying 'a feeling in the group, and certainly there's a very heavy feeling in my head, that we've really let things slide horribly and it's beginning to drive me crazy'. He looked ahead to our next UK tour as 'another bit of pressure, because there's not really enough time between now and 19th January or whenever it starts to perfect anything. To create an hour of something that's really good is very difficult.' It might have been difficult but at least he set to with a will. Roger had worked up an outline for a new album. He had some ideas, a number of songs in development – 'Time' had a verse and chorus, though no lyrics – and he had created an unusual 7:8 bass riff that seemed quite radical.

The discussions that developed *The Dark Side Of The Moon* took place at a band meeting held round the kitchen table at my house in St Augustine's Road, Camden. This was unusual, since we could see each other every day in the studios or on the road, but we must have felt we needed a change of environment to concentrate on getting our next project under way.

As well as Roger's songs, we had several fragments from earlier rehearsal sessions, and a number of more finished items. But there was as yet no coherent theme to help Roger develop his initial work. As we talked, the subject of stress emerged as a common thread, although at the time we weren't experiencing any particular angst: it was, in fact, one of the most stable periods in our domestic lives.

Roger was now living in Islington, on the New North Road. At the bottom of his garden, he had put up a workspace that was a half-step up from a potting shed. In fact, potting was done there, but rather than the common garden variety, Judy was creating her ceramics in one half of it. In the other Roger had constructed a home studio, which was modelled on the Ron Geesin approach: three Revox tape recorders, set into a workbench to facilitate the swift transfer of sounds from one machine to the others. Rick was installed in Leinster Gardens in Bayswater with Juliette and their children. I was in St Augustine's Road with Lindy. Only David had moved out to Royden in Essex, having abandoned his bachelor pad in Chelsea.

Despite all the tours, I definitely felt involved in life in Camden. Lindy and I had become friends with a number of our neighbours, and there were occasional street parties for major national events. I was certainly aware of the community, as Roger was of his; he became a committed Arsenal fan. With Judy and Lindy we would get together socially a couple of times a week, and spent a lot of time in each other's houses; I have a clear memory of being in Roger's house with Lindy when she was heavily pregnant with our first daughter Chloe.

However, despite this stability, we assembled a list of the difficulties and pressures of modern life that we particularly recognised. Deadlines, travel, the stress of flying, the lure of money, a fear of dying, and the problems of mental instability spilling over into madness... Armed with this list Roger went off to continue working on the lyrics.

Compared to the rather piecemeal approach of our previous albums, which had often been conceived in an air of desperation rather than inspiration, this felt like a considerably more constructive way of working. Continuing band discussions about the aims and aspirations of the record helped to fuel the process.

Using the specific lyrics that Roger devised, the music evolved in the rehearsal studio – and subsequently throughout the recording sessions. This gave Roger the opportunity to see any musical or lyrical gaps and to create pieces to fill them.

Once Syd left the band in 1968, the onus had fallen on Roger to write the majority of our lyrics. David and Rick were still only occasional lyricists – Rick once said that 'if the words came out like the music, and we didn't have anything else to do, then quite a few would be written'. On *The Dark Side Of The Moon* Roger took on the task with considerable style: his words gave the album our most open and specific lyrics to date – although he would later occasionally be disparaging about them, calling them 'Lower Sixth stuff'. For the first time we considered it appropriate to print them in their entirety on the album sleeve.

An early, performable version of *Dark Side* was produced within a few weeks. The first full roll-out of the piece, already called 'Dark Side Of The Moon, A Piece For Assorted Lunatics' (although it would oscillate between this title and 'Eclipse' at various times), was at the Rainbow Theatre in North London, during a four-night series of dates in mid-February 1972. The Rainbow, a former cinema, was England's version of the Avalon or Fillmore ballrooms in San Francisco, and its darkened auditorium hiding an ornate but peeling decor created a distinctive and funky ambience that harked back to our early days at the Roundhouse. It was a relief for Pete Watts and the road crew to be able to set up just the once for the four gigs: by now, we had some nine tons of equipment in three trucks, seven auditorium speakers, a new PA and a 28-input mixing desk with four quad outputs. There were gratifyingly full houses to hear the results: a couple of ads in the back of *Melody Maker* had proved sufficient for all four shows to sell out.

However, although the live version of *Dark Side* was quite

advanced, the actual recording of the piece spread throughout 1972, as it was constantly interrupted not only by our touring commitments but by a whole host of other projects: the *Obscured By Clouds* film track, the release of our own *Live At Pompeii* film, and a number of concerts with Roland Petit's Ballet de Marseille. Luckily *Dark Side* proved to be resilient enough to survive all these distractions. We did not feel oppressed by this mountain of work – on the contrary, it was evidence that we were active, professional musicians. After the doldrums we had encountered around the time of *Atom Heart Mother*, we had a revitalised sense of purpose.

Obscured By Clouds was the first of the interruptions. After the success of *More*, we had agreed to do another sound track for Barbet Schroeder. His new film was called *La Vallée* and we travelled over to France to record the music in the last week of February. The film was straight out of the aftermath of the 'Summer of Love'; it mixed a story about a band of hippies from Europe travelling in Papua New Guinea with some ethnographic reportage about the local Mapuga tribespeople (one reviewer made a connection between this documentary feel and the Robert Flaherty film on the people of Aran which had featured Steve O'Rourke's father).

We did the recording with the same method we had employed for *More*, following a rough cut of the film, using stopwatches for specific cues and creating interlinking musical moods that could be cross-faded to suit the final version. Standard rock song construction was optional: one idea could be spun out for an entire section without worrying about the niceties of choruses and middle eights, and any idea in its shortest, most raw version could work without the need to add solos and frills. I was able to try out a very early pair of electronic drums – not as advanced as later syndrums, more like electronic bongoes – on the opening sequence.

This method of evolving and modifying themes played to our

strengths, but we had no scope for self-indulgence since the recording time available was extremely tight. We only had two weeks to record the soundtrack with a short amount of time afterwards to turn it into an album. What impresses me now is that what we actually ended up with was fairly well-structured. A whole series of songs were produced, but my perception is that the song titles were hurriedly allocated under pressure to meet the film schedule.

The recording took place at Strawberry Studios, based in the Château d'Hérouville, just north of Paris, known by Elton John fans as Honky Chateau. This was a delightful and spacious recording studio in the countryside, but I can only remember being able to enjoy the location on the very last day. We locked ourselves in, put our heads down and played, wrapped up the soundtrack recording and went home. Later we had an altercation with the film company, and so, rather than releasing the soundtrack as *La Vallée*, we used the title *Obscured By Clouds*. Gratifyingly, we discovered later that the film had been retitled *La Vallée* (*Obscured By Clouds*) to tie in with our album.

We still had to remix the material for an album release, but before we could do that we had another tour to Japan. This time we had chartered a DC8 and even after loading all our equipment on board there were still plenty of spare seats. Wives and girlfriends were obvious co-travellers, but the remaining places were filled with passengers who had increasingly tenuous connections with the band, but the kind of careers that apparently allowed them to drop everything and join us at very short notice – usually a bad sign.

Until this point we had generally been unaccompanied on tour, and having the families and camp followers along for the ride noticeably changed the atmosphere. My memory is that the shows suffered as a result, and that the mood in the band room was less focused. This was exacerbated by the difference in the pace of the tour, not the intensive city-to-city routine of the States, but maybe five dates in three weeks. All this made the tour feel more like an upmarket school outing, a holiday visit rather than a working trip. We were in Japan shortly after the Sapporo Winter Olympics and headed there to enjoy some time on the pistes. At Sapporo there was Alpine music piped through a Tannoy system along the chairlift to get us in the mood, and instead of Glühwein, it was rice and sake. We had difficulty finding ski boots big enough, especially for Arthur Max, who had something like size thirteen feet. We had brought Arthur in to look after our light show, when we remembered just how inventive he had been with the lighting at the Fillmore East in 1970.

Another – comparatively straightforward – American tour followed. It was part of a band's life that you had to try and build the audience base in the States. We were by now several years into the process, and although we had not yet had a really successful album, we were able to fill the larger auditoria. Once formally engaged in the process of 'cracking America', it goes on forever.

After America and a few dates in Europe we at last had an opportunity to begin serious recording work on *Dark Side* – and for the whole of June we were able to spend time in Abbey Road. We approached the task assiduously, booking three-day sessions, sometimes whole weeks, and would all turn up for every session, everyone anxious to be involved in whatever was happening. There was an air of confidence in the studio. Since *Meddle* we had been our own producers, and so we could set our own schedule: at this point we were tending to work on the album track by track until we were happy with each piece.

The atmosphere seemed more youthful than it had been on our earlier visits to EMI. There was a new generation of engineers and tape operators – the apprentice engineers – who had grown up with rock music. As in the new breed of commercial studios, they realised the importance of a good relationship with the musicians. Gone were the days of studio managers roaming around to check that you weren't using their editing scissors or fiddling with the plugboard.

At the beginning of the *Dark Side* recordings we were assigned Alan Parsons, who had been assistant tape operator on *Atom Heart Mother*, as house engineer. After joining EMI's tape duplication facility, Alan had set his mind to becoming a recording engineer, gaining experience on the Beatles' *Abbey Road* and *Let It Be* albums, before working as a full-time engineer with Paul McCartney and George Harrison on their solo material, and with the Hollies on their singles 'He Ain't Heavy' and 'The Air That I Breathe'. Having come through the EMI apprentice system, Alan had acquired – as all EMI trainees did – a remarkably thorough knowledge of all the aspects of working in a recording studio. He was a bloody good engineer. But he also had a very good ear and was a capable musician in his own right. This, combined with his natural diplomatic skills, helped enormously and meant he could make an active and positive contribution to the album.

I loved the sound he could get on tape for my drums. In rock music, getting this right is still one of the great tests for any engineer. Since the drum's original use was to spur on troops to warfare, rather than winning over a maiden's fair heart, it is hardly surprising that many a battle has been fought over the drum sound.

The kit – virtually the only remaining acoustic instrument in a standard rock context – consists of a number of different constituent parts which insist on vibrating and rattling through a remarkable range of sounds and surfaces. Worse, hitting one element will set up a chain vibration in the others. In the days of four-track recording, the engineer needed to capture, but keep separate, the firm impact of the bass drum and the hi-hat for marking the time, the full fat sound of the snare drum, the tuned tones of the tom-toms and the sizzle or splash of the cymbals. Setting up the mikes to capture this is one of the black arts of the business, and is a pretty good way of detecting the best practitioners of them. Alan's full range of engineering skills were self-evident as we began to piece the record together.

'Speak To Me' was conceived as an overture and was what we understood an overture should be – a taster of things to come. This was constructed from cross-fades of all the other pieces on the album, which I put together roughly at home and then finally assembled in the studios. Initially we had tried creating the heartbeat that opens the piece from hospital recordings of real pulses, but all of them sounded far too stressful. We returned to the possibilities of musical instruments, and used a very soft beater on a padded bass drum, which strangely sounded far more lifelike, although the average heartbeat rate of 72 bpm was too fast and we slowed it down to a level that would have caused any cardiologist some concern. An enormous piano chord held for over a minute with the loud pedal firmly down was then run backwards underneath the piece to provide the build-up into the next section.

'Breathe' represented the first half of an experiment in reusing the same melody for two songs, or more precisely inserting two completely different sections in the middle of two verses, so that the song reprised after 'On The Run' and 'Time'.

'On the Run' was a substantial rework of an instrumental bridge from the live version, and was in fact one of the last pieces added since it was only at this point we had access to an EMS SynthiA, the successor to the VCS3. The VCS (the Voltage Controlled Studio) was an English synthesizer that had been devised by Peter Zinovieff and a team from the BBC Radiophonics Workshop, whose *Doctor Who* theme tune had helped bring purely electronic music to a wider audience, and we had used it on some of the other *Dark Side* tracks. However, it lacked a keyboard. The SynthiA came with a keyboard on the lid of its carry case. For 'On The Run' this meant the bubbling sound could be played very slowly and then electronically speeded up. For the track we also ran riot in the EMI sound effects library, and had another excuse to go back into the echo chamber behind Studio 3 to record the footsteps.

That sound library certainly earned its keep while we were ensconced in the studios: there was always an element of procrastination in heading off to explore its potential, and there were a number of sounds which we were always very fond of, but could never use. 'The Overstuffed Closet' was a big favourite: the sound of someone opening a cupboard from which all kinds of paraphernalia could be heard falling out. And we all liked 'Gunga Din', in which an irritating trumpet player was assailed by an increasingly heavy arsenal of weapons trying to wipe him out. After each rifle shot, burst of heavy machine-gun fire or aerial bombardment he would play on, each time enfeebled but persistent.

However, for the clocks that introduce 'Time', we used elements from a quad demonstration recording Alan had made a month or two before the *Dark Side* recordings. He had gone to an antique clock shop and recorded a horologist's delight of chimes, ticks and alarms. The main intro for this song was devised because a set of roto-toms happened to be in the studio and we completed it in just a few takes. The roto-toms consisted of drumheads stretched over a frame on a threaded spindle. By turning the head it could be tuned just like a tympani drum, so that a controlled series of tones could be used.

'Great Gig' was a piece of Rick's, with the vocal section soaring over the top. There were a number of suggestions about who to use: mine was the avant-garde mezzo-soprano Cathy Berberian (who I was listening to a lot at the time) but she might have been a bit radical, even for us. Clare Torry, who did the track in the end, was pursuing a career as a solo singer – Alan had worked with her in the past and recommended her. We were looking for a more European sound than the soul singers we used for some of the other backing tracks, and directed primarily by David and Rick, she delivered some terrific performances. She was embarrassed by having let herself go so much during one of the takes and came into the control booth to apologise, only to find that everyone was delighted. After our experience on *Atom Heart Mother*, it is surprising that we had ventured back into the realm of additional musicians, but we were well served by all of them: Clare, the other singers – the late Doris Troy, Leslie Duncan, Liza Strike and Barry St John – and Dick Parry, a Cambridge acquaintance of David, who added the rougher timbre of his tenor sax to 'Us And Them' and 'Money'.

Roger and I constructed the tape loop for 'Money' in our home studios and then took it in to Abbey Road. I had drilled holes in old pennies and then threaded them on to strings; they gave one sound on the loop of seven. Roger had recorded coins swirling around in the mixing bowl Judy used for her pottery, the tearing paper effect was created very simply in front of a microphone and the faithful sound library supplied the cash registers. Each sound was first measured out on the tape with a ruler before being cut to the same length and then carefully spliced together.

'Us And Them' was a lyrical piece which had been created by Rick. There is a saying that music is 'the space between the notes' and Rick's music on this particular track proves the point with some style. 'Any Colour' really provides a touch of relief on a record so tightly arranged, contributing to the dynamic pacing, as a pause before 'Brain Damage'. Although lead vocal duties on the rest of the album were handled by David, the vocal on the verses of 'Brain Damage' is Roger's, as it is on 'Eclipse', and it shows how well Roger's voice suited the songs he wrote.

The last track, 'Eclipse', was a piece that had benefited enormously from live performance prior to recording. The original versions of this lacked any real dynamic, but with gradual development on stage – where we needed to end the piece on a grander note – it acquired sufficient power to make a suitable finale.

The snippets of speech that punctuate the album were a late addition, recorded one night just before the final assembly of the album. Roger suggested the idea of incorporating spoken words and in half an hour we had devised a way of generating this. Roger drafted a series of questions about madness, violence and mortality – and I think I wrote them out on a set of cards. These were placed, face down, on a music stand in Studio 3. We then invited into the studio whoever we could find around the Abbey Road complex: our crew, the engineers, other musicians recording there – anyone other than ourselves. They were asked to sit on a stool, read each card to themselves and then simply give their answers into a microphone.

This naturally induced a certain amount of paranoia, as a studio is a lonely place when everyone else is grouped in the control room peering through the soundproof glass. As it happened, some of the professional performers were a lot more stilted than the amateurs, who seemed quite happy to chat away at length. Paul and Linda McCartney, for example, were recording *Red Rose Speedway* with Wings, and took up our invitation. It was very brave of them to accept at all, and in hindsight unfair of us to expect them to reveal their innermost psyches to a group of near strangers with a tape recorder set up. They were guarded, very reserved, and we didn't use any material from their session. We must have had a very clear idea of what we did want, since it would have been unthinkable otherwise for us to turn down two such famous voices. In contrast, Paul's guitarist Henry McCullough ('I don't know, I was really drunk at the time') and his wife were frighteningly open: they went straight into a story of a recent and somewhat physically violent argument they had had, like some particularly aggressive edition of a *Jerry Springer* show.

Among the other voices were Peter Watts's wife Puddie and our road manager Chris Adamson, who was recognisable by his slightly Northern accent. Roger the Hat, an itinerant roadie of the old school who had worked for us on a number of occasions, supplied a memorable session. His particular segment would have made an album in its own right. One story, which he delivered with all the deadpan precision of a constable in the witness box, concerned the day another driver had unwisely cut him up. 'I remonstrated with him,' said Roger the Hat. 'He was rude. He was very rude. But retribution was at hand… I 'it him.'

Some contenders were rejected for audio reasons: Robbie Williams, in his second week of work as a crew member for us, could not be used because his mellifluous bass voice was too deep and theatrical. Others sadly couldn't be fitted in, however good the lines. But Gerry O'Driscoll, the Irish doorman at Abbey Road, was the undoubted star. He delivered a wild torrent of jokes and homespun philosophy, tinged with a touch of melancholy. His voice closes the album in the fade-out at the end of 'Eclipse', and his line 'There is no dark side in the moon. Matter of fact, it's all dark' helped clinch the final title for the album.

After the recording came the cross-fades, and there were a lot of them. In a pre-digital age these sequences, where one piece fades out as another fades up, were still a fairly serious manoeuvre. Giant tape machines would be trundled in from all parts of the building and hooked up into the mixer. As the cross-fades usually involved seven- or eight-foot tape loops as well, a forest of mike stands was required to provide temporary spindles to ensure that the loops did not get tangled. After a while the whole room started to look like a deranged Heath Robinson contraption.

Even with Alan's engineering expertise, he didn't possess enough hands to manage all the necessary tasks, so starting points would be carefully marked on the tape, and band members positioned with fingers poised on various buttons. The machines would be stopped and restarted while trembling hands worked the faders. A single mistake would mean starting the whole process from scratch. The importance of all this synchronised teamwork was to get the correct levels for one track finishing, another starting and all the sound effects and dialogue fading up and down underneath. Once the transition had been successfully achieved it was then spliced into the master tape.

Sadly, we lost the benefit of Alan's skills when we invited him to engineer the next album, offering him a small amount of money but pointing out how privileged he was. To our astonishment he turned us down. Pityingly we shook our heads and then watched as he had an enormous hit record with *Tales Of Mystery And Imagination* as the Alan Parsons Project and launched his own career as a performer.

We had intended to oversee all the final production decisions ourselves, but in the end we brought in an outside producer for the mix, right at the end of proceedings in February. Chris Thomas had a background in music rather than engineering, and had written to George Martin asking if he could work as his assistant – eventually George gave him an opening in his production company. Chris had been working on the Beatles' *White Album* at one point, when George had to head elsewhere, leaving Chris in charge for a short, alarming, but exciting period. Chris had a number of links with Pink Floyd. He had seen us on many occasions – including the violent night at the Feathers at Ealing, at UFO and performing *Dark Side* at the Rainbow in 1972. He knew Steve O'Rourke socially, and had produced Quiver's second album, following in David's footsteps.

There is, of course, more than one way to mix any given track. There is no definition of right and wrong. Some prefer a mix that has an ensemble feel to it in the way a classical orchestra can produce a balanced sound in which no one instrument features more than another. At other times it may benefit the piece to have one clear solo voice, instrument or sound riding above everything else. On *Dark Side* this type of argument raged about vocals, sound effects, guitars and rhythm section. At times three separate mixes were done by different individuals, a system which in the past had tended to resolve matters, as a consensus normally developed towards a particular mix. But even this was not working.

These were the early warning signals of fundamental disagreements within the band. Lines were being drawn in the sand, indistinctly and involuntarily, but being drawn nonetheless. At the risk of simplifying things too far, David and Rick felt more comfortable with a purer musical solution. Roger and I were drawn towards experimenting with the balances, and making more of the non-musical elements. David always preferred a certain amount of echo, Roger preferred the sound to be much drier.

Chris, having few preconceptions, simply did it the way he thought sounded right. However, he said he wanted input from us all. What he remembers is that, at a time when release date deadlines were looming and things could have been rather fraught, the atmosphere was good, efficient and – for the music business – extremely disciplined, allowing him to clock off at eleven in the evening before heading off to work on a Procul Harum album for the rest of the night.

The work involved was immense, considering the amount of overdubs, overlays, inserts and cross-fades required. And since the tape was constantly rolling, it always suffered some degradation, which had to be painstakingly treated and returned to health. That Alan and Chris between them delivered a sonic finish that still offers stunningly good sound quality over thirty years later is a testament to the engineer's art.

When the recording was complete, it was immediately apparent that, despite the disparate elements of spoken words, sound effects and songs, the album had emerged as a homogeneous whole. It was also refreshing to be able to return to the finished piece with fresh ears after letting Chris get on with completing the work on the final mixes.

The album's release date was set for 3rd March 1973. In the meantime we had seen the release of *Pink Floyd Live At Pompeii*, more touring in Europe and North America – including an appearance at the Hollywood Bowl and one date in Canada when we discovered one of our backing singers had disappeared, the reason being that she had been arrested with her boyfriend for holding up a grocery store. And we had also seen the final fruits of our original conversation with the choreographer Roland Petit.

Live At Pompeii had turned out to be a surprisingly good attempt to film our live set a year or so before. We had been approached by the director Adrian Maben, whose idea was to shoot us playing in the empty amphitheatre beneath Vesuvius. Adrian described the concept of the movie as 'an anti-*Woodstock* film, where there would be nobody present, and the music and the silence and the empty amphitheatre would mean as much as, if not more than, a crowd of thousands'. Opening and closing the set with 'Echoes', we played as if to an audience, intercut with shots of bubbling, steaming and flowing lava, or of the band stalking across the volcanic landscape. At a time when rock films were either straight concert footage or attempts to copy *A Hard Day's Night*, the idea was appealing.

The elements that seem to make it work – none of which we had thought much about during the filming in October 1971 – were the decision to perform live instead of miming and the rather gritty environment created by the heat and the wind. Only a few sequences were added later in a studio – the versions of 'Careful With That Axe' and 'Set The Controls' along with the blessedly short reworking of 'Seamus' with Mademoiselle Nobs.

It had been a fairly cheap and cheerful trip. Peter Watts and Alan Styles had the slog of driving the equipment all the way down through Europe. There were no families in tow to go sightseeing with, as we only had a limited number of days to fit in the work. Even so, as films often can, we overran our original schedule, and had to cancel a university gig; however, as the rearranged date came after the release of *Dark Side*, I think in the end the organisers were actually quite happy to have had the delay, since by the time we appeared they could charge four times the ticket price, while being able to pay us the original contracted fee.

At Pompeii, we were filming in the early autumn but it was still quite hot, shirts-off weather. It was hard work, with no leisurely nights out sampling the local cuisine and wine list, but the atmosphere was enjoyable, with everyone getting on with their jobs. At the end of the amphitheatre sessions, we headed off up the mountain to shoot some cut-ins among the steam of the hot springs, and had a brief chance to explore Pompeii itself.

We were, though, beset by a couple of technical hitches. One of the reels of film was mislaid, and the director had to insert a lengthy sequence featuring nothing but the drumming on 'One Of These Days', since the palette of available shots and camera angles was severely limited.

After one showing at the Edinburgh Festival, a premiere was planned at the Rainbow Theatre in the autumn of 1972, but at the last minute Rank, the landlords of the building, invoked a clause preventing any event that was 'competitive' with their own activities. Roger declared the fiasco itself 'rank', and I liked the promoter Peter Bowyer's comment that he would wait for the wounds in his back to heal before considering any other similar events.

Live At Pompeii proved to be very disappointing in financial terms, especially as it got lost in the wash of *Dark Side*, and so for a long time we received very little reward for our efforts. So much so, that when, years later, a New York film mogul approached Roger at a show to tell him he had made millions from the film, he was surprised that instead of Roger congratulating him, he was escorted from the premises… We later learnt that a lot of the paperwork relating to the film had been lost in a fire, proof, as I have learnt over the years, that offices of those handling such matters are prone to levels of self-immolation, flooding and invasion by locusts that even Old Testament prophets would have found unbelievable.

In our quest for upmarket artistry, we had more luck with Roland Petit. Our original discussions in 1970 had been about his idea of creating a ballet based on *À la recherche du temps perdu* by Marcel Proust. The work consists of multiple volumes of detailed reminiscences about his life. I know this only because along with the rest of the band I tried to read it; at a time when science fiction was our principal literary diet this was not an easy task. I still like to think I got further than anyone else, but certainly none of us made it beyond volume three. This project was eventually cancelled on numerous grounds. The reading time alone would have been too time-consuming, and the subject matter too challenging for much of our audience.

Roland, however, had not given up on us and had finally got us involved with the Ballet de Marseille, although we had taken the easy option of not writing any original music for the shows, by reusing versions of 'Careful With That Axe, Eugene' and 'Echoes', the latter with a story line loosely based on *Frankenstein*. Working with the Ballet was a relaxed expedition. We enjoyed being in

Marseilles, David's fluency in the language was a useful asset with both the corps de ballet and local waiters, and the atmosphere of civilised sophistication, in contrast to the routine of tours and studios, may have appealed to a certain intellectual snobbery in us. In the programme for the ballet, the deputy mayor of Marseilles kindly described us as *'ces millionaires du disque, idoles de la jeunesse populaire comme de la jeunesse dorée'*.

For the shows we played on a raised stage, overlooking the dancers performing in front of us. The major hurdle facing them was that they had worked out the choreographed steps based on our existing recordings. However, in the case of 'Axe' each performance varied in length, since the attraction of the piece was the chance to improvise. We rapidly had to engineer a version of constant length, a task exacerbated by our legendary inability to count bars reliably.

As luck would have it Leslie Spitz was with us in France. Leslie was a four-poster bed salesman from the dodgier end of the Kings Road in Chelsea and an expert ligger. His greatest triumph had been getting a seat on board our chartered aircraft on the Japan tour earlier that year. No one had seemed quite sure why he was there, or who had invited him, but we were far too polite to ask. As a payback for that freebie, Leslie was drafted in to count the bars. He was issued with a pile of cards which had the numbers of the bars written on them and – crouched beneath the piano – he was expected to turn up a card every four beats. The result was less than metronomic, as Leslie was easily distracted by loud music and lithe ballerinas, but it did help, and anyway we knew when we were meant to finish because the dancers stopped moving.

It actually all turned out to be a success. The dancers, I think, enjoyed what was really quite a different and populist piece, and they also assembled a surprisingly good football team to play against us after rehearsals. The dance director watching all those expensive legs rushing about in football boots had a fit. After the Marseilles concerts we later took the show to Paris for a few performances in January and February 1973.

The aftermath to all this was an extraordinary lunch at Rudolf Nureyev's house in Richmond. Marcel Proust had reared his head again, but this time in film format. Nureyev, Roland Petit and Roman Polanski were there along with Roger, Steve and myself. Feeling slightly self-conscious in a truly exotic atmosphere of fine art and lavish decor, we were astonished at the rather louche youth who greeted us and then left us to amuse ourselves until the others arrived and Nureyev made an appearance, which of course he did in style – swathed in Oriental drapery.

Lunch seemed to involve a lot of wine and very little Proust. I think there was talk of resurrecting the Frankenstein project as a quasi-porno film but my memory is a little fuzzy on this. After the meal, in tabloid style, we made our excuses and left before we were drawn too deeply into this *demi-monde*. We never did get to deal with Proust, Frankenstein, Nureyev or Polanski again although Roland did retain the ballet in the company repertoire for some time, performing to tapes rather than live music.

During our sojourn in Marseilles there were serious machinations on the business front, as our US record deal was sorted out. Our first albums had been released on Capitol's Tower label, which was principally a jazz and folk label, and not a good fit. Capitol, EMI's US operation, had then started up a new label called Harvest under the leadership of Malcolm Jones, and we were intended to be the label leaders along with other underground British bands. That hadn't worked for us either. Although the staff were enthusiastic, we felt a lack of genuine belief in our commercial potential among the higher echelons, and our sales performance in the States had been particularly poor.

Steve O'Rourke had made it clear to EMI that we were not prepared to continue with Capitol. We were proposing to withhold *Dark Side* from the USA since our contract was expiring after five years, and we were not prepared to waste what we thought to be our best album yet on a record company that wouldn't support us sufficiently.

After Steve had gone in and batted heavily for the fact that the results just weren't good enough, even EMI had seen that there was a problem in the US. Bhaskar Menon, who had recently been appointed the chairman of Capitol Records, heard about our unhappiness, and he took the trouble to travel over to Marseilles to see us. His flying visit made all the difference. Bhaskar was still only in his thirties, a graduate of Oxford and the Doon School in India. He had met and impressed Sir Joseph Lockwood, who had brought him into EMI. Later Bhaskar would himself become chairman of EMI.

Bhaskar convinced Steve that he could deliver what was needed in America and we agreed to let him have the record. It was a shame that he hadn't been brought in earlier. Unknown to Capitol – and Bhaskar – we had already given up on the company earlier in the year and signed a new deal with Clive Davis at Columbia for the American distribution of all our releases following *Dark Side*. In our usual non-confrontational way we just forgot to mention it.

A tour to America in early 1973 also gave us a chance to bring to the fore the lighting skills of Arthur Max. He had served a good apprenticeship. After training as an architect – always a good qualification for working with Pink Floyd – he had found himself at Woodstock operating a spotlight continuously for three days (he said) for Chip Monck, one of the pioneer rock lighting and stage designers. Arthur's arrival coincided with a time when we were growing out of our early light shows. There is a limit to what can be achieved with yet another oil slide, and with bigger venues and longer projection throws the finale was all too often a brilliant frozen moment as yet another glass slide cracked to be followed shortly after by the projector burning out.

Arthur was interested in the power of stage lighting and spotlights rather than oil slides; he was particularly talented in finding ways to exploit theatrical lighting. Our shows immediately gained more visual innovation and he was expert at making the most of the available facilities of an auditorium and exploiting existing technology from other sources. For our version of 'Echoes' with the Ballet de Marseille, Arthur interpreted the Frankenstein mood we wanted by installing a welding kit backstage and each evening donning mask and gloves to provide the added effect of genuine argon sparks.

I think Arthur was also responsible for introducing the Genie tower to our shows. These towers were one of the more important innovations in rock staging. Arthur had seen these hydraulic towers being used to change light bulbs in a factory, and adapted the principle to allow them to carry racks of spotlights. For shows that had insufficient set-up time for rigging regular stage lighting, or were out on a field on a stage made out of flat-bed trailers, these towers were a godsend. The fact that they could also be raised as an opening to the show was the icing on the cake. This was also the period when we brought in the circular screen backdrop that has remained a staple of our live shows.

One of Arthur's greatest shows for us was at Radio City Music Hall in March 1973. This auditorium was a wonder of technology when it was first built and for many years the technical details of the stage riser was classified information, since the technology had been taken direct from the fighter plane lifts on American aircraft carriers.

The stage itself contained six sections, each of which could rise twenty feet and then roll forward. There was also a steam curtain in front of it; this was a tube drilled with holes that sent out a sheet of steam to obscure the stage. This enabled us to start the show with the audience filing into the auditorium, faced by a completely bare stage. When the show began, the steam evaporated, and behind it our set slowly rose with us and all our equipment in place, with flashing police lights attached to the Genie lighting towers. Unlike the bad old days of the Top Rank revolving stages, this was how it should be done.

Unfortunately, Arthur had one major failing: his temper. Roger and I (his two principal contacts in the band) have not spoken to Arthur in over twenty-five years following his final resignation. I've rarely come across anyone who could get so fired up quite so quickly. Apart from sacking each venue's own follow-spot operators on a regular basis, he would scream so much abuse at them during the performance that it would have been foolhardy for him to linger after the show for a post-mortem as it could have been his own. Arthur was also prone to leaving our employment in the middle of a show. Steve would frequently arrive back in the interval to announce that Arthur had dashed his headset and intercom to the ground and left the building in a fit of pique. Eventually we could no longer handle this level of unpredictability and Graeme Fleming, Arthur's second in command, and a far more phlegmatic character, took over. Arthur went on to become an enormously successful movie art director, working with Ridley Scott and collecting a BAFTA award and an Oscar nomination for *Gladiator*.

The release for *Dark Side* was set for March 1973, and we were delighted with the package. Apart from the additional posters and stickers the main image was also perfect. Storm had turned up with a series of ideas and as soon as we first saw the prism design we all knew it was the right one. However, we failed to attend the press launch at the London Planetarium. We were not happy that the record label planned to use a sound system that we didn't consider good enough. After all the work we had put in to *Dark Side*, we didn't want it played to the press on a sub-standard PA system. The row probably all boiled down to a question of money, but we refused to relent and missed the fun. We weren't a favourite with the music journalists as it was, since none of us had worked that hard to cultivate any kind of relationship with them.

So I have to rely on Roy Hollingworth's report of the launch for *Melody Maker*. After cocktails at 8 p.m., the journalists were ushered into the Planetarium: '…like standing on the inside of a hollowed-out concrete egg. The egg filled, and the lights dimmed. Laughter from one quarter. A bum pinched no doubt. And then it began… The thick thump, the staggered bumping of a heartbeat filled the blackness, gaining in volume and intensity until it packed against your whole body.'

So far, so good. But after fifteen minutes the audience seemed to be losing interest. 'Quite a few people were beginning to chatter and light cigarettes. And then, as people found more fun in being funny, the shape of a bunny rabbit appeared on one wall. This was done by holding a cigarette lighter behind a hand, and performing tricks with the fingers. Later I witnessed a swan in strangled flight, and a brace of doves. Then some enterprising fellow scooped the impromptu magic lantern show with an enormous portrayal of a naughty thing.' Our decision to stay away may have been wiser than we thought.

The record sold fast. We had a gold disc by April in both the UK and the US. Everything happened very quickly. That May we presented a complete *Dark Side* show at Earls Court. All the elements came together, as we presented the piece in its most developed version. The music had been rehearsed enough to be tight, but was new enough to be fresh. The lighting, thanks to Arthur, was dramatic. There were additional effects including a fifteen-foot spotlit plane that shot down a wire over the heads of the audience to crash on stage in a ball of fire in sync with the explosion in 'On The Run'. Films accompanied the music, including animation for 'Time' by Ian Eames and the *Crystal Voyager* surfing footage that we had first seen in Australia in 1971. Sadly, none of these shows was filmed or recorded.

Everyone has their own opinion about why *The Dark Side Of The Moon* sold – and still sells – so spectacularly well. Even for someone intimately involved with the album, the statistics make staggering reading. For example, total sales have been in excess of 35 million and it has been calculated that one household in four in the UK owns a copy in one form or another. At the time of writing *Dark Side* has been on the US album charts almost continuously since 1973.

My view is that there was no single reason, but a number of factors working together and multiplying the effect. The primary reason – which is true of any great album – is the strength of the songwriting. *Dark Side* contained strong, powerful songs. The overall idea that linked those songs together – the pressures of modern life – found a universal response, and continues to capture people's imagination. The lyrics had depth, and had a resonance people could easily relate to, and were clear and simple enough for non-native-English speakers to understand, which must have been a factor in its international success. And the musical quality spearheaded by David's guitar and voice and Rick's keyboards established a fundamental Pink Floyd sound. We were comfortable with the music, which had had time to mature and gestate, and evolve through live performances – later on we had to stop previewing work live as the quality of the recording equipment being smuggled into gigs reached near-studio standards.

The additional singers and Dick Parry's sax gave the whole record an extra commercial sheen. In addition, the sonic quality of the album was state of the art – courtesy of the skills of Alan Parsons and Chris Thomas. This is particularly important, because at the time the album came out, hi-fi stereo equipment had only recently become a mainstream consumer item, an essential fashion accessory for the 1970s home. As a result, record buyers were particularly aware of the effects of stereo and able to appreciate any album that made the most of its possibilities. *Dark Side* had the good fortune to become one of the definitive test records that people could use to show off the quality of their hi-fi system.

The packaging for the album by Storm and Po at Hipgnosis was clean, simple, and immediately striking, with a memorable icon in the shape of the prism. The packaging also featured the Pyramids, which were, for Storm, a cosmic version of the prism. It is one of Storm's credos that photo shoots should ideally be real rather than faked, and so he set off for Cairo, with wife Libby, baby son Bill and Hipgnosis partner Po in tow. Come the shoot, the entire party were struck down by the Cairo cooking, leaving Storm to head out alone in the dead of night, since a full moon was a requisite part of the photograph. He found himself in a restricted area, with a squad of machine gun-toting soldiers heading his way, frightening him with thoughts of some kind of *Midnight Express* imprisonment. A small transfer of baksheesh resolved the problem, quieted Storm's nerves, and allowed him to complete the shoot unmolested.

The record companies handling the album (particularly Capitol in the States under Bhaskar Menon's instructions) threw every ounce of heavyweight marketing muscle they possessed behind it. A totally committed record company is a fearsome and powerful machine and without doubt their efforts contributed to the album's success.

And last, but possibly not least, one music critic commented that it was a great album to make love to – some sex clubs in

Holland and Sweden, so I am told, used it to accompany their own performances.

I think we all knew that *The Dark Side Of The Moon* was a very good record when we finished it – definitely much better as a complete piece than anything we had done before, but I certainly had no real inkling of its commercial potential, and was as surprised as everyone else when it simply took off.

When Lindy and I decided to move home from Camden to Highgate, I went along to my bank manager to request a bridging loan. He asked me what I could offer as security. I said, 'Well, I've got a Number One album in America.' He was not impressed, and said he was looking for something a little more concrete...

HARD LABOUR 7

AFTER THE success of *The Dark Side Of The Moon* we were brought back down to earth when we had to start tackling yet another album. On this occasion, *Dark Side* actually added to the burden, since we were particularly anxious to avoid accusations of cashing in on the album's success by simply replicating it. We clearly felt that after one album was released, we really should get back into the studio to start on the next one, even though at that point we were not locked into a contract that demanded we churn out one or two albums a year. In fact we were under no obligation to deliver within any timeframe. I do not remember any huge pressure from EMI to deliver *Dark Side II: The Lunatic Returns*, but this may well be a tribute to Steve O'Rourke's managerial ability in deflecting brickbats and any other missiles sent out by the record company.

We returned to Abbey Road in the autumn of 1973, following a tour of the States in June and a welcome summer break. Lindy and I had stayed in a house near Vence in the Alpes-Maritimes, not far from L'Ousteroun where Roger would later stay during the recording of *The Wall*, and close to where Bill Wyman had a house. It had been a complete change, incredibly quiet, and a chance to relax completely with the family.

At Abbey Road we began work with a blank sheet: there were no fragments of songs or unused out-takes left over after *Dark Side*. The sessions started out quite well. Our suspicions should have immediately been aroused.

Preliminary discussions threw up the idea of a record created entirely out of sounds that had not been produced by musical instruments. This seemed suitably radical, and so we started out on a project we called 'Household Objects'. The whole notion seems absurdly laboured now, when any sound can be sampled and then laid out across a keyboard, enabling a musician to play anything from barking dogs to nuclear explosions. In 1973 it took us two months to assemble – slowly and laboriously – what could now probably be achieved in an afternoon. However, the length of time involved was not a problem for us. In fact it was a blessing. We found the project was a brilliant device to postpone having to create anything concrete for the foreseeable future, since we could busy ourselves with the mechanics of the sounds rather than the creation of the music.

Almost everything we've ever recorded in a studio has been extracted by someone at some point and subsequently bootlegged. However, no such recordings exist of the 'Household Objects' tapes for the simple reason that we never managed to produce any actual music. All the time we devoted to the project was spent exploring the non-musical sounds, and the most we ever achieved was a small number of tentative rhythm tracks.

We investigated the domestic sound world in a variety of ways: percussion was created by sawing wood, slamming down hammers of different sizes or thudding axes into tree trunks. For the bass notes we clamped and plucked rubber bands, and then slowed the resulting sounds to lower tape speeds.

Like some adult playgroup we set about breaking light bulbs and stroking wine glasses, and indulged in various forms of water play including stirring bowls of water before pouring them into buckets. We unrolled lengths of adhesive tape, sprayed aerosols, plucked egg slicers and tapped wine bottle tops. Chris Adamson remembers being sent out to local hardware shops to find brooms of various bristle strengths, and asked to track down a specific kind of elastic used to power the propeller of a model aeroplane. After a number of weeks, musical progress was negligible. We could sustain the pretence no longer, and the whole project was gently laid to rest.

Group momentum was pretty well non-existent. The early days of total commitment were beginning to dissipate. Some of us had started families and were experiencing the responsibilities and distractions that young children provide. In my case, my daughter Chloe was two, while Rick had two kids, Gala and Jamie. In the extended Pink Floyd family, Steve O'Rourke had two daughters, Katy and Shena. Peter Watts had two children, Naomi and Ben. Roger did not have children yet, but interestingly, he was one of the prime movers in making sure that we never went on tour for too long. Three weeks away in the States seemed plenty. The schedule and style of touring were hardly conducive to family life on the road. One rental car at the airport was still enough for band and management to get to hotel and gig; even one additional person would automatically break up this tight-knit unit, and require a second rental car, doubling transportation costs.

Off the road, we were increasingly conscious that life existed outside the band. All of us were working with other musicians either as performers or producers. Amongst the mass of demo tapes musicians sent, David had received one from a schoolgirl whose songwriting and voice stood out above the rest. He encouraged her career over a period of time, and was rewarded by seeing her achieve great success with her first single 'Wuthering Heights' and album *The Kick Inside*: it was Kate Bush.

I collaborated on an album with Robert Wyatt of the Soft Machine. Our long relationship with the Soft Machine dated back to the underground days of the Roundhouse and UFO, and the US tour in the late Sixties, when I remember their vocalist Kevin Ayers, in a hotel room at the Chelsea in New York, dangling upside down off the side of the bed as part of the digestion process demanded by whichever macrobiotic diet he was then following.

In May 1973 I had received a postcard from Robert suggesting I might like to produce his solo record. The day the card arrived I heard that he had fallen from a window, and been paralysed from the waist down. A one-off benefit for Robert was organised in November that year at the Rainbow Theatre: Soft Machine opened the show, and then we played, performing a cut-down version of the Earls Court gigs, including the plane descending over the audience... but this was not a testimonial for a wrecked career.

Within six months of his accident Robert was ready to start work again – although unable to use a full drum kit, he could still handle vocals, keyboards and percussion. Recording for his solo album, *Rock Bottom*, took place during the winter of 1973 at The Manor, Virgin's house studio near Oxford, a studio which had been set up specifically for rock music, providing accommodation, a relaxed atmosphere, and total freedom to record away from the constraints of scheduled sessions. Bootleg, a huge and immovable Great Dane, was also in attendance. Exposure to Robert's fertile stream of ideas was the most rewarding musical experience I had enjoyed outside the band.

It also allowed me to return to *Top Of The Pops* – for a rinse, trim and blow-dry – since we produced a single as well as the album and, slightly to our surprise, it entered the charts. This was a rather offbeat version of the Monkees' 'I'm A Believer', which featured a fabulously avant-garde violin solo by Fred Frith of Henry Cow. Although the appearance was slightly soured by the BBC's reluctance to show Robert in his wheelchair, the director was eventually shamed into giving way, and a good time was had by all. Since not all the original musicians were available, and it was of course mimed, we had to bring in some extra help. This included Andy Summers on guitar, who was at a bit of a loose end since the Police had yet to be invented.

Pink Floyd continued to spend most of the rest of 1974 delaying the evil moment of making a record. In the same way that we had released *Relics* when *Meddle* was taking its time to emerge, we once again succumbed to the blandishments of the record company and released a compilation album. *Piper At The Gates Of Dawn* and *A Saucerful Of Secrets* were sandwiched together as a double album called *A Nice Pair*, in a cover that contained a selection of visual jokes and puns (Storm's idea of an out-of-focus pair of spectacles remains a personal favourite).

We also embarked on a short tour of France in the summer of 1974, a tour which contained an element of penance for some previous greed. Two years earlier we had committed to an advertising photo for the French soft drinks company Gini. This had been shot in Morocco for use in France only, and we thought the experience had been conveniently left behind – apart from the occasional twinge of guilt about falling for such easy money. At this time touring for most bands was still seen primarily as a way of promoting records to boost album sales, with the odd chance to get some income from the larger venues. Promotion was usually limited by the promoter's budget to a rash of flyposting and a few radio plugs from the band.

However, we had forgotten that inserted in the contract with Gini was a clause which ensured that, instead of being left to our relatively low-key promotional devices, we would on this occasion be accompanied by a circus of Gini-promoting extras, mainly consisting of an ad agency's view of 'trend setters'; for this read Page Three models and Easy Rider bikers. Like an unfortunate cat with a can tied to its tail, we were followed everywhere we went in France by a frightful gaggle of groovy people in dark glasses and leather jackets, sporting gigantic Gini bitter lemon signs. Steve spent a lot of time negotiating the exact distance we could keep them apart from us, but even so our hard-earned credibility with our French fans was left in tatters whenever we came to town.

The general feeling was that our crew had the most fun. They had no qualms about enjoying the company of our co-travellers, and in fact were deeply grateful to the band for giving them access to the bevy of models who accompanied us on tour, and with whom they could while away the duller hours of a roadie's life.

Roger and I tried to erase this particular memory during September and October by working on a set of films for a tour we were due to start later in the autumn. For the early *Dark Side* shows we had used clips from the surfing documentary *Crystal Voyager* and Ian Eames's animation for 'Time', but now we wanted to have a complete sequence of films to project throughout the show. The films, a mix of library footage and specially shot sequences to accompany the songs, were in place for the beginning of a major British tour – our first in two years – which opened in the Usher Hall, Edinburgh, at the beginning of November.

Phil Taylor, who had worked for a number of other bands, came in to work on the 1974 tour, and he now describes it as 'shambolic'. He had arrived during rehearsals for the tour, which were taking place at the Unit Studios in King's Cross – next to the Wimpey bar – where we were working on some new songs including 'Shine On' and 'Raving And Drooling'. The definition of a 'rehearsal studio' is actually a large room with nothing in it, in which you can make a lot of noise.

This was a gloomy period for the band – although the audiences were hopefully unaware of this. The weather didn't help: a wintry rain and low clouds accompanied us from Edinburgh to Cardiff. Although, for the first time, we had the funds available to develop our stage show in the way we wanted, there was a good deal of dissatisfaction with what we were doing, or perhaps how we were going about it. We now came to realise that what we had thought was a good idea – never touring for more than one month – had a downside. In a three-week tour, the first week or so of a tour would effectively be a mobile production rehearsal; by the second week the performances would start to gain some cohesion; and by the final week we would be thinking less about the music and more about going home.

Our dissatisfaction was exacerbated by personnel problems. Peter Watts had left us after seven years as chief roadie. He had become increasingly – and then totally – unreliable. However, since the four of us in the band were not completely in tune with each other, and we had no clear chain of command, our handling of the situation was inept. Peter was fired – at least once – by one band member in the morning, only for another of us to reinstate him the same afternoon. What I didn't realise for some time was that Peter had developed a serious drug habit. I clearly had a rather naive view of the crew's appetites. Many years later I discovered that one long-serving crew member had initially joined, not out of devotion to the music, but to pay off a drug debt he owed another member of the crew. When the situation with Peter became impossible, we tried to behave with more understanding than we had been able to with Syd, and arranged for Peter to undergo treatment at a clinic, which, though not totally ineffectual, did little to solve the core problem – sadly, Peter died of an overdose in 1976.

When Peter left, the lighting director Arthur Max had been promoted to crew chief, but the highly strung temperament and ego that made Arthur such a talented lighting designer made him impossible as a team leader. However, there was no obvious alternative candidate from the remainder of the crew, a disparate bunch of technical boffins and equipment humpers. Arthur's personality added an extra twist to the general air of tension and chaos. Phil Taylor encountered Arthur Max at his most dogmatic. Arthur was in charge of all technical aspects including the sound, which he knew little about. Phil asked Arthur, 'What should I do?' to which Arthur simply shouted, 'Don't ask me about it, just do it!' On one occasion Arthur wanted to film the show, and so he flooded the stage in bright white light, which rather starkly eradicated any of the light show.

We had also taken on a studio engineer at short notice who had no experience of working in a live concert environment, and whose job was made more difficult by a number of factors, some technical, some of his own making. The halls we were now playing after the success of *Dark Side* were a step up from the university circuit, and often tended to be large echoing civic halls with difficult acoustics and nowhere convenient to put the mixer board. The very elaborate Bereza mixing desk that we had ordered (customised for our performance needs) arrived late, had severe teething problems, and was like no desk this particular engineer had encountered before.

He also made the mistake of failing to establish a congenial rapport with the rest of the crew: one night they rigged up an array of fireworks beneath the new, miracle, mixing desk. When the luckless engineer switched the desk on, the explosives ignited, leaving him considerably shaken, since he thought he had blown the brand-new equipment to smithereens... Now marked down as a natural victim, his days on the road were numbered. After three shows we felt obliged to replace this luckless sound engineer with Brian Humphries, the engineer we'd first encountered at Pye Studios when we were recording the score for Barbet Schroeder's film *More*. Brian had been recording the show for a radio broadcast and when he finished his work, we hoicked him out of the BBC van and placed him behind the desk. He was familiar with both band and crew, and his experience in the studio, and on the road with Traffic, at last gave us confidence that the sound quality would be acceptable. However, showing a new sense of caution, we did ask Chris Thomas to sit with Brian and evaluate him. Brian either showed he could handle the pressure, or failed to notice Chris was there.

As a band we were also demonstrating a distinct lack of commitment to the necessary input required. We seemed to be more interested in booking squash courts, for example, than perfecting the set. As a result our shows were a wildly erratic mix of the good and bad (and occasionally ugly) both technically and musically. The exception to this state of affairs was provided by the two backing singers, Carlena Williams and Venetta Fields, who always performed wonderfully, looked great and went to sleep whenever the band started arguing or sulking.

After the way the Earls Court performances in May 1973 had gelled so perfectly, the problems we had experienced on the tour added to our frustration, and to the sense that we were all pulling in slightly different directions. Inevitably we were castigated by some of the music press, notably receiving a mugging from Nick Kent of the *New Musical Express*, who, also being a particularly fervent Syd Barrett devotee, was unrestrained in his attack. The trouble was that we recognised that some of his criticisms were valid, and in fact his comments may have had some influence on drawing us back together.

I think it might be true to say that we were close to calling it a day. Steve O'Rourke always maintained that each member of the band came to him separately at some point to vent his irritation, going as far as threatening to leave. Roger certainly could see there were easier ways of achieving his ends and David was thinking of alternatives. Even Rick, who was better known for thinking about thinking, was reaching the end of his tether... I thought I'd hang on, wash up the teacups and liberate the typewriter on my way out.

Eventually we managed to pull ourselves into some semblance of order. Brian Humphries was confirmed as the live sound mixer during our four shows at the Empire Pool, Wembley, in mid-November. Andy Bereza got the new wonder desk he had invented to work. Arthur Max was reallocated to his natural habitat behind the lighting desk and the PA team of Robbie Williams and Mick Kluczynski were promoted to tour managers. Meanwhile the band had enough of a discussion to make some positive decisions and address the problems of playing together. But we were all grateful when Christmas arrived, and the tour ended in Bristol. As a final coda I had rather imperiously arrived at the hotel in yet another second-hand bargain – this time a Ferrari 265 GTB4. I spent most of the next morning changing the spark plugs in order to get the Ferrari to start, followed by yet another journey from hell, with memories of the Bentley, as the brakes failed to do more than offer the gentlest hint of retardation even when pressed hard enough to engender leg cramps.

We did get back to work in the studios in January 1975. It was far from easy. The increased isolation of multi-track recording created a marked shift in the atmosphere as the whole process grew increasingly drawn out and demanding. From my point of view, the drum parts had become more structured and had to be learnt more carefully. In the early days I had been able to stay closer to arrangements that had been developed for live shows. The separation of each drum onto a different track meant it took even longer to get a result. This was part and parcel of general improvements in studio technology, but it did nothing to help the sense that we were not a band playing together.

After his work on the tour, we brought Brian Humphries in as engineer. It was still highly unusual for anyone to import a non-

EMI engineer in to Abbey Road, and Brian encountered a few teething problems as he familiarised himself with the set-up, once accidentally and irreversibly flooding the backing track with echo, a track Roger and I had spent many hours perfecting.

There were a few niggling differences between us, none significant in their own right, but enough to make life in the studio a lot less constructive than it had always been before. Punctuality became an issue. If two of us were on time and the others were late, we were quite capable of working ourselves up into a righteous fury. The following day the roles could easily be reversed. None of us was free of blame.

The success of the previous album had also brought its own dark side. We were all a little more conscious of how much had been contributed by each member of the band, and the credit (and share of the benefits) being doled out. There was more money involved now. Our publishing had been reorganised under the guidance of Peter Barnes with the setting up of Pink Floyd Music Publishing in 1973. For a group to own its own publishing company was still unusual – even the Beatles only owned part of Northern Songs – as was the ability to collect direct from overseas partners. This decision was justified when it was found that EMI had forgotten to collect a six-figure sum in overseas income over the previous three years.

The royalties from the record sales of *The Dark Side Of The Moon* were starting to flow through, although it was a gradual process. Lindy and I upgraded our house, moving from Camden to Highgate, but the fact we still had a relative lack of worldly goods was proved by the fact we managed the move with the help of a transit van and one of the road crew – no fleet of pantechnicons required. As the four of us acquired larger properties, we were able to draw on the skills of a group of creative designers, carpenters and artisans who not only worked on the house improvements, but also became involved in working on our shows. I was also finally able to indulge my passion for motor racing and started up a car restoration business with the Aston Martin specialist Derrick Edwards.

Despite any problems, we did now have the beginnings of a piece, 'Shine On You Crazy Diamond', devised in rehearsal in 1974, and developed during both rehearsals and shows that year. Roger had added lyrics to a poignant and mournful guitar theme of David's and the song had been a staple part of the autumn tour of the UK, opening the first half with two other songs of Roger's, 'Raving And Drooling' and 'Gotta Be Crazy', which we decided not to work on, but set to one side for the time being – Roger already had come up with the overall idea of 'absence' for the album, and it was clear that those two songs had no place within the concept.

The intro to 'Shine On You Crazy Diamond', the opening track of the new album, contained the only remnant from the 'Household Objects' sessions: we had used an old party trick of filling wine glasses with varying levels of water and then running a finger round the rim to create a singing tone. These tones were then put on to sixteen-track tape and mixed down in chord clusters so that each fader controlled an individual chord. In fact, although we didn't use it, the glass harmonica, an instrument using a keyboard to control spinning glass plates, had been invented to achieve the same effect.

We took a break from the studio work on these new pieces to undertake a tour of the States in April 1975. Some lessons had been learnt – our stage show benefited from a much higher professional input. Previously our special effects had been a dangerous mixture of imagination and passing acquaintance with the pyrotechnic arts. During one earlier gig at the Cobo Hall in Detroit, an over-enthusiastic application of flash powder coupled with a stage weight containing an air bubble in the casting nearly ended our careers in one bang. At the salient point in 'Careful With That Axe', instead of the boom and flash we expected there was an explosion of monumental proportions which blew out the cones of virtually every speaker we had, leaving the remainder of the show sounding rather thin. Alarmingly, pieces of shrapnel flew overhead hitting at least one member of the audience who fortunately refused to be hospitalised, and took a T-shirt in lieu of damages. Our road manager Chris Adamson remembers that the blast sent Roger's bass speakers ten rows into the empty seats behind the stage, and the road crew spent the following day rewiring all the cabinets before the next show.

On another occasion, at a gig at the Boston Gardens, squads of fire marshals were positioned around the venue to prevent us letting off unauthorised pyrotechnics. Show time arrived with no pyro in sight. In fact, it had all been secreted in boxes ready for individual members of the road crew to abandon their innocent demeanour and make a strategic dash to detonate a particular charge. The marshals began to rumble this tactic, but the crew were one step ahead. As one sprinting roadie was rugger-tackled by a hefty marshal, another explosion revealed that this had been a diversionary ruse. It was only our manager's Irish name and connections in Boston that stopped us all being locked up.

However, for the 1975 American tour we had fortunately acquired the services of Derek Meddings, the doyen of special effects, who was responsible for some of the best ever explosions in the James Bond movies. It was invaluable having access to Derek's know-how. His Bond connection gave us so much more clout with the fire marshals: they realised we knew what we were doing. His involvement also underlined the increasing sophistication and professionalism of the road crew.

In May and June we returned to the studios to push on with *Wish You Were Here*. We heard that the veteran jazz violinist Stephane Grappelli and the classical violinist Yehudi Menuhin were recording downstairs in Abbey Road and someone offered to make the introduction. It seemed an obvious idea to ask them to play. We thought they might have something to add to the title track, which – being essentially acoustic – seemed the most suitable vehicle. Both were pleased to be asked, and Stephane volunteered to take up the challenge. Yehudi preferred to stand listening to Stephane's sinuous jazz violin. It was just an experiment, and instead of running anything off onto two-track to keep, we simply recorded over the multi-track when we needed it for something else, once we had decided the addition of the violin didn't work.

A more enduring guest appearance was by Roy Harper. Roy was a blend of poet and troubadour in the tradition of great English eccentrics. He was part of Peter Jenner and Andrew King's Blackhill stable and a fellow EMI artist, and he was recording his album, *HQ*, at Abbey Road. We were having problems deciding how to sing 'Have A Cigar'. Roger was not happy with his vocal delivery. Rick and I thought David should sing the track, but he too was not sure he could do it justice. Roy had popped in to the control room – we would occasionally drop in to each other's sessions – and volunteered to sing the part. At the time, this seemed a good solution, although I think Roger in particular later regretted not doing the vocal, especially as he was increasingly feeling that it was important that he should sing the songs he had written.

It was during these sessions at Abbey Road, on 5th June, that we had one totally unexpected visitor. I strolled into the control room from the studio, and noticed a large fat bloke with a shaven head, wearing a decrepit old tan mac. He was carrying a plastic shopping bag and had a fairly benign, but vacant, expression on his face. His appearance would not have generally gained him admittance beyond studio reception, so I assumed that he must have been a friend of one of the engineers. Eventually David asked me if I knew who he was. Even then I couldn't place him, and had to be told. It was Syd. More than twenty years later I can still remember that rush of confusion.

I was horrified by the physical change. I still had a vision of the character I had last seen seven years earlier, six stone lighter, with dark curly hair and an ebullient personality. My memory was less of the wasted Syd who'd left the band in 1968, but much more of the character we knew when he came down to London from Cambridge, who played that distinctive Fender Esquire with its reflecting discs, had a wardrobe full of Thea Porter shirts and was accompanied by his beautiful blonde girlfriend.

Now he didn't seem like a man who appeared to have any particular friends at all. His conversation was desultory and not entirely sensible, though to be fair I don't think any of us was particularly articulate. Why he was there I've no idea. He wasn't invited and I hadn't seen him since he'd left the band in 1968, although in 1970 Roger, Rick and David had worked on Syd's two solo albums, Roger and David on *The Madcap Laughs* and David and Rick on *Barrett*. Syd was still living in London – he took a suite at the Hilton Hotel at one stage – and had obviously heard we would be at work in Abbey Road. His arrival suddenly and unexpectedly brought back a whole part of the life of the band. Guilt was one feeling. We had all played some part in bringing Syd to his present state, either through denial, a lack of responsibility, insensitivity or downright selfishness.

To have met Syd in the street would have been disconcerting, but coming across him without warning in the studio environment was particularly alarming. The fact that it wasn't just any studio but Studio 3 at Abbey Road, the site of most of his greatest work, and at one time his territory as much as anyone else's, added to the poignancy. It is very easy to try and draw parallels with any Peter Pan returning to find the house still there and the people changed. Did he expect to find us as we had been seven years earlier, ready to start work with him again?

We tried to continue the recording session, playing back the piece we were working on (legend has it that this was 'Shine On You Crazy Diamond' – the track most influenced by Syd's presence, or absence – although I'm not sure it actually was), but all of us were a little disturbed by his arrival. Syd listened to the playback, and was asked to comment. I don't remember him voicing any particular opinion, but when it was suggested that we run the track again Syd asked what the point would be since we had only just heard it...

Phil Taylor was there on the day Syd visited. He found himself in the canteen at Abbey Road, sitting at a table with David and Syd. David asked Syd what he was up to. 'Well,' said Syd. 'I've got a colour telly, and a fridge. I've got some pork chops in the fridge, but the chops keep going off, so I have to keep buying more.' Later Phil, driving away from the studios, saw Syd looking for a lift, but wasn't sure he could handle the conversation and ducked down as he went past.

Apart from the weirdness of his arrival at that stage and in that environment, we should credit his presence as a catalyst to the piece. The lyrics were already written, but Syd's visit underscored the melancholy of them, and maybe influenced the final version of the song. I still find the most affecting moment on the whole record is where the last notes fade out and Rick introduces a wistful rubato line, on high notes, from 'See Emily Play'.

After the success of *Dark Side*, we were able to pursue some more elaborate ideas with Storm and Hipgnosis. Storm presented four or five ideas tying into themes contained within the album – including the man swimming through sand, the frozen dive, the burning businessman and the flying veil – and rather than have to plump for one we decided to retain them all.

When the recording was complete, we turned our attention to the live shows. Deciding that we would bring in a director to shoot more specific footage for the back projections, we signed up the Hungarian director Peter Medak, whose previous films had included *A Day In The Death Of Joe Egg* and *The Ruling Class*, and he reshot 'Money' and 'On The Run'. Using a professional film director reflected our desire to move up another gear, and we used the same logic in asking Gerald Scarfe to create the animation.

We had first met Gerry through his brother-in-law Peter Asher, who we had known since the Sixties, when he was part of the duo called Peter and Gordon which had a hit in America with 'Lady Godiva' and 'World Without Love'. Peter was always helpful when we asked his advice, even if we didn't follow it; after his own performing career ended he became a very successful manager looking after James Taylor and Linda Ronstadt.

I had seen a wonderful hand-coloured piece of animation that Gerry Scarfe had done called 'Long Drawn-Out Trip' for a BBC programme, and when we were looking for new ideas for film he immediately sprang to mind. As Gerry is a very civilised man with clear opinions on politics and life, and the kind of black sense of humour that fitted in with ours, we soon established a good working relationship. He created images and film sequences amongst which were a human figure being eroded by the wind, and a surreal armadillo-like monster, both of which accompanied 'Welcome To The Machine'. As with Derek Meddings, Gerry's involvement was proof that commercial success had given us the chance to work with the best people in their fields.

During June 1975 we had returned to America on tour. We were trying to incorporate more and more complex effects. Of these, the inflatable pyramid was perhaps our most spectacular disaster. Roger, drawing on the architectural education the British taxpayer had kindly funded, had conceived a pyramid-shaped stage with an inflatable roof, thus solving all the design problems of the size of stage we required as well as providing protection from the weather at the same time. We applauded his vision, and thought it would look marvellous. The icing on the cake was, that as a climax to the show, the pyramid would gracefully ascend into the heavens on the end of a rope cable, delighting the assembled multitude below. Roger's design demanded pillars at each of the four corners reaching over forty feet high, a base size of some six hundred square feet (the size of a decent house), an overall height of eighty feet and a volume of helium sufficient for a Zeppelin. The slightest breath of wind would set the entire structure shuddering and wobbling in a manner not dissimilar to the way London's Millennium Bridge flexed when it was first opened.

The first show was in Atlanta, where the strength of the wind was outside our safety parameters and sufficient for the whole thing to fail. We tried hard to remedy the problem by sending the whole rig for repair and redesign during a series of indoor shows, but, bugged by poor weather, the difficulties of transporting the helium, and further high winds, when we got to Pittsburgh two weeks later, we eventually – like Captain Hornblower faced with an out-of-control mainsail – instructed someone to cut the thing free.

The device ascended to a few hundred feet before inverting, allowing the balloon in its peak to emerge like a teardrop through the base. 'My God, it's giving birth,' one chemically affected American shouted as it emerged. Now of course the fabric had insufficient lift – so as the teardrop headed for the stratosphere the world's biggest wet blanket settled ungracefully into the car park to be ripped to shreds by some scavenging souvenir hunters. At the end of this show, we were able to walk to the front of the stage, drop down to the ground and stroll without any hassle to our nearby hotel. This brought home the fact that our pyramid was more recognisable than we were – which was just how we liked it.

One small, but telling, clue that these tours were getting bigger and bigger was the size of the crew breakfast. I happened to be in one of the crew's rooms when breakfast arrived. The fact that it was after a show at two in the morning was one oddity, but it was the scale of the meal that impressed me. The breakfast was clearly designed to avoid eating again within the next twenty-four hours. Steak, eggs, bacon, sausage, hash browns, waffles, muffins and pancakes were accompanied by a platter of fresh fruit, cereal, French toast and syrups. Juice, coffee and a selection of liqueurs finished off the repast.

Our own appetite for stage effects was equally excessive, and continued through to Canada where, following our final North American show, some over-zealous crew member, encouraged by Alan Frey, our long-serving American agent, decided the easiest way to dispose of the remaining explosive was to attach it to the stadium's illuminated scoreboard and fire it off. The explosion was devastating. The board erupted in smoke, flame and scores of a thousand goals a side. Not only did we have to pay for a replacement scoreboard but also a great deal of glass for the neighbouring houses. Fortunately we made our excuses and left before the locals tracked us down.

We then rushed back to England on a completely crazed timetable for a technically challenged show at Knebworth. Time was too short or we were too frazzled. Part of the problem was that the generators were unstabilised. During the afternoon it became clear that all Rick's electric keyboards needed retuning. However, we managed to miss the significance of this and as darkness fell and our stage lights were operated, Rick's keyboards were changing pitch in unison with the sound. It sounded awful. It transpired that every time the master volume was turned up, the keyboards went out of tune. Below the stage, Phil Taylor, Robbie Williams and the technician from the generator company, in a scene reminiscent of *Das Boot*, strove to churn round the generator handle in an attempt to control the damage. Phil recalls that their efforts were 'manful, but hopeless' as the keyboards continued to see-saw between sharp and flat.

Rick walked off in despair at one point, and somehow or another we staggered through the show using only one piano and one less sensitive keyboard, and a more modest light show. Yet although we were painfully aware of the technical problems below and on stage, we managed to distract the audience with a great effect, when – instead of using model planes as we had done on other shows – we managed to co-ordinate a fly-past by two original Spitfires low over the crowd as the show opened.

THE BALLOON 8
GOES UP

PERHAPS INFLUENCED by the stately grandeur of Knebworth, this was the period we embarked on a little light empire building. We bought a building at 35 Britannia Row, just off the Essex Road in Islington. Britannia Row was a three-storey block of church halls which we in due course set about converting into a recording studio and storage facilities for our ever-expanding quantity of stage equipment. We were not dissatisfied with Abbey Road, but we were spending so much time in the studios that it seemed worthwhile creating an environment we could customise for our needs. It was also the mood of the times for bands to build their own recording studios: Pete Townshend had Eel Pie Studios and the Kinks owned Konk Studios.

The original deal we had agreed with EMI – where we had taken a cut in our percentage in exchange for unlimited studio time at Abbey Road – had lapsed, and so we were conscious that we might start incurring escalating studio costs. Somehow we convinced ourselves that Britannia Row would be a money-saving move. Indeed, we probably had dreams of a successful commercial studio, despite the substantial capital outlay it entailed.

At the time Roger and I were the only London-based band members – David was still living north of London near Royden in Essex and Rick was now up in Royston, south of Cambridge. So the location of Britannia Row in London N1 was reasonably convenient for David and Rick, quite convenient for me (I was living in Highgate, a few miles north-west), and annoyingly handy for Roger, whose place in Islington was only a couple of hundred yards away. Inconveniently for him, with the demise of his marriage to Judy, he was soon on the move to south-west London.

Of the three floors in the building we had bought, the ground floor was required for the studio. This meant that the main storage facility had to be above, which in turn entailed installing a chain hoist system to lug tons of equipment up and down, augmented with a fork-lift truck that teetered dangerously between the street and an unprotected trap door. The top floor became an office and home to a billiards table, which was one of the first pieces of equipment Roger insisted we needed. This helped him through the duller moments of recording; and thereafter billiard tables have tended to manifest themselves wherever he records. Should he tire of the lure of the green baize, he could sustain himself with the substantial fare offered by the studio caretaker – Albert Caulder, the father of one of our former roadies, Bernie – who devised a magnificent hamburger generously laced with garlic.

Our master plan for Britannia Row was to glide into becoming kings of the rental business on the assumption that other bands would be desperate to lease our equipment. Regrettably most of them did not need the wildly elaborate kit that we insisted on building for our shows, and most of the lighting towers and quadraphonic mixers stayed lurking in the back of the storeroom until they were, like loyal but elderly family pets, gently dispatched to a better world. As time went on, one by one the others slipped away from commercial involvement in both the rental and property side of the business, until I found myself the only remaining shareholder. Fortunately, in 1986, the management team of Brian Grant and Robbie Williams took it over. When last heard of it was flourishing, and has counted Pink Floyd among its clients.

If the rental company turned out to be a self-imposed millstone round our necks, the studio facility was much more interesting.

We had asked Jon Corpe, our old friend from the Regent Street Poly, to design the studio. Jon's plans incorporated a breeze block called lignacite for the structure. Lignacite – a composite of sawdust, sand and cement – is acoustically far less reflective than brick, which meant we could use it as the final finish for the studio instead of the usual bizarre blend of pinewood, crazy paving and carpet that was the preferred decor of the day.

Our intention was to build a shell in the full knowledge that any acoustic imperfections could be tuned out afterwards with pads and soft materials. We dug out the ground floor enabling us to drop a complete block structure within the framework of the existing building. This studio structure was floated on rubber insulating pads set onto a concrete slab. This was necessary to avoid the inevitable noise injunctions from the neighbours as well as stopping the rumble of trucks and buses trundling down the nearby New North Road. Like most recording studios, we seemed to suffer more complaints about tired and emotional people spilling out of the premises late at night, rather than noise escaping from the carefully constructed dungeons.

We also wanted to design a studio that could be used by any one of us on our own without an expert engineer or tape operator on hand to help. This meant designing a system that was simple enough for visiting players to be able to locate their headphone sockets without sending in an assistant to point out the relevant place. This worked surprisingly well. Everything was clearly labelled in layman's terms: the headphone socket would be called 'headphones' instead of the indecipherable code that tended to be the norm in the big commercial studios.

Our decision to avoid any excessive cosmetic decoration gave the place a fashionably austere feel. It was also our natural inclination – the Pestalozzi warden's house that Roger, Jon Corpe and I had designed for a project as architectural students was so forbidding no right-minded person would have wanted to live there. Roger was reported as saying 'It looks like a fucking prison' when he first saw the finished result at Britannia Row. 'That's appropriate, I suppose...' There was no natural light and after some hours the place could take on the grim and claustrophobic qualities of a nuclear bunker – although obviously much more stressful, particularly in the small control room, which was extremely cramped and had an uncomfortable seating arrangement along the back wall, perhaps to discourage visitors. At the time, the studio itself was still the most important area of activity in the recording process; more recently, with the ability to plug digital instruments and samplers straight into the mixing desk, bands tend to spend most of their time in the control room, rendering large studios obsolete, and large control rooms obligatory.

The construction work had taken up most of 1975, but by the end of that year we had been able to test out the equipment on a couple of jobs, one of which involved working with Robert Wyatt on some Mike Mantler songs. We had a mixing board and a 24-track tape machine from the American company MCI which, although not the most expensive available, was professional quality. This is where we recorded *Animals* in 1976. Although studios owned by bands might be an opportunity for considerable self-indulgence, Britannia Row represented a more minimalist, or perhaps parsimonious, approach.

Brian Humphries was in charge of the engineering. Although Brian had worked on our film music, our live shows and *Wish You Were Here*, the oppressive lack of space at Britannia Row, combined with the effects of life on tour, seemed to take an especial toll on him, as he began to show signs of wear and tear as the album progressed. This was exacerbated by the fact that Brian never totally realised that among a band noted for their left-of-centre sensibilities, it was wiser to keep his own somewhat more right-wing views to himself, especially when Roger was in earshot. For some reason, he used one particularly horrible scrap of duster throughout the whole job to clean off the marks on the mixing desk; it became his comfort blanket. Roger later had it framed and presented it to Brian after the completion of recording.

Much of the material for *Animals* already existed in the form of songs that Roger had previously written. 'Dogs' had been performed even before the *Wish You Were Here* album, on the Autumn 1974 tour of the UK, as a song called 'Gotta Be Crazy', and elements of 'Sheep' had appeared on the same tour as 'Raving And Drooling'. The music had thus been in gestation for well over a year, and had benefited from some toughening-up in front of the audiences on the tour.

Towards the end of recording Roger created two pieces called 'Pigs On The Wing' to open and close the album, designed to give the overall shape of the album a better dynamic and enhance the animal aspect of it. An unwanted side effect was that it opened up the question of the share-out of publishing royalties (which are based on the number of tracks, not their length) since it gave Roger two additional tracks, and meant that the longer piece 'Dogs', co-written with David, was not split up, but left as a single track. This was the kind of issue that would later prove contentious.

With a tour in the offing, we had been discussing the need to augment the band on tour, using another guitarist to play some of the pieces that David had overdubbed in the studio, and Steve invited a guitarist called Snowy White along to meet us. Snowy had played with the former Fleetwood Mac guitarist Peter Green as well as Cockney Rebel, and had just finished touring the States with Al Stewart when he received a message that Steve had been trying to get in touch, after Snowy had been recommended to Steve by Hilary Walker, who worked with Kate Bush.

Snowy remembers arriving in the control room at an

unfortunate moment. While Brian was on a break, Roger and I had assumed engineering duties, and successfully erased David's recently completed guitar solo. This was a perfect moment for me to recognise Roger's seniority... Snowy was given a cursory interview by David ('You wouldn't be here if you couldn't play, would you?') and later Roger ('Since you're here you might as well play something'), who gave Snowy a shot at a solo on 'Pigs On The Wing', a part made redundant when the track was split in two for the final album. However, Snowy had the consolation of the whole track – including his solo – appearing on the eight-track cartridge version, and thus appreciated by the select minority who purchased it. Snowy later appeared on the *Animals* tour, walking on every night to open the show with the bass intro to 'Sheep', confusing the front few rows of the audience as they tried to work out which of the Fab Floyd this character was, since there were no programmes or announcements to explain his appearance.

My memory of this period is that I enjoyed making this album more than *Wish You Were Here*. There was some return to a group commitment, possibly because we felt that Britannia Row was our responsibility, and so we were more involved in making the studio and the recording a success. Given that it belonged to us, we really could spend as long as we wanted in the studio, and there was no extra cost involved in unlimited frames of snooker or billiards.

Compared to some of our earlier efforts, *Animals* was really quite a straightforward album. My view is that it was not as complex in its construction as *Dark Side*, or *Wish You Were Here*. After recording the numbers the assembly seemed a relatively painless process, but maybe we had just got quicker at doing it. I have to say I don't have any particularly strong memories of the recording sessions themselves; it's much more to do with Britannia Row as a place.

Some critics felt that the music on *Animals* was harder and tougher than anything else we had done. There were various reasons why that might have been so. There was certainly a workman-like mood in the studio. We had never encouraged a stream of visitors to our previous recording sessions, but at Britannia Row the lack of space meant there was really only room for the crew in the cockpit.

Any harder edge may also have been a subconscious reaction to the accusations of 'dinosaur rock' that were being thrown at bands like Led Zeppelin, Emerson, Lake & Palmer and ourselves. We were all aware of the arrival of punk – even anyone who didn't listen to the music could not have failed to notice the Sex Pistols' explosion into the media spotlight. Just in case we had missed this, locked in our Britannia Row bunker, Johnny Rotten kindly sported a particularly fetching 'I hate Pink Floyd' T-shirt.

Punk was perhaps also a reaction to the decision by record companies to concentrate on what they thought of as guaranteed earners rather than taking risks with new acts – whereas in the 1960s they would have signed up anything with long hair, even a sheepdog. Nearly thirty years later the same is true once again. If a record company pays a huge amount of money for an established act, it is odds on that they will recoup the investment; they could spend the same amount on a dozen new bands and lose the whole lot. Financially it is perfectly understandable, but it does not foster fresh talent. One of the messages of punk was that it was possible to make records for thirty quid and some change. Although we could sympathise with the sentiments, we were, however, on the wrong side of the divide, as far as the punk generation were concerned. 'Of course, you don't want the world populated only with dinosaurs,' I said at the time, 'but it's a terribly good thing to keep some of them alive.'

Britannia Row made an unlikely Winter Palace, but the punk movement was the moment when we found ourselves on the wrong end of a cultural revolution, just as we had been very much on the right end of it during the underground days of 1966 and 1967. The ten-year cycle had turned, and will doubtless turn on. The cool blissed-out hippies of yesteryear are now harassed and stressed-out parents who mutter about the banality of *Pop Idol* and the incomprehensible lyrics on *Top Of The Pops*. They have, inevitably, found themselves turning into their parents – although now they, at least, are excruciatingly aware of the irony...

A year or so after the release of *Animals*, I got a call from Peter Barnes, our publisher. He wanted to know if I would like to produce an album for the Damned at Britannia Row. I don't think I was first choice. They really wanted Syd to produce them, which would have been remarkable, but impractical. I enjoyed the experience, probably rather more than they did. Unfortunately they were having a nasty dose of musical differences at the time, so there were conflicting messages about what they wanted to achieve.

The band contained a curious mix of outlooks. Rat Scabies and Captain Sensible were of the punk persuasion, but of the two I found the Captain considerably more alarming. Though Rat might set fire to something in fun on the spur of the moment, the Captain would have spent some time beforehand carefully assembling highly flammable materials. Dave Vanian was a dedicated Goth, while Brian James was the one who seemed to want to move the band into new musical areas. The Captain was not taken with this philosophical change. The suggestion of a particular bass line using a glissando slide was rejected out of hand, and the idea of more than a couple of takes was seen as heresy. We finished the album, and mixed it in the time Pink Floyd would have taken to set up the microphones.

Nick Griffiths, a former BBC engineer, who had joined us at the very end of the *Animals* recording, engineered these sessions. Nick remembers that one of the Damned crew took it upon himself to write all over those expensive Lignacite walls. The only solution was to painstakingly grind away the graffiti. Even the band were embarrassed, and although the vision of Rat Scabies and Captain Sensible donning rubber gloves is unlikely, they certainly issued orders for the scrawling to be scrubbed off.

In December 1976 the recording and mixing of *Animals* was complete, and work started on the album cover. Hipgnosis had presented three ideas, and just for once none of them appealed. So the cover emerged from a concept of Roger's, executed by Storm, based around Battersea Power Station, an odd vision of the future on the banks of the Thames, which was nearing the end of its active service. Initially completed in the early 1930s, and designed by Sir Giles Gilbert Scott – designer of Britain's iconic red telephone box, now also superseded – the building in fact consisted of two linked power stations; it was the second of these, constructed in 1953, that provided the skyline of London with its four towering chimneys. At the time Roger was living in Broxash Road, just off Clapham Common, and so was driving across London to reach the studios in Islington on virtually a daily basis, a route which took him past the looming chimneys of the power station, and provided the seed for the idea used on the cover.

A maquette for an inflatable pig was made by Andrew Saunders – with involvement from Jeffrey Shaw – and then the actual object was built for us by a German company. Ballon Fabrik had learnt their craft constructing the original Zeppelins, but in a nice display of swords into ploughshares, they subsequently built a number of inflatables for us. We ended up in early December at the disused power station with a giant porcine balloon (which was known as 'Algie' for some reason) – some thirty foot long, full of helium and very truculent – straining at its tether. As an extra precaution we had a trained marksman on standby in case Algie made a run for it.

Photography was scheduled for 2nd December, but the weather was inclement; we also had some rigging problems, so we decided to reconvene the following day. Unfortunately, although the weather had improved by early the next morning, the marksman had not arrived and was not in position by launch time. There was a sudden gust of wind, the steel hawser snapped, and Algie was off, ascending into the heavens at about two thousand feet a minute, a lot faster than the police chase helicopter scrambled to intercept it. This was not a deliberate stunt and we were well aware that apart from losing an expensive piece of kit we could cause a major aviation disaster. Lawyers were summoned, emergency plans mapped out, and scapegoats nominated.

One of my favourite memories from the whole incident is the meeting involving our lawyer Bernard Sheridan, at which Linda Stanbury, our PA at the time, indoctrinated in the mentality of tour paperwork and overhearing the news that the pig was heading towards Germany, groaned 'But it hasn't got a carnet…' (The bureaucracy of touring was daunting. Endless lists of equipment, forms in triplicate every time the trucks were loaded up. The team could not cut any corners. At any border crossing, the customs control might decide on a whim to go through the whole damn lot. The annoying thing was that even the customs didn't seem to know how the forms worked. On one occasion we had a run-in with the authorities when Belgian customs tore off the wrong part of a form, or stamped the wrong section of a carnet, and it took three years to convince the Belgian authorities that we had not had a mammoth car boot sale of three articulated lorries' worth of equipment. The encouragement of free movement within the European Community has led to at least one advantage.)

Thankfully the pig descended of its own accord, and was recovered by a farmer in Kent with no damage done. There was a story of an airline pilot spotting the errant pig as he came in to land at Heathrow, but being afraid to report it in case flight control thought he had been drinking. Sadly I think this is apocryphal. The awful truth is that the image of the pig was stripped into the final cover later on, because the best image of the power station, in a moody cloudscape, had been taken on an earlier recce day, when Algie was absent.

A number of inflatable pigs were to become tour regulars. At some of the outdoor shows one would float over the audience before being pulled in to disappear behind the stage. Later an identical, but cheaper, cousin would rise in its place and, filled with helium with a propane stomach, explode in a conflagration that on the Hollywood scale of disaster effects was well up at the *Die Hard* end. At one venue, the propane was replaced with a mix of oxygen and acetylene as an experiment, producing such an explosion that Mark Fisher's ears still ring, not from the blast, but from the dressing-down he received from Steve O'Rourke.

We also had some fireworks which when they detonated released sheep-shaped parachutes which then gently floated down. The company which made these for us had polished the technique for a Saudi Arabian sheikh whose picture was similarly released for his birthday celebrations – this particular company told us they inherited the job when their predecessors, at the sheikh's enthronement, had inadvertently used a picture of his cousin, who had just been deposed...

The *Animals* tour was our first 'branded' tour. Previously material from a new album would naturally have been included in any gigs on tour, but this was the first time that we were conscious of going out on the road specifically to promote a particular album. The tour opened at the Westfalenhalle in Dortmund on 23rd January 1977 and after Europe in February and the UK in March we headed over to the States for three weeks in April and

May, and a further three weeks in June and July.

We had underestimated our promoters' enthusiasm for the pig motif. In San Francisco, Bill Graham had organised a pen full of the animals backstage, and none of them seemed very happy to be there. David's wife Ginger, who he had met on one of our US tours a couple of years earlier, was a strict vegetarian and animal lover, and she was aghast. She leapt into the pen demanding their freedom, and refused to leave until oaths had been sworn as to their future welfare.

Marcel Avram, our long-time German promoter, presented us with a piglet in Munich. Once again a home had to be found for the new arrival, and with various apparently hungry Germans eyeing the piglet greedily, our tour manager Warwick McCredie was drafted in to take it back to the hotel for the night. We were staying at a particularly smart Hilton close to the venue, but Warwick managed to smuggle the piglet in without detection. The real problem was that Warwick's room had mirrored walls, and the pig kept seeing a myriad of other pigs staring at him. He did not care for this. During the night the piglet cracked most of the glass at floor level, as well as spreading a film of excrement along every surface. The next morning I saw Steve peel off to the reception desk as we hurriedly left after surveying the full horror. I never could quite bring myself to ask him about the conversation that ensued.

The larger stadiums that we now were playing brought with them a range of new problems. At smaller theatre venues, the audience is admitted just before show time, but at a baseball stadium the sheer size of the crowd and the resulting car park requirements mean that the stadium has to be opened three or four hours before the start. The increased scale of the venues also required more elevated levels of fitness, not to mention mountaineering skills, from the road crew. We now had a team known as 'the quad squad', the SAS of humpers, who were charged with lugging our quad speakers to the furthest and highest corners of stadiums and auditoria.

We have rarely used a support act on tour. There are a number of reasons for this. In the early days, there was a certain element of combat between the bands appearing on a bill – and the first acts on would aspire to out-perform the headline act, to 'blow them off the stage'. In our case, our additional props, like the Daleks, also meant that resetting the stage after another band was a lengthy process. In later times, it was more a question that any support act would simply destroy the mood we were trying to create, by over-exciting, boring or alienating our audience. As far as stadium shows were concerned, not having a support act meant that the audience could get to see the main event early in the evening around 8 p.m., rather than sitting through two or three other bands' sets. Even so, with nothing much to amuse them, stuck either under a baking sun or pouring rain, the crowd could get restless. There were always a few who tended to load up on alcohol or drugs – and then promptly pass out when the band hit the stage. It could sometimes be a distraction, as we tried to spot members of the audience nodding off or completely comatose.

We were becoming increasingly conscious of crowd control, security and safety. With up to 80,000 people swilling around it's like being elected mayor of a small town for the night, with all the attendant responsibilities including car crashes, petty theft, children being born… There's even some live music if you're lucky. We were learning the facts of life of touring, including the realisation that although you may be able to relate to the first thirty rows of people, it is extremely difficult to capture and hold the attention of the invisible ranks at the back of the crowd.

The shows on this tour varied in quality. Although we were still improvising a little, this was limited – but this was not in itself the main problem. The lack of consistent quality was due to other reasons. These were short tours and we were not spending enough rehearsal time on key aspects of the show like seguing from one number to the next, or syncing with the projected films. And my memory is that some of the staging was as erratic as the music, since we never allowed enough time for stage rehearsals. We also always underestimated the weather factor. The wind and the rain were constant threats, and could both play havoc with our sound levels and quality, all of which would affect our concentration and the mood of the audience.

However, on the *Animals* tour, one feature of the stage set had been developed for the inevitable onslaught of bad weather at open-air stadiums: a set of mechanical umbrellas. These could be raised from under the stage and then opened, and although the motors operating them proved unreliable, they looked terrific bursting from the stage and then flowering out. As we progressed into using more and more gear suspended from trusses such devices became obsolete, but on this tour we could still rely on the audience being surprised by the sudden transformation of the stage into a Continental pavement café. We did try similar individual umbrellas again on the *Division Bell* tour, but David threw his to the ground in a fit of pique as he said afterwards he felt daft standing under a dripping plastic palm tree, and Rick nearly collapsed with asphyxiation as smoke became trapped in the inverted fish bowl we had thoughtfully created for him.

One consistently effective feature in the shows was the use of cherry-pickers either side of the stage – an idea instigated by Arthur Max. These are the kind of hydraulic lifts used to change the bulbs in street lamps, but instead of a simple cradle, each unit had a spotlamp mounted on it, which was manoeuvred by a black-clad operator squatting behind it. With the addition of revolving beacons, the cherry-pickers made a great opening for any show, as they rose slowly from below stage level. The lights could also be dropped down alarmingly close to the band, close enough to singe the lead guitarist's hair on at least one occasion.

Despite the larger venues, and the increase in paraphernalia on stage, the crew we were using was about the same size as it had been on the tours a couple of years earlier. We were still sending out for burgers (tour catering was not yet an exact science) or feasting on whatever the promoter decided to provide – usually burgers, or a huge plate of cold cuts.

There were no office facilities at the venues in 1977. Most of the ever-increasing mass of bureaucracy and legal, technical and financial issues was being dealt with out of the hotel rooms of Steve, Robbie and Graeme Fleming, and most of the paperwork had to fit into the rather smart aluminium briefcases that had become the style statement for the upper echelons of the road crew.

For the musicians there was a realisation that the big tours can also be much lonelier – they only discover your body slumped in the hotel bedroom when you don't show up on the bus two days later. And it's easier to become isolated from the rest of the band. In the days when we were all driving around in one van, we simply had to avoid falling out with each other every day otherwise it would have been impossible to carry on. But on the larger tours there is a tendency for people to split into smaller groups.

With the rise in status from club to stadium, the local promoters – in a spirit of goodwill and the hope you will stay with their organisation – are always proposing activities that range from sailing, dune buggies and speedboating to a trip to Disneyland or a visit to the local fish market at 5 a.m. next morning. Often, late at night, one of these outings will be suggested as an excursion for the following day. Everyone agrees, enthused by champagne and canapés, and the arrangements are made – but by first thing the day after, it has usually lost its appeal. So a fleet of limos arrives at the hotel entrance only to find three tired and embarrassed tour party members ready to be picked up, rather than the promised forty.

If you do go out en masse without a promoter or record exec on hand to pick up the bill, an outing involving drinking can easily become a terrifying financial experience as the more experienced participants make their excuses and slip away early, leaving the luckless victim holding the tab, and filled with a grim determination never to socialise again, certainly not in an overpriced hotel bar.

The end of the *Animals* tour marked another low point. David now says that this was one period when he really felt that it might be all up for Pink Floyd. His view is that we had achieved, and sustained, the success we had originally wanted as a band, and accordingly were finding it difficult to see what more we could do.

We returned to the UK to find that the top floor of the Britannia Row building was beginning to silt up with accountants, as business matters became increasingly obtrusive in our lives. By this time we were all turning up at business meetings with briefcases, almost certainly covered in the hide of animals nearing extinction. This may have made us feel like businessmen, and we were certainly given the impression that we could put off the next album forever because of the revenue we were earning. It sounded so easy: you talked a bit, had lunch and doubled your money.

One of the great attributes of the men in chalk-stripe suits, like doctors, is a good bedside, or deskside, manner. Noel Redding, the bass player with the Jimi Hendrix Experience, always felt he had been turned over particularly badly by the contractual vagaries of the industry, and had a quote handy for anyone wanting to enter the music business and asking his advice: 'Study law. Buy a gun…'

We should have taken heed. We had been seduced in the

afterglow of *Dark Side* into an involvement with a company of financial advisers called Norton Warburg. In 1977–8 the earnings from *Dark Side* and *Wish You Were Here* were flowing through, and tax in the UK for high earners was 83 per cent, and 98 per cent on invested profits. Norton Warburg persuaded us to enter a scheme that would save tax; venture capital was the buzzword, and the proposal was to turn us into a working company by investing Pink Floyd money in a variety of enterprises. The annoying downside was that even should they turn out to be successful, we would have to get rid of them to avoid attracting the interest of the revenue men (and women) by unholy profit-making, since that was the way the deal was constructed.

As it was, this was unlikely to be a concern, since many of these business ideas were so flawed that no banker in their right mind would even consider them. During this period we were involved in carbon-fibre rowing boats, pizzas, and a restaurant on a floating barge. There was a failed hotel that went into fudge manufacturing, a children's shoe company, the Memoquiz (a precursor of the Game Boy), a car hire business and a skateboarding firm called Benji Boards. In one case, we were puzzled when a company we had been told had been unofficially sanctioned by Rolls-Royce to deal in second-hand cars, seemed to have a number of delivery problems: cars either did not arrive or if they did were worse than the group Bentley in which we had escaped near death on the Jimi Hendrix tour of 1967. Eventually two of the directors of this particular company served a period of time at Her Majesty's pleasure.

However, we had little time to investigate, as our thoughts and energies had turned to producing an album to follow *Animals* – and we needed some new material. We were faced by one particular problem. Two of the potential composers in the band, namely David and Rick, had been working on solo projects and so had little if any spare material to present to the band.

David's solo album, called simply *David Gilmour*, was released in May 1978 – on the album he worked again with Willie Wilson who had been a fellow Joker Wild before David joined us in 1968. Rick had also been working on his own solo album, *Wet Dream*, with a band that included Snowy White on guitar. I had briefly worked with Steve Hillage on the production of Steve's album *Green*, which was engineered by John Wood, the engineer on our original 'Arnold Layne' recording session at Sound Techniques Studios in January 1967.

Whenever any member of the band went off to do any kind of solo work, it never became an issue, as it so easily could have done, and has with other bands – the difficult days of the Mick Jagger/Keith Richards relationship in the 1980s focused around exactly that issue. All of us have done our own albums, and produced other artists, and rather than prove a source of tension or jealousy, it seems that it has actually provided a useful safety valve.

Luckily, Roger solved the shortage of material. While we had all been otherwise engaged, he had been working alone in his home studio. Roger's demos varied wildly in quality. Some were so good that we could never improve on them in the studio, and would revert to the original. Others were really just rough sketches, over-modulated and distorted. Roger actually disputed this, claiming that they were all of excellent quality, and has threatened to play them in their entirety to me again to prove his point – consequently, I graciously concede to his view.

WRITING ON THE WALL 9

THE MOMENT that sparked *The Wall* happened at a show in Montreal's Olympic Stadium during the *Animals* tour of 1977. This was a gigantic sports stadium, overlooked by a futuristic tower, that had been constructed for the Olympic Games of the year before. The tower soared up to enormous heights, and by its very scale the venue was not conducive to a warm and fuzzy rapport with the fans.

There was a relatively small but over-excited group in the audience close to the stage, who were probably high on chemicals and definitely low on attentiveness. Being right at the front they were audible and defined our sense of the audience's mood. During the break between a couple of numbers, this group were shouting out suggestions for songs. When Roger's eye was caught by one particularly vocal member of the claque yelling, 'Play "Careful With That Axe", Roger,' he finally lost patience, and spat at the offender.

This was more than unusual, it was weird. Roger had always been the spokesman on stage since Syd's departure, and handled the introductions, the gaps in proceedings when the projectors broke down or the hecklers with some aplomb, and often with some droll observations. This incident just indicated that establishing any kind of bond with the audience was becoming increasingly difficult.

Roger was not alone in feeling depressed about this show. Over the years we had evolved a definitive final encore, where we played a slow twelve-bar blues while the crew gradually removed all the equipment and instruments, leaving one lone, silent musician to walk off stage. On this occasion, David was so upset by the mood of the concert that he refused even to take part in the encore.

Although the spitting incident was unnerving at the time, it did serve to set Roger's creative wheels spinning, and he developed the outline for a show based around the concept of an audience both physically and mentally separated from their idols. Whether the confrontation in Montreal had any life-changing impact on the hapless spat-upon fan remains unknown; suffice to say that he has never employed a lawyer, nor claimed any royalties for creative inspiration.

The Wall as a piece represents a large amount of material spread across a range of media: the record, the concerts – enhanced with film, stage effects and props – and a movie. This had been Roger's intention from the outset. He had already shown his fondness for exploring the possibilities of multimedia, but *The Wall* took things considerably further. The whole project also covered a large amount of time, a period of work that actually lasted from mid-1978, when Roger was creating the initial version, until 1982, with the release of the movie.

Roger had learnt from experience that one maxim for work was to know when the time was right to push an idea ahead. At some point during 1978 he clearly felt that it was that time and set to work in his home studio. By the time he played the results to us – I remember going to his house on at least one occasion to listen to them, and he also brought the tapes into Britannia Row – he actually had two records roughed out, one being *The Wall* and the other *The Pros And Cons Of Hitch-hiking*.

Although it later underwent an enormous transformation, and in fact Roger ended up rewriting the whole piece in France, the *Wall* demo contained sufficient clarity and enough concepts – some only in outline form, others relatively well fleshed out – for us all to understand that this had much more potential than just an album. Equally we all felt less inspired by *The Pros And Cons Of Hitch-hiking*; it seemed better left for Roger to do on his own (which he did in 1984). *The Wall*, it was obvious even then, was a major new work – and I think we could all imagine ourselves performing it. It was also a huge relief for us to be presented with such a complete concept so early in the process.

On one of the demo tracks I could hear myself cursing down the phone. Roger had needed a ringing telephone tone as a rhythm, and assuming I was out, had called my home number without bothering to check whether I was there or not. I had picked up the phone and initially thought it was a crank call, since it seemed there was a madman crooning on the other end of the line – hence my swearing. Some time later, it transpired that this had been Roger singing away. Meanwhile, both of us remained confused for some time.

Steve O'Rourke also listened to the demos: he was the only one able (or honest enough) to remember selecting *Pros And Cons* as his favoured piece. This continued the time-honoured tradition of allowing us to sneer at the management's musical taste, but in Steve's defence it must be remembered that the demos of *The Wall* did not yet contain any of the well-known songs, such as 'Run Like Hell' or 'Comfortably Numb'.

The level of contributions by other members of the band would become a bone of contention. Perhaps the very completeness of Roger's demo made it difficult for David or Rick to contribute much. But certainly David later felt that his musical contribution, especially to 'Run Like Hell' and 'Comfortably Numb' was not being fairly recognised. This potential volcano of future discord was, however, still dormant when we started making rough versions of some of the tracks for *The Wall* at Britannia Row during the autumn of 1978.

When work began we were short of an engineer. I think we felt that Brian Humphries was now completely exhausted, and suffering an extreme case of Floyd burn-out. Alan Parsons was now the Alan Parsons Project and Nick Griffiths was felt to be still a relatively unknown quantity, so we started looking and asking round for a young but talented engineer with a track record who could bring a different approach to our sound. In the end Alan recommended James Guthrie, who had been producing and engineering a number of bands including Heatwave, The Movies and Judas Priest as well as a band called Runner. James's track record, particularly an instantly identifiable shimmering audio edge he had brought to his work with Runner, suggested that he could add a fresh, brighter feel to our work.

Steve O'Rourke asked James to come in to his office. James had little knowledge of who Steve managed or what he wanted to talk about. He says that Steve had two projects he wanted to discuss. One was Tom Robinson, the other Pink Floyd. 'I calmly picked my jaw up from the ground, composed myself and nodded professionally, but my heart was racing. Steve said that the band had listened to some of my work and were interested in meeting me. He stressed that this would be a co-production. I thought, "These guys have been producing themselves since I was in school. I have no problem with that."' James met Roger whom he recalls as 'courteous and serious, carefully analysing my every word and gesture'. They discussed Roger's concept for *The Wall* and James was sent a copy of the demo.

The infinitely patient James was a complementary counterbalance to the extremely energetic and often irascible Bob Ezrin. Although we had produced *Dark Side* and *Wish You Were Here* ourselves, Roger had decided to import Bob as a co-producer and collaborator. Bob was an established producer who had worked on a number of Alice Cooper albums and Lou Reed's

Berlin. He had been introduced to us via Roger's second wife Carolyne, who had worked for Bob, and in fact had taken him along to the show in Hamilton, Ontario, where we exploded the scoreboard.

On the same occasion Bob had also brought along a friend who was a psychoanalyst as well as a fan of the band. After seeing Roger cut his foot after the show in a mock fight with Steve, the psychoanalyst had suggested it might be a good idea if he joined the tour as a permanent crew member… James Guthrie has astutely remarked that once he had been deemed trustworthy, it was like becoming accepted in a family, 'albeit a very dysfunctional family', as he recalls me once saying.

Bob clearly remembers his first visit to meet us at Britannia Row. He was late, because not thinking to lay on a car from the airport for him, we had simply told him to rent a car and fight his way across central London. Eventually locating the studios, the first person Bob met was a haggard Brian Humphries, coming down the stairs. Brian looked awful; he saw Bob and said, '*They* did this to me…' When Bob entered the room we were in, he was greeted by the sight of Roger pointedly tapping his watch. Bob maintains he later took Roger to one side and said, 'I already have a father; don't ever do that to me in public again.' Steve O'Rourke arrived to find a somewhat tense atmosphere, a whole conference of producers, and Bob threatening to walk out. Oil was poured and Bob placated.

As we settled into recording, we started looking for new ambiences. We tried to achieve something of a live auditorium sound, by recording some of the drums in a vast open space at the top of Britannia Row, the glass-roofed, wooden-floored room which housed Roger's precious billiards table. Since the room was totally lacking in any soundproofing or noise deadening, the other occupants of the building may not have totally appreciated the experience. Not only could they hear nothing but the drums, deprived of any backing track and out of any musical context, but once the drums started, they had no idea of how long this devilish racket would last.

Still, unlike early rehearsals, we owned the building and so were not receptive to grievances, rather like the guy in the Continental Hyatt House in Los Angeles (known as the 'Continental Riot House') who after a request to his neighbour to turn down the noise found three men trying to break down his door in order to kill him. A phone call down to reception elicited the rather unhelpful advice that, 'This hotel caters to the music business. We don't accept complaints.'

For the first time the drum sound on *The Wall* was kept intact throughout the recording process. The drums and bass were initially recorded on an analogue 16-track machine, and mixed down to two tracks on a 24-track machine for the overdubs, retaining the original recording for the final mix. This avoided the inevitable degradation that occurs with the tapes being constantly played for the addition of the other instruments and vocals.

However, although Britannia Row had been adequate for recording *Animals*, it now became clear that it was not up to the task for *The Wall*. We had already installed a large quantity of replacement equipment. This was primarily due to Bob and James wanting to upgrade it to their own demanding standards, and it seemed that everyone who arrived to work on the production side also brought along their own preferred piece of kit. We soon had a new Stephens 24-track in place, and the existing monitors were also swiftly replaced.

After all this work and respecification, we had to up sticks and change our recording venue anyway, as external events overtook us. This was the period when our business affairs outside the band exploded. We had brought in a financial adviser in the shape of

Norman Lawrence to administer the Britannia Row studios at the suggestion of Norton Warburg, the company who had been handling our investments. Norman, although ostensibly a Norton Warburg man, began to notice that there was something very wrong in the whole set-up, and started to investigate.

The truth that emerged was that Norton Warburg had been siphoning off funds from their investments company, an apparently gilt-edged set-up, to underwrite the disastrous venture capital side, all those skateboards, pizzas and dodgy cars. Eventually the company founder Andrew Warburg fled to Spain, returning to England in 1982, where he was arrested, charged, and served three years. A lot of people lost their money. Because Norton Warburg had been approved by reputable organisations such as American Express and the Bank of England many people had put their entire life savings or pensions in. The widows and pensioners were not going to have any further opportunities to go back to work. We were lucky that we still had the potential to work again.

All of these business problems had little to do with our music. But the ramifications had a significant impact on the decisions we had to make about our next album. We discovered that we had lost in the region of £1 million between the four of us. The losses in the venture capital companies were frighteningly large, and since we had been investing pre-tax funds – the whole point of the exercise – we now had a huge tax exposure, which, according to our financial advisers, could have been anywhere between £5 million and £12 million.

The problem was exacerbated by the fact that rather than having a single venture capital company, we had decided that each of us would have our own individual one. The ramifications of that decision quadrupled – at the very least – the tax implications. The suggestion was put to us that we should become non-resident in the UK for one year so that we could earn some money and replenish the dwindling coffers, and provide some time for our accountants and tax specialists to salvage something from the wreckage. The whole experience cast an enormous cloud over us. We had always prided ourselves on being smart enough not to be caught out like this. We saw ourselves as educated, middle class, in control of everything. We had been utterly wrong.

The answer was exile. Showing an alacrity that the Great Train Robbers might have admired, within two or three weeks we were packed and on the way. It seemed by far the best option. The tax residence rules meant we had to leave the UK before 6th April 1979 and not come back until after 5th April the following year, not even for the briefest of visits. This exile option was actually seized on with glee by a number of rock bands, who were grateful to benefit from the government's apparent largesse. In our case, it was simply essential. On later tours we were able to take advantage of a rule that involved staying abroad for at least 365 days, but with some visits back allowed (a wheeze originally introduced by the Labour government of the 1970s to encourage exports and benefit oilmen working out in the Middle East).

The prospect of not only one year of tax-free income to pay the debts, but also the opportunity to make a new start on our music without the distractions of lawyers and accountants, was irresistible. In any case Bob felt that the comfortable family home life that we were all enjoying in the UK was another factor in slowing down the process of making a hard-edged rock opus. We almost welcomed the chance to go overseas to escape. Like naughty children abandoning an untidy playroom, we were able to leave the financial mess behind for the professionals to clear up.

While we worked abroad, our advisers dismantled the partnership we had for touring – a throwback to the ideals of Blackhill – and restructured everything in negotiation with the gentlemen and ladies of the Inland Revenue. At one point, Nigel Eastaway remembers, we had 200 sets of accounts on hold, waiting for agreement with the revenue, an indication of the size of the problem. We could hardly get into Britannia Row for the serried ranks of accountants – but the deal they structured just about covered their costs. Steve O'Rourke and Peter Barnes also negotiated a major publishing deal with Chappell's to help provide additional revenue.

The studio in France we started working in, and where most of the groundwork for *The Wall* was carried out, was called Super Bear. Both Rick and David had worked there on solo projects the previous year and liked the atmosphere. It was located high up in the Alpes-Maritimes about thirty minutes' drive from Nice, set apart from a small village, with its own tennis court and pool and plenty of lounging space. We interspersed recording with tennis and occasional trips to the fleshpots of Nice – the lengthy drive there discouraged too frequent trips.

While Rick and I stayed at Super Bear itself, Roger and David rented villas nearby. Meanwhile Bob Ezrin installed himself at the sumptuous Negresco Hotel in Nice. An invitation to dinner with Bob was like dining with royalty. In the hotel restaurant, Bob was on first-name terms with the maitre d', who was all over Bob, as the expression goes, like a cheap suit in the rain. After savouring magnificent Michelin three-star cuisine, we would thank Bob effusively as he generously signed the bill. It was only halfway through the drive back into the hills, subdued probably by the effect of the vintage wines proffered by the sommelier, that we realised that we were in fact the ones picking up the tab.

Bob's timekeeping was, to say the least, erratic, but in a strange way his constant lateness – each day he had another more elaborate and increasingly less credible excuse – served to focus our energies as he became the target for our tongue-in-cheek resentment. It was great, just like being on tour again.

I had laid down the drum tracks early on at Super Bear, and so spent most of the time as an interested observer. Roger had rented a large villa above Vence – and I moved in, since the studio accommodation, although delightful, was a curious mix of boarding school and Espresso Bongo. Each day we used to drive the forty miles from the villa to the studio. Between us, Roger and I used two sets of tyres on my Ferrari Daytona in eleven weeks.

With the drum parts complete I was excused boots to go to Le Mans. I gave Roger my gold Rolex – a present from EMI after ten years' not-so-hard labour – for safe keeping (he did return it) and Steve and I set off on a boy's own mission for the weekend. Actually, it was quite a big adventure. This was my first real experience of motor racing, and as deep ends go it was Captain Nemo territory. Earlier in the year I had managed a brief test session in the two-litre Lola that I was to drive with the Dorset Racing Team, but had never got to the sort of racing speeds achievable on the five-mile Mulsanne straight, or experienced racing at night. It is, to say the least, exciting to be travelling at around 200mph, and then to be passed by a Porsche doing another 40mph more.

The fact that a number of my competitors were world-class sports car champions added to the experience, and the paddock was a motorsport equivalent of backstage at Woodstock. Le Mans is an extraordinary race, one of the last opportunities for the amateurs to compete with the big boys, and still have the chance of a result. The Lola ran faultlessly, and my only real scare was during qualifying when I poked my head too far above the windscreen. The slipstream caught the edge of my helmet and I thought my head was about to be wrenched off. Fortunately the only ramification was neck ache for the following week. We not only ended up with a finish – deemed an achievement in itself –

but also gained a 2nd in class and won the index of performance. Steve's Ferrari finished a few places ahead. This was without doubt the best form of rejuvenation prior to returning to Berre-les-Alpes.

While I had been let off quite lightly, Rick had a much harder time of it. At some point in the summer, shortly after Le Mans, Dick Asher at Sony/CBS had proposed a deal, offering to increase the percentage points we would earn if we could deliver a completed album in time for an end-of-year release. Roger, in consultation with Bob, did a quick calculation and critical path, and said it might just be possible. The decision was taken to use another studio fifty miles or so away called Miraval. This was owned by the jazz pianist Jacques Loussier, and was in a faux château. Apart from anything else you could dive off the walls and swim in the moat. Although all studios trumpet their unique features, this facility had to be one up on any number of jacuzzis. Recording was divided up between both studios, with Bob oscillating between the two locations. As well as dealing with the physical divide, Bob was grappling with the job of bridging a developing rift between David and Roger. Yet somehow he managed to ensure that as well as handling this role, he also got the best work out of both.

The keyboard parts, however, were still to be recorded. The only way to achieve the proposed release date was for Rick to curtail his summer vacation; we had previously agreed to record through the spring and early summer and then have a break. As my drum parts were laid down early this was not an issue for me. But when Rick heard, via Steve, that he had to do his keyboard parts in the summer holidays, he refused point blank. When this was relayed back to Roger, he was stunned and furious. He felt he was doing an enormous amount of work, and that Rick was not willing to make any effort to help.

The situation was made worse by the fact that Rick had wanted to be a producer on *The Wall* – as if we didn't have enough already – and Roger had told him that was OK as long as he made a significant contribution. Alas, Rick's contribution was to turn up and sit in on the sessions without doing anything, just 'being a producer'. This had not gone down well with Bob either, who felt this particular broth already had too many cooks, and Rick had been relieved from production duties. Nonetheless Bob volunteered to help Rick with the keyboard sections, but for any of the many possible reasons, Roger was never satisfied with Rick's performances.

Whatever bond Rick had enjoyed with Roger in the previous fifteen or so years was terminally broken, and Rick's downfall was swift. Steve was happily cruising to America on the *QE2* when he was called by Roger and told to have Rick out of the band by the time Roger arrived in LA, where the album was due to be mixed. Rick, said Roger, could stay on as a paid player for the *Wall* shows, but after that he was no longer to be a band member. If this was not done Roger threatened to pull the plug on the whole enterprise. This sounded like a madman with a gun pointed at his own head.

However, rather than fight, Rick acquiesced, perhaps with relief. I think a number of factors contributed to this decision. The demotion from production responsibilities, along with the difficulties, even with Bob's help, of providing keyboard parts that satisfied Roger were exacerbated by the crumbling of his marriage to Juliette, and like all of us he was worried about the financial implications if we did not finish the album. As it transpired Rick's decision was quite beneficial for him: as a salaried performer on *The Wall* he was the only one of us to make money from the live shows. The remaining three of us shared the losses...

I still find it hard to really cover some of the events of this period properly. Roger was probably still my closest friend, and we were able to enjoy each other's company. But our friendship was increasingly put under strain as Roger struggled to modify what had been an ostensibly democratic band into the reality of one with a single leader.

After the initial recording was completed, operations were transferred to Los Angeles for the mixing phase. Orchestral overdubs had been arranged and conducted by the composer and arranger Michael Kamen. Brought in by Bob Ezrin, Michael recorded the arrangements at the CBS studios in New York, only meeting the band at the end of the sessions. In the car park outside the Producer's Workshop in LA where the mixing was being carried out, various effects were recorded including the screech of tyres for 'Run Like Hell'. This involved Phil Taylor slewing a Ford LTD van around the car park with Roger inside, screaming at full volume.

Meanwhile, back in Britannia Row, Nick Griffiths was getting on with a long list of other sound effects he had been asked to gather together, ranging from the Brit Row staff chanting 'Tear down the wall!' to the sound of trolley-loads of crockery being smashed. For one SFX Nick had travelled around the country for a week to record buildings being demolished. He was rather disappointed to find that the demolition companies were so professional that they were able to bring down huge buildings with small amounts of explosive at the weak points and there really wasn't much noise to record. In the middle of this, he took a call from the States at two in the morning London time. Roger and Bob were on the line, and Nick felt rather fearful, in case he had messed up the effects. However, they only wanted to ask if he could record two or three kids singing some lines from 'Another Brick In The Wall' in a rather pathetic voice. Nick said, 'Of course' but also remembered a favourite album by Todd Rundgren, which featured an audience in each of the stereo channels. He suggested recording a whole choir of children. Yes, he was told, but do the three kids too.

Nick popped down the road from Britannia Row to the local school, where he found the music master Alun Renshaw extremely receptive. Nick agreed a loose deal whereby in exchange for recording some of the schoolchildren, we would record the school orchestra. The slave tape carrying the backing track arrived by courier from LA, along with photocopied lyrics. 'That's a bit strong,' Nick thought as he read them early one morning after a long night in the studio.

He set up some mikes, recorded the three children on their own as planned, then invited the rest of the kids in. While Nick engendered enthusiasm by singing along and jumping up and down in the studio, the recording was wrapped up in the forty minutes he had available – the length of the lesson that the school had given the children off. The tape was packed up, mixed quickly and sent back to LA. A few days later Roger rang to say he liked it – and the next time Nick heard the track it was on the radio.

Following the success of the single, in Nick Griffiths's words 'all hell broke loose'. The press had camped on the studio doorstep, anxious to report on the apparent exploitation of angel-faced schoolchildren by unscrupulous rock stars, only to find we were safely 7,000 miles away. Following instructions not to talk to them, Nick had to squeeze out of a back window to escape on a couple of occasions. Eventually a deal was struck with the school, and it was decided that the whole school should benefit since the recording had been done in school time.

That 'Another Brick' appeared as a single was partly due to the influence of Bob Ezrin, who curiously had always wanted to produce a disco single. We, on the other hand, had abandoned the idea of releasing singles in a fit of pique in 1968 when 'Point Me

At The Sky' failed to dent the charts. Bob maintains that such was the lack of enthusiasm to make a single that it was only at the last minute that the piece was tailored to the requisite length. The tempo was set at a metronomic 100 beats per minute, which was considered the ideal disco beat, and so the concept of a hit disco single was forced through rather to our bemusement, a bemusement made even stronger when we ended up as the UK Christmas Number One for 1979.

✓ The album – a double – had been through a number of traumas during the final mixing. I had arrived in Los Angeles a month after David and Roger (Rick had retreated to his house in Greece). Since the mixing was down to Roger, David, Bob and James, I had used the time to work on a record with Carla Bley and Mike Mantler in upstate New York. This was recorded in the relaxing environment of Woodstock in upstate New York, and the sessions produced a collection of Carla's songs, which were released as *Nick Mason's Fictitious Sports*, for ease of release and size of advance. By the time I arrived the mix was all but finished – under great time pressure, with mixes unusually being sent directly to master – but the most extraordinary sense of paranoia permeated the studio. Relationships with CBS/Sony were not good. Roger, in a negotiation with them over publishing rights, had been outraged when, because *The Wall* was a double album, they tried to reduce the amount he would get per track. When Dick Asher offered to toss for the decision, Roger's response was to ask why he should gamble on something he rightfully owned. The record company capitulated. Steve was also deep in negotiation with CBS, who were fighting their own battle to try and avoid paying independent promotion men to launch a record. This battle raged for a short period and was lost by the record company when the radio stations in the US simply refused to play even a Number One record if it wasn't promoted independently.

We threatened to withhold *The Wall* from CBS and they countered by threatening to take the album by force. The studio was broken into at the time. It was probably kids, but in the mood of paranoia, everyone thought it must have been a SWAT team of crazed record executives. In reality no one could have ever assembled the mountains of tapes into any semblance of a record without the entire production team's cooperation. However, we were only allowing admittance to people briefed with a secret password. I can now reveal the magic open sesame. It was 'I'm from CBS Records'…

Relations between the band and the record company were not improved by the head of promotion at CBS, who having received the first few tracks rapturously at a pre-listening session in Palm Springs, heard the finished version and claimed in outrage that it was a travesty of the record he'd first been played.

As always there were some political and financial repercussions as the album climbed the charts. We had lawyers representing all and sundry trying to scramble aboard the gravy train. One voice heard on the album after we recorded a random turning of the TV dial belonged to an actor who thought the success was primarily due to his contribution. We offered him a settlement with the option of doubling the amount if he gave it all to charity. He took the half for himself.

Work on the live show had overlapped with the mixing. The final evolution of the show's concept was that the audience should enter the auditorium to find a partially constructed wall standing at the sides of the stage. As the show began, it would be introduced by a compère, a combination of MC and radio DJ designed to heighten the unreality of the performance and to unhinge the audience's expectations.

With all the bombast of a rock show – fireworks and special effects – the show would open with a band who appeared to be us rising from below the stage. In fact this was a look-alike group known as the 'surrogate' band – Pete Woods on keyboards, Willie Wilson on drums, Andy Bown on bass and Snowy White on guitar – each equipped with life masks (one of the benefits of basing ourselves in Hollywood was that these were easy to get made). As the pyrotechnics and effects headed towards a climax, the first group of musicians froze, and the lights revealed the real band behind them. The surrogates would later appear on stage as auxiliary musicians, without their life masks – in this incarnation they were known as the 'shadow' band. All their instruments and costumes were grey, rather than the black we were using.

As the show progressed, the wall was gradually constructed, so that the first half ended with the final brick ready to be placed in position. Every night the crew managed to complete the wall within 90 seconds or so of the standard time. We had a certain amount of cushion built into the music so that the final brick would be placed in position to coincide with the final line of 'Goodbye Cruel World', the last song in the half. Once completed, the wall, made of 340 fireproof, reinforced cardboard boxes, each approximately 4 feet wide by 3 feet high and 1 foot deep, reached a height of 33 feet and a width of 260 feet. The second half then opened with the intact wall in front of the band. The wall was used to screen segments of the animated films made by Gerald Scarfe. At one point a drawbridge section of wall opened up to reveal a hotel room scene. At another, during 'Comfortably Numb', Roger appeared in front of the wall, while David emerged on top to play the solo.

The boxes were made of cardboard so that they could be flat-packed for transporting to the next show and assembled on site. The hollow bricks could be linked together by a team of wall builders using the hydraulic Genie towers, which rose as the wall grew, to get themselves in the right position. Once built the wall was supported on a series of tippers that could be controlled to tip in or out (not wishing to lose the front rows of the audience), as the wall was dismantled.

The climax of the piece came as the bricks began to tumble – this involved elaborate mechanics to avoid litigation, hospitalisation and the prospect of a one-night-only show, since the bricks, even made out of cardboard, were very heavy indeed. After the collapse, we would perform the final number acoustically like a group of strolling players.

Fisher and Park had started work on turning Roger's ideas into reality the previous Christmas. Mark Fisher – following on from his work on the inflatables for the *Animals* tour – had in fact travelled down to the South of France during the recording of the album, well ahead of schedule, which meant that when the green light was given to the show, it was a matter of creating 3D versions of the drawings rather than starting from scratch under pressure. (Mark was another architect – he had attended the Architectural Association school of architecture in London in the late 1960s, and in fact hired Pink Floyd for an event there in 1966, where, he remembers, we were paid less than the Bonzo Dog Doo-Dah Band.) Yet even with this lead time there were innumerable mechanical problems to resolve. The technical rehearsals were held in the States. This was the most practical solution. There was good logistical support, and a suitable location at Culver City Studios in LA was available for a complete two-week period at the right price. The teething problems emerged. The Genie towers for the wall builders were extraordinarily noisy, and the first experiments in wall demolition nearly destroyed all the equipment on stage. Large steel cages were hurriedly designed and built to protect the equipment, and some magic space-age lubricant sourced. Rehearsals continued, and by the beginning of

February we were in the Los Angeles Sports Arena for two weeks' final rehearsal before the first show on the 17th.

The night before we opened, we had a semblance of a show. But during the final rehearsal we had to admit that although most of the staging was working, the stage lighting was simply sub-standard. A frantic search ensued, first for a scapegoat, closely followed by a saviour. Steve contacted Marc Brickman, who had been noticed by Roger working on Bruce Springsteen's shows.

Marc had taken the phone call from Steve and – since he knew someone in the Floyd organisation – thought it was his friend pretending to be Steve, and ringing to say he'd got Marc tickets for the show the next night. Yes, said Marc, he'd love to go. No, said Steve, you don't understand. Marc, who was originally from Philadelphia, had been involved in lighting since his mid-teens, working in the music business with artists like Johnny Mathis as well as Bruce Springsteen, and more recently had been in Los Angeles working on TV shows. He remembers taking the initial call from Steve at 1 p.m. and coming down to the show at 3 p.m.

Gerry Scarfe and Roger walked him through the show and explained that there was a rehearsal at 7 p.m. the same day. When Marc came back that evening, Roger said, 'We didn't think we'd see you again…' There was a slightly awkward meeting after which Graeme Fleming was dismissed (i.e. fired) and Marc was dismissed (i.e. to continue his new duties). Given the time pressure, he was grateful that Robbie Williams and Mark Fisher offered him plenty of help.

Our opening night was given additional drama when a drape caught fire after the opening explosion. The drape proceeded to smoulder away until Roger had to call a halt and wait while riggers armed with fire extinguishers scampered into the roof and put it out. By then audience and performers were united in communal alarm and the show could go on. Since the shouted command

'Stop!' was an integral part of the show, it took Roger some time to convince the well-drilled road crew that this time it was an emergency.

At one point someone had suggested that the show would tour, rather than be a static event in just a few cities. The concept of a giant inflatable slug with sufficient space for the entire show plus audience was promoted briefly, but fortunately for designers, crew, performers and health and safety experts it never saw the light of day... We returned to the simpler idea of one of the shorter 'world tours' in rock history: seven nights in LA, five at the Nassau Coliseum, NY, six performances at Earls Court in August 1980, eight in Dortmund in February 1981 – and five more nights at Earls Court to provide footage for the film version.

Nearly all the shows were relatively serene. The only hitch came when Willie Wilson, the surrogate band drummer, collapsed a few hours before one of the shows was due to start. Fortunately, Clive Brooks, my long-time drum technician, is a very capable drummer in his own right. A veteran of an English blues band, the Groundhogs, Clive stepped in and played all the parts required for the next two nights. Ever since then I can sense the eager anticipation in his voice if I ever betray the slightest sign of ill health on tour.

The show was much more rehearsed than anything we had previously done and was technically well developed. In this way it was a precursor for the tours that David and I later organised, and Roger's solo work. We also found that the regular structure of the show helped to carry us through any 'bad' nights. The success of the show made it a great pleasure to play, but the lack of opportunity to improvise or change the music began to pall a little. That said, the requirements of building the wall meant that one stuck brick or overhasty builder could influence the length of each half, and we had various fillers or cuts for key moments.

By the five nights at Earls Court in June 1981 the show was well honed. However, they also turned out to be the last time Roger, David, Rick and I would play together for nearly a quarter of a century. As far as group relationships were concerned things had deteriorated even further than during recording. The clearest indication of this could be seen in the backstage area of Earls Court, where each band member had an individual Portakabin. Roger's and Rick's both faced away from the enclosure... I think that we also had individual after-show parties, carefully avoiding inviting each other.

A few months later, filming of the movie started with Gerald Scarfe and Michael Seresin as co-directors, and Alan Parker as overall producer, but after a week it was clear this system was not going to work. Alan was elevated to director, Michael departed, Gerry was reassigned to other duties, and we started again. Changing the command structure so early on was something of an omen. The stories are legion of the disagreements that occurred on the film. Alan Parker had a strong vision, but so too did Gerry and Roger. Gerry certainly felt quite isolated, as Alan Parker and the new producer Alan Marshall represented one self-supporting faction, and Roger and Steve O'Rourke another. Alan Parker, according to Bob Geldof, subscribed to Michael Winner's dictum, 'Democracy on the set is a hundred people doing what I tell them', a philosophy shared by some of the other principals on the project. Despite this recipe for disaster, I think the results were a victory for ability over organisation. Gerry's animation managed to make the transition from stage show to big screen, as did Bob Geldof, in the lead role of Pink.

Bob and Roger both tell the story of a taxi ride which Bob and his manager took to the airport, during which Bob's manager was telling him that an offer had come in for him to play the role of Pink in the film, and that he really ought to consider it as a great career move. Bob erupted, along the lines of 'Fuck that. I fucking hate Pink Floyd.' As Roger remembers, 'This went on until they reached the airport. What Bob didn't know was that the cab driver was my brother. He called me up and said, "You'll never guess who I've just had in my cab…"' Luckily Bob changed his mind and accepted the role.

He had convinced everyone in the screen test with a scene from *Midnight Express* and the phone scene from *The Wall*. Cajoled by Alan Parker, Bob underwent the change from restrained novice to melodramatic thespian in a couple of hours. The trouble was that it was only later he realised there was barely any dialogue in the film for him.

Filming wasn't helped when the details of Bob's contract got bogged down with his management. When the person responsible finally appeared at London airport, it was only to be arrested and taken off for questioning. Bob gallantly started work despite various contractual matters remaining unresolved.

Despite his reservations, Bob, says Alan Parker, gave the role his best shot, prepared even to have his eyebrows shaved for the part. As a non-swimmer Bob found that, according to Alan, 'the drowning scenes in the rooftop pool came easy to him, as they were most authentic'. Bob only complained once, when during a cold night-time shoot at an old biscuit factory in Hammersmith, he had to strip before being covered in pink slime and asked to metamorphose into a fascist.

In his autobiography, *Is That It?*, Bob also tells the story of one scene in the film in which an American actress, keen on method acting, had to show that she was frightened of Pink. She asked Alan Parker what her motivation for doing this was. Alan sighed and told her, 'The money'. Apparently the scene was wrapped on the next take…

The battlefield sequences were shot at Saunton Sands in Devon.

This is a particularly useful beach, which has supplied us with a number of backgrounds including the beds on the cover of *A Momentary Lapse Of Reason*. One of the half-scale Stukas performed admirably with a registered pilot to control it. The other was claimed by the sea when it crashed. I remember one early morning on the sands when, through the smoke and haze of battle, we were cheered by the sight of a tea trolley being manfully manoeuvred across the dunes by one of the location caterers to ensure we were safely reinforced with tea and bacon sarnies.

The other notable piece of location work was at the Royal Horticultural Hall in London, where two thousand skinheads had been recruited to form the crowd for a cross between a rock show and a political rally. A penchant for drinking their wages at the nearby and rather exclusive pubs, coupled with a hatred of uniform – even if on the backs of unfortunate extras – ensured a lively, bordering-on-dangerous, atmosphere. Gillian Gregory, the choreographer, had the impossible task of trying to teach the skinheads very straightforward dance movements. After two hours of simplifying the routine and scaling down the difficulty factor, she finally gave up. The military precision she had been aiming for was sadly impossible to achieve: watching the final version you know they are meant to be doing something in unison; the question is what.

Alan Parker has one particular recollection of Steve O'Rourke. During post-production Steve took a phone call in Alan's office, a bungalow in the Pinewood gardens, from Roger in the main building. Steve turned to rush back, but 'with his bad eyesight he failed to see the closed glass doors, which he ploughed through and shattered. Steve was badly cut, concussed, and lying on the floor. He opened his eyes to see my secretary Angie, gently picking the shards of glass out of his face. He immediately fell in love and eventually married her.'

My belief is that Alan was the best man for the job. And on occasion he did listen to what was said or suggested by others. I still have a small film canister that he sent to me. We had argued for some time about a particular shot of the boy on the beach, which I thought a bit on the whimsical side. In the can was a roll of film of this sequence and a note saying 'OK, you win'. Alan remembers few creative disagreements with Roger over the material – he remains very proud of the finished film – but says that the problems that arose from a clash of two strong egos did often make him miserable. The sign on Alan's door at Pinewood said, 'Just Another Prick On The Wall'.

Steve as executive producer was responsible for ensuring that we survived the financial disasters of film making. 'As for the accounts,' says Alan, 'someone said that Steve O'Rourke had written the cost of the animation off in so many books they could fill a shelf at Foyle's.' We were initially at risk for the start-up costs on the film of $2 million (all our *The Wall* record earnings), but eventually David Begelman at MGM came through with the guarantee for $10 million that we needed. Bernd Eichinger at Neu Constanin provided a further $2 million and Goldcrest, through Lazards, financed the actual production. Regrettably for Goldcrest it had gone into liquidation by the time we were to pay them back their profit element, though we did give Jake Ebberts, who was the president of Goldcrest, two free tickets for the show in Canada when he called in 1994.

Alan Parker recalls that when he and Steve first offered the film to MGM (he had recently made *Fame* for the company), David Begelman 'told me he was entrusting their many millions of dollars of investment to me even though he had absolutely no idea what the film was about. What's more neither did his eighteen-year-old son, who was a Pink Floyd fan. Steve O'Rourke and I shook Begelman's hand on the deal, and I said, "Don't worry,

David, you can trust us because we treat other people's money as if it's our own.'" Steve then told Alan in the lift that that remark was probably inappropriate as David Begelman had been ousted from a previous job as chairman of Columbia Pictures after being accused of embezzling a cheque for $60,000.

There never was a film soundtrack album, partly because it was inevitably so faithful to the original record, but there were some interesting versions of songs where Bob Geldof was able to bring his own interpretation to bear.

Various premieres took place in 1982, including a late-night showing at the Cannes Film Festival that was fun, particularly as it coincided with the Monaco Grand Prix, and I was able to take a guest in the shape of James Hunt. The sound system at the old Palais du Festival had been upgraded with a little help from the Britannia Row stores. As the music started, plaster began to crumble from the ceiling, creating a curtain of dust and paint. Alan Parker remembers that Steven Spielberg attended the Cannes screening and, 'as the lights went up at the end, he looked across at me with enormous pity and shrugged, as if to say, "What the fuck was that all about?"'

There were various shows, too, in LA and NY, including one US press conference where the producer, Alan Marshall, when asked about the meaning of the film said, rather succinctly, 'It's about some mad bastard and this wall, innit...'

COMMUNICATIONS
FAILURE
'10

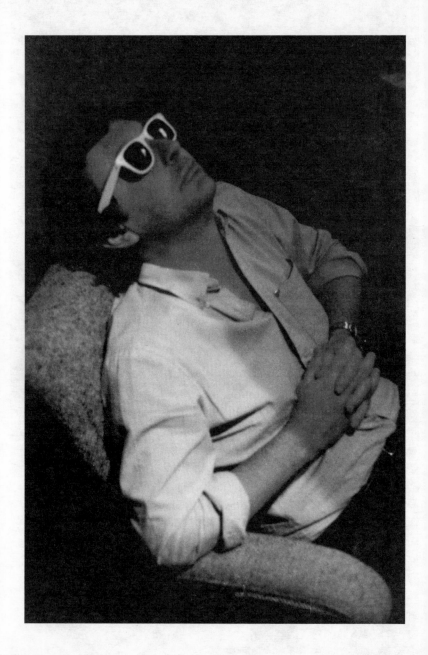

AFTER ALL the work on *The Wall* was complete, my overriding feeling – and by now a pattern may be emerging – was less of elation than exhaustion. Given that we had only performed the show thirty-odd times in two years, it was difficult to blame this on physical exertion. It was more a feeling that the whole project appeared to have been going on for an eternity. However, perhaps another reason for my lethargy and lack of enthusiasm was caused by the thought of confronting each other once again.

Following the end of the tour and the film, the four-man Pink Floyd that had existed since 1968 was no more. Rick was enjoying self-imposed exile: he was living in Greece, the home of his second wife Franka, and relishing a taste of lotus eating. Rick's absence in the sun only served to underline the fact that we were locked into a cycle of non-communication.

In July 1982 *The Wall* had gone on general release. We had all been involved in promotion to a greater or lesser extent. I remember being sent to Spain as the sole ambassador for the premiere there – since I think all the others were in America for openings in New York and California – and smiling through gritted teeth for the cameras. Meanwhile I waved in what I thought was a regal way from the royal box in Madrid and modestly admitted that it had not been entirely my own work…

Back in London Roger had started work on an album that underwent a number of changes in fairly quick succession. My recollection is that the original scheme was to incorporate a number of tracks that were left over from the *Wall* project. There were some songs that had been included on the film soundtrack but had never made it onto the original album, and these were to be augmented with new material.

This is borne out by the fact that the original working title for *The Final Cut* was 'Spare Bricks', an idea that was dropped as the record gestated into something rather different. I think various factors contributed to this change of tack. Roger was dissatisfied with the original piecemeal approach and by now had a much clearer idea of what he wanted to tackle. *The Final Cut – A Requiem For The Post War Dream* was a much more focused piece. Although still linked to elements contained in *The Wall*, it dealt with Roger's feelings about the death of his father at Anzio in the Second World War. The fact that for the initial years of the war Roger's father had been a conscientious objector added more poignancy. The underscore to this was the failure of post-war Britain to provide the better world that so many had died for.

The other unlikely candidate for a muse was Margaret Thatcher. In 1982 Britain, under Thatcher's premiership, declared war on Argentina over sovereignty of the Falkland Islands in a conflict most expertly described by Jorge Luis Borges as 'two bald men fighting over a comb'; the atmosphere in Britain at the time was alarmingly jingoistic and I think this particularly upset Roger. *The Final Cut* became a real tool for expressing his horror at these events.

I could hardly fail to sympathise with these political sentiments, but I think David's view was that it was becoming unsuitable as a band album. David wanted time to produce some material of his own. Roger, now totally motivated, was not interested in waiting. He wanted to press on, and once he has the bit between his teeth he leaves little time for prevarication by anyone else. In addition, he appeared doubtful of David's ability to produce anything in the foreseeable future.

Certainly, the imposition by Roger of a deadline to complete the album seemed to staunch David's creativity. I'm not sure that this was a conscious power play by Roger. I suspect that he might have been angry or simply impatient with David's apparent lack of speed in producing material, or it may be that in Roger's head he was already moving into his solo career, and merely wanted David and me to assist him in his aspirations. During the *Wall* recordings we had maintained some semblance of democracy, but even this semblance was under threat. The matter rapidly became 'an issue', and like a menacing U-boat, poked a periscope up above the murky waters of our relationship.

The upshot was that the album consisted entirely of Roger's writing. David's input was minimised – apart from his guitar solos, which even Roger was not foolhardy enough to try and influence – and most significantly Roger decided to take on the bulk of the vocal duties himself, leaving David to sing one song, 'Not Now John'. In the past, the inflection of David's vocals had inevitably made some subtle changes to the melodic structure of Roger's songs. So this change, and the loss of Rick's trademark keyboard sound, meant the disappearance of key elements from what had become an established 'Pink Floyd sound'.

Another missing link was Bob Ezrin. In bandspeak this parting of the ways might be described as 'musical differences', but in reality it could have been due to one of a number of incidents: Roger was still seething over an unfortunate interview Bob had granted an American magazine just prior to the *Wall* shows. A journalist friend (friend no more) had weaselled out of Bob – and published – a full description of the show, including the exclusive revelation of the tumbling wall as the grand finale. Bob was as mortified as anyone by this betrayal, but to add fuel to the fire the journalist also gave glowing credit to Bob for rather more than he deserved, or at least more than we felt he deserved.

Bob now got a call from Steve threatening litigation and suggesting that, being in breach of contract by talking to the press, he might not be seeing any of his hard-earned royalties. Bob was shaken by all of this. From being one of the inner circle he was suddenly out in the cold. It was made clear to him that he would not even be welcome at the shows. I think now that we just had no idea of how terrifying our combined disapproval could be. With the record just beginning to show every sign of being a huge hit Bob could not even enjoy this moment of glory.

Eventually the whole issue was dropped, but a couple of years later the dust was still pervading the atmosphere rather than settling, and Roger was certainly not ready to take Bob back on board – even assuming Bob wanted the ride. For my money this was a shame. Bob's mind may be addled but he's always prepared to speak it…

The gap left by Bob was, in part, filled by Michael Kamen, who was not only a highly rated – and later an Oscar-nominated – composer but a very able keyboard player. Michael had originally studied oboe at the Julliard School in New York, and began composing film music in the 1970s. After *The Wall*, he went on to score, amongst other movies, *Brazil*, *Mona Lisa*, *Die Hard*, *Licence To Kill*, *Robin Hood: Prince Of Thieves* (for which he got his Oscar nomination) and *Mr Holland's Opus*, and created the music for the TV series *Edge Of Darkness*.

This solved the practical problems left by Rick's departure. However, Michael had no interest in a confrontational approach to making records. Indeed he had no need to. He would simply get on with producing wonderful work in whatever situation he found himself. His work on *The Wall* had been done without any face-to-face contact, and band politics were simply not in his remit.

Much of the work for *The Final Cut* was done at Mayfair

Studios in Primrose Hill in north London. Apart from its convenient location close to a restaurant we all rather liked, James Guthrie was anxious to work there. In Bob's absence, James had been the obvious choice as engineer and co-producer, especially for his ability to breeze through the tricky business of working with all of us. In 1981 he had helped us re-record 'Money' for the compilation release *A Collection Of Great Dance Songs*. Dave had programmed the groove on the recently released Linn Drum Machine, and then I went into the studio to overdub live drums. Unfortunately, there were some discrepancies between my timing and the machine's, and James felt he needed to confront me directly. He explained that there were some consistency problems in both timbre and timing. He recalls that I listened intently to his comments, nodding and weighing each word carefully, and then responded, 'Mmm, timing and consistency never were my strong points. I was always much better at the after-gig parties.'

A number of other studios were used for specific overdubs, including Olympic, RAK, Eel Pie, and Roger and David's own home studios, both of which were now equipped to professional levels. Roger's studio name, the Billiard Room, indicated the contents augmenting the 24-track recorder...

Part of this was a desire to avoid returning to Britannia Row, which although now in much better shape technically, still lacked a number of qualities that James felt were essential. It was also probably a wise decision to use neutral studios rather than Britannia Row: in the confines of our own nuclear bunker things might have become terminally explosive on the inside rather than the outside. The only real technical hitch we experienced at Mayfair was the assistant who overslept and kept us locked out on a weekend just before Christmas, when we had all made a particular effort to come in – for his own safety he was advised not to return in the New Year.

On one occasion during the recording of *The Final Cut*, James remembers a rather fraught session at the Billiard Room, with Roger attempting to perfect a particular set of vocals: 'Roger was in his customary position, perched on the edge of the billiard table, headphones on, and singing. Most days, Roger was in his stride and able to capture a moving vocal performance fairly quickly. Today was an off day. Pitch was not coming easily, and the tension began to build. Michael was just not in the mood. He had not said a word for quite some time and his attention was clearly elsewhere. He scribbled with great focus on a legal pad.'

Eventually Roger, distracted by Michael's apparent lack of interest, stormed into the control room and demanded to know what Michael was writing. 'Michael had decided that he must have done something unspeakable in a past life, something he was now karmically paying for by having to endure take after take of the same vocal performance. So he had written over and over on his legal pad, page after page, line after line, "I must not fuck sheep". He was not sure exactly what he had done in this past life, but "I must not fuck sheep" seemed like a pretty fair guess.'

Some years later, when Michael was on tour as part of Roger's band, the touring party were issued with T-shirts. All of them had 'Am I really cost effective?' written on them in mirror writing (to remind them first thing every morning), while the band had individualised messages on their T-shirts. Michael's particular one read 'ЧƎƎHS ꓘϽUꟻ TOИ TꙄUM I' … Both Michael and James, perhaps surprisingly, belong to the extremely exclusive band of collaborators who have survived to work again with all of us.

My own part in the proceedings was pretty minimal for a while. I was spending more and more time motor racing: in 1981 I had failed to get to Le Mans, *The Wall* shows having taken precedence. Steve, however, had done a remarkable piece of jet-setting by driving in the start of the race, before rushing back to Earls Court for the show on the Saturday night, and then returning to the circuit to drive in the latter half of the race on the Sunday morning. To make up for this, I had organised one particularly smart piece of promotion in the form of encouraging Wilfred Jung, the president of EMI Germany, to sponsor the Dorset Racing Lola 298 to run at the Nürburgring 1,000-km race in 1981 in full *Wall* livery. This was actually not very difficult since Wilfred was the most ardent motor race fan. I think we both felt that this was exactly how to cement artist–company relations. The following year I had returned to Le Mans sharing a drive with Steve. Between sponsor hunting, practice sessions and a disastrous part-ownership of a Grand Prix team, it's a wonder I ever found time to get to the studios…

Still, I spent some days laying down a few drum tracks and a certain amount of time turning up to show willing and to remind everybody I existed. These undemanding tasks were only augmented when it became clear that another ingredient was failing to live up to expectations: the holophonic sound effects were not working. At the start of recording we had been approached by an Italian audio boffin called Hugo Zuccarelli. He claimed he had devised a new holophonic system that could be recorded simply onto stereo tape. We were sceptical since some previous forays into the wonderful world of quad during the 1970s had proved to be far too complex. The quad recording process required vast amounts of track space and seemingly endless adjustments to the control knobs to place the sounds in the quadraphonic spectrum. Not only was the process extremely complicated in nearly all aspects, but also the number of lunatics prepared to position their armchair precisely in the centre of their living room to get maximum enjoyment from the experience was insufficient.

However, Hugo Zuccarelli's holophonic – or 'total sound' –

system was different. It really worked. I still don't know exactly how because it only used a pair of stereo mikes contained within a dummy head. This provided some spatial sonic quality that when heard back through headphones replicated the way the human ear works in daily life. Hugo's first demo cassette was truly startling: I remember one effect where a box of matches was shaken and moved around your head so it seemed to be behind, above or below. If you closed your eyes while listening on the headphones it was quite disorientating and completely convincing.

We immediately decided to use the system for all the sound effects on the album, and I was volunteered to escort the holophonic head (which answered to the name of Ringo) to various locations to capture the sound of church bells or footsteps. Roger was particularly taken with the Doppler effect of traffic going by, and the musical effect that was created as the passing vehicle's tone changed. Finally my motor racing experience paid off: I spent many a happy hour capturing the sounds of the Queen's Highway, and trying to record screeching tyres on the skidpan at the Hendon Police Driving School (a total failure since even with their brakes fully locked the cars glided over the oil slicks in eerie silence).

Roger also wanted warlike plane sounds. Through a high-ranking air force contact, I was granted permission to record a number of Tornadoes at RAF Honington in Warwickshire. It was an extraordinary experience to stand at the end of the runway trying to set a level for a sound so intense that as the afterburners were lit up the air itself was crackling with sonic overload. I also drew on the old pals' network to persuade a friend who was flying Shackletons to record one of the planes in flight. The thought of a half-day spent circling the ocean looking for non-existent submarines did not thrill me, but Ringo manfully accepted the mission and was returned for breakfast and medals, along with twelve hours' worth of droning aircraft noise on tape. I do still have a twinge of guilt that I had so much help from friends within the armed forces, and that all that work ended up on a protest record. I hope they have now all forgiven me.

It was a pity that before I'd even started work on *The Final Cut*, Roger felt it necessary to announce aggressively that since whatever I did 'was drumming', I couldn't claim either extra royalties or credit for any of this work. This really did seem like behaviour beginning to border on the megalomaniac, particularly since I posed no threat to his plans. I decided to look on the bright side: at least it was a way of escaping from the fraught atmosphere in the studio.

If I was not having much fun, David was certainly not having an easy time either. Roger was studiously ignoring any of David's suggestions, which is why he probably wanted Michael on board to augment the musical input. In many ways Michael was probably as much a substitute for David as for Rick or Bob, given his melodic strengths and his experience in writing, and arranging. It may well have been paranoia, but it did look as though David was being frozen out. By the time *The Final Cut* was finished Roger was effectively running the show. I think we had always worked on the basis that the writers should have the final say on how the work should be produced. With no writing contribution at all from David his role was inevitably eroded.

However, I have no recollection of discussing whether it should be released as a Roger Waters solo album. In any case, such a plan would probably already have been too late. The record company were expecting a Pink Floyd album, and would not have taken kindly to being presented with a Roger Waters solo work. I would have resisted it because it would, I think, have signalled the end of the band, and I do have an unfortunate tendency to operate in the belief that 'if we do nothing, maybe the problem will go away'. And the option of us starting all over again on a group album at some point in the future seemed unthinkable. We should of course have resolved these issues at the time, but we somehow dodged them completely.

Although we possessed a remarkable ability to enrage and upset each other, while still maintaining a straight face, we never acquired the skill of talking to each other about important issues. After *The Dark Side Of The Moon* there had been a pronounced tendency for all of us to deliver criticism badly – and to take it even worse. Roger is sometimes credited with enjoying confrontation, but I don't think that's the case. I do think Roger is often unaware of just how alarming he can be, and once he sees a confrontation as necessary he is so grimly committed to winning that he throws everything into the fray – and his everything can be pretty scary. On the positive side I think it is an enormous asset to his golf, tennis and poker playing... David, on the other hand, may not be so initially alarming, but once decided on a course of action is hard to sway. When his immovable object met Roger's irresistible force, difficulties were guaranteed to follow.

What ensued was a massive argument about credits; eventually David's name disappeared, although it was agreed that he would still be paid. Michael Kamen remained as co-producer – along with James Guthrie.

Why were we prepared to go along with what felt like Roger's takeover? We accepted so many things as inevitable that, looking back, seem unnecessary. Such craven compliance might have been the result of gradual changes wrought in the band structure over the previous decade. Perhaps lacking confidence in his own writing abilities, David may have felt that if we confronted these issues we risked losing Roger and being unable to continue. Or in

Rick with Mini-Moog synthesiser on top of his faithful Hammond organ.

In performance with Roland Petit's Ballet de Marseille, November 1972.

Close to the volcanic crater of Etna, during the filming of *Live At Pompeii*.

Lighting director Arthur Max prepares to debrief, or possibly behead, another team of follow-spot operators.

One of the comic-book spoofs from our Winter 1974 tour programme, in which Steve O'Rourke was always depicted as the baddie.

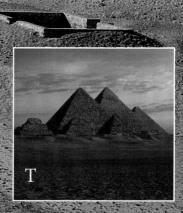

The *Dark Side* tour
road crew and stage
set-up.

Storm Thorgerson
with David.

David and Roger on the Winter 1974 tour of the UK.

With David and Roger is Aubrey Powell, aka Po, Storm Thorgerson's partner in Hipgnosis.

Robert Wyatt, Soft Machine drummer, song-writer, raconteur, rock'n'roll's answer to Lenin…

David and Rick on the steps outside the front door of the Abbey Road Studios during the *Wish You Were Here* sessions.

Roy Harper with David at Abbey Road, during the period Roy volunteered to handle the vocals on 'Have A Cigar'.

Syd Barrett at Abbey Road Studios, 5th June 1975.

Britannia Row studios, inside (with sound boffin Bill Kelsey) and out.

The pyramid stage in various phases of assembly, 1975

Algie rises over Battersea Power Station in December 1976 while (opposite) the marksman takes aim.

On this particular occasion, Roger was, unusually, at the end of the queue for T-shirts.

On stage during the *Animals* tour, 1977.

Portrait by Bob Jenkins.

the aftermath of Rick's departure maybe we feared being marginalised and then negotiated out individually. It pains me to admit it, but whatever the reasons, the tendency to cast Roger as the ultimate villain, though tempting, is probably misplaced.

I remember this period as particularly tense, with a sense of struggling to hold things together. My own life was not exactly in apple-pie order. After the year away I was dealing with my own dramas. I was breaking up my marriage to Lindy and about to hurtle into a new relationship with my present wife Annette. Given my penchant for avoiding confrontation in emotional issues and real life it would smack of understatement to say this was not an easy time. It was particularly dreadful for Lindy and my two daughters Chloe and Holly, although I have a bad feeling that I probably felt that I was the one really suffering.

By the time of the album's release in March 1983 another Floyd connection had been severed. Due to some heavy budgetary overspend on one video shoot, Storm and Po had disbanded Hipgnosis (citing 'visual differences' perhaps) and despite Gerald Scarfe's involvement in *The Wall*, Storm might reasonably have expected to pick up the job. However, both Gerry and Storm were passed over, and Roger chose to design the cover himself. He used Willie Christie to take the pictures – I think this was a slight embarrassment for Willie, since he happened to be Roger's brother-in-law as well as an excellent photographer – but the absence of Hipgnosis did add another few decibels to the impression of the 'Last Post' being sounded for the Pink Floyd that once had been.

I don't think Roger feels entirely happy with *The Final Cut* – 'deeply flawed' is one comment he made, I believe – but there must be many things about it he is happy with. The fact that it is dedicated to his father spells out how personal the record was to him, and in a way how disenfranchised from it the rest of us were.

For me the record represents such a difficult time in my life that this overrides any real judgement of the pieces. As with all our records the final finished disc is as much a diary of a certain number of months of my life, rather than a musical piece that I can view objectively.

Music is capable of tapping directly into a particular phase of your life, and you can maintain affection for dreadful songs for years and years ('Extraordinary how potent cheap music is' as Noel Coward put it). For recording musicians, the odd thing is that this time-frame is out of kilter, as the reality of an album actually exists in a period up to a year *prior* to its release. For me, *The Final Cut* is the latter half of 1982, rather than 1983...

After *The Final Cut* was finished there were no plans for the future. I have no recollection of any promotion and there was no suggestion of any live performances to promote the record. It would have been hard to imagine a show that could follow *The Wall*, anyway. But it was another factor in how David and I viewed the future. Both David and myself regarded playing live and touring as an integral part of being in the band. If being part of a Roger-led Floyd meant that there would be no live shows ('due to indiscipline, all touring has been cancelled this term') and only aggravation in the recording studio, the future prospect seemed distinctly unappealing.

Consequently, David and Roger both went off to work on solo projects. David's *About Face* album and tour concentrated more on playing and less on spectacle. Much of the material played was from his solo albums, but the tour and album helped us later on in a number of ways: they showcased David at his very best as a musician, and the strong relationship that he was able to build up with the press and the record company stood us in extremely good stead when we most needed it four years later. It might also be the case that it brought home to him the necessity of putting on the full theatrical show if one wanted to fill the big arenas.

Just before his tour reached the Hammersmith Odeon, David approached me and suggested it would be nice to have Rick and myself make an appearance at the end of the last London show to join him on 'Comfortably Numb'. It sounded fun, and I turned up in the afternoon to have a run-through and check out playing someone else's kit. This felt a little strange, particularly as I hadn't played the piece for four years, but Chris Slade, the drummer on David's tour, couldn't have been nicer. After years of drummers grumpily surrendering their kit saying, 'Don't use the snare', it proved the case that the more able the drummer the more relaxed the attitude... The song sounded wonderful and we loved playing it. I hate to lapse into metaphysical parlance, but I think we did feel some particular magic performing together again, and I think this was a moment that contributed to the subsequent events of 1986.

Roger, meanwhile, was reviving the *Pros And Cons Of Hitchhiking* project that he had prepared demos for years earlier as an alternative to *The Wall*. The album was released shortly after David's Hammersmith shows, following which Roger proceeded to put on what was his version of a Pink Floyd tour, utilising new animation from Gerry Scarfe as well as elements from Fisher Park. I went to see his show at Earls Court, and found the experience had an astonishingly depressing effect on me. The first half was made up of Floyd numbers and gave me the impression of being a (rather elderly) Peter Pan at the nursery window – that was my part being played by someone else. In retrospect this one event probably had as much to do in galvanising me as anything else. I realised I could not quite so easily let go and watch the train roll on without me.

Rick was working with Dave Harris on a project called *Zee* (they released an album almost simultaneously with Roger), and I became involved with a short documentary film that neatly combined music and motor racing. In fact it tied in perfectly with a collaboration I had formed with a friend of mine, Rick Fenn, the 10cc keyboard player with whom I had set up a small company to provide music for commercials and films.

The idea for *Life Could Be A Dream* involved a deal with Rothmans and their team of World Sports Car Championship Porsche 956 cars. I would drive with the works team in some of the 1,000-km races with a camera on board. As an added bonus I would get a drive at Le Mans with René Metge and Richard Lloyd (by pure coincidence, Richard had in a previous life been a Decca producer and had been responsible for recording Rick's first song with Adam, Mike & Tim). With a soundtrack, we thought this might have some commercial potential. I must admit, sadly, that I had very little compunction about wearing all the tobacco company logos – and paid careful attention as to how to field difficult questions about smoking. We then went on to make an album, which included a single called 'Lie For A Lie' that David generously provided vocals on. Even with his help it failed to get close enough to the charts to tarnish the paintwork, let alone dent it.

There was little chance of Pink Floyd performing together in this period, although in 1985 there was a vague possibility of us appearing at Live Aid. Eventually David was the only one of us who made it, playing guitar with Bryan Ferry, which had the added bonus of introducing him to keyboard player Jon Carin.

I used the greater amount of spare time to learn how to fly, finally conquering the fears that had been engendered by too many knuckle-whitening flights on tour. This obviously set a trend and somewhere along the line David also got his pilot's licence – as did Steve O'Rourke. We ended up sharing planes for a number of years, and frightening ourselves far more than we ever did on all those commercial flights.

This phase of solo projects – which might have offered the four of us a useful breathing space – in fact only served to create another source of dissatisfaction. Roger had decided, around this time, that he would renegotiate his individual deal with Steve, and he wanted to keep these negotiations confidential. Steve felt, both on moral grounds and also probably for financial reasons, that he was obliged to inform the rest of us. This betrayal – as Roger saw it – coupled with his belief that Steve had tended to represent David more strongly throughout the tetchy *Final Cut* negotiations, led Roger to want to replace Steve as his manager.

We did meet and talk; we even had a relatively relaxed meeting in 1984 at a Japanese restaurant, soothed by sushi and sake, to discuss all the things we weren't going to do – and then Steve joined us to hear about it. Roger was doubtless misled by our general bonhomie and acquiescence into believing that we accepted Pink Floyd was almost over. David and I meanwhile thought that after Roger had finished *Pros And Cons*, life could continue. We had, after all, had a number of hiatuses before. Roger sees this meeting as duplicity, rather than diplomacy – I disagree. Clearly, our communication skills were still troublingly non-existent. We left the restaurant with diametrically opposed views of what had been decided.

RESTART... AND
RESTORATION 11

IN 1986 DAVID and I decided to try and make another album, without Roger. There had not been any specific single moment of revelation when we resolved to go ahead. David had in fact made up his own mind quite early on, and had been working on a number of demos. There then followed a number of half-conversations, when Steve O'Rourke might have said, 'Do you want to...?' or David might have asked me, 'Well, should we or not?' Eventually these discussions gathered their own momentum, and we finally agreed, 'Let's do it.' Once the decision was made it was irreversible. It was a little like losing Syd in 1968: the alternative options only seem alarming in hindsight. We did not know exactly how it was to be done, but we felt it must be possible. Despite my personal track record as rock 'n' roll's resident vicar of Bray, I was totally committed to the decision. I am still slightly surprised by this show of will. So much of our previous work had consisted of Roger's songwriting and direction, and yet I had great faith in David's ability to awaken any dormant abilities relatively quickly, as well as confidence in his vocals and guitar work, which had contributed so much to the band's sound.

I don't think we considered whether there would be any legal ramifications, but we were certainly aware of the risks. At a time when the press was still interested in the fight with Roger, there was a disturbing possibility that we might give them a field day by releasing an album that proved the gainsayers correct by revealing ourselves as no more than money-grubbing forgers. Another potential horror was that we might be defeated by our erstwhile colleague in a shoot-out among the megastore shelves, always a significantly powerful drive, and a sad indictment of our real motivations compared to the dream of bringing beautiful music to lovely people. The damage to our egos was potentially more damaging than any financial disasters.

Throughout the recording process the ongoing struggle with Roger continued unabated, and provided its own roller-coaster entertainment. Endless phone calls with lawyers were replaced by lengthy meetings, often held in the Dickensian surroundings of the Inns of Court. In the hope of finding a clinching piece of evidence, hours of discussion revolved about the dullest aspects of our history, namely the legal niceties of what we thought we might have agreed to verbally eighteen years earlier. Litigation is a remarkable experience, as you select your gladiators for their fighting skills and then sit back to watch them perform. It is probably the most overpriced form of entertainment I have ever encountered, and also the most nerve-racking.

Away from the legal front line, there had been some discussion and attempts at reconciliation. I had dinner one night with Roger, who said that he would settle for being released from Steve's contract. Unfortunately, Steve was a significant part of our enterprise and I think we felt that we were bound together, perhaps more than necessary. Part of the problem was that nothing was written down. There was a verbal agreement – just as binding as a written one, so the lawyers tell us – between Steve and the band, which meant that any actions by one individual had to be ratified by the rest of us. Discussions were muddied by a lack of understanding, certainly by me, of what the implications really were – as a result the issues remained unclear and any trust uncertain. In retrospect, we should have settled with Roger then and there.

However, I did think I understood Roger's predicament. On the one hand he felt that he was Pink Floyd, and had carried the band on his shoulders for ten years or more as a writer and director of operations. But as long as the band existed as any sort of entity, it represented a real obstacle to his solo career, since the record company would always be waiting for a Pink Floyd release. Any of his solo work would be seen as intermediate filler material and would be unlikely to receive the kind of promotional support that would accrue to a band album.

What Roger really needed was for the band to be formally dissolved to clear the way for his own solo career, and he probably assumed that this would happen if he withdrew his services, given that Rick was no longer technically a member, I had done little beyond motor racing and becoming a garage proprietor, and even David had become more of a producer and guest guitarist with other musicians than a band member. What no one anticipated was David's response to what I think he felt was the lack of credit and exposure for his contributions and ideas. The division of spoils – and more particularly credit – is often unfair, but he had perhaps suffered the most injustice. Even I, not prone to confrontation, felt aggrieved that after twenty years I thought I was being told to quietly lie down, roll over and retire.

Although in the past I had usually sided with Roger, who was after all one of my oldest friends, I was mortified at the suggestion that I had contributed nothing and was unemployable without him now. The quote I am credited with that I particularly like is 'Roger was fond of saying no one's indispensable and... he was right'.

In retrospect, Roger probably made a tactical error in going to law – and at one point we were all set to go to court. However, since 'patience' is not a word that appears in Roger's thesaurus, his innate desire to act rather than wait meant he was driven to bring everything to the boil – and achieved the opposite result to the one

he intended. For David in particular, one of the great spurs was
the fact that Roger, hearing about the plans for a new album, had
told him 'You'll never do it.'

Roger had already intimated that he thought that Pink Floyd
was finished, and his falling out with Steve had escalated. With
everyone feeling angry, we dug trenches to maintain our
respective positions and refused to budge. Roger broke the phoney
war by announcing to the world that the band 'was over'. This was
a surprise to the rest of us. And it proved another incentive to
make the album.

The motivation was there in ample quantities. Now we turned
our attention to the how, who and where of going ahead. When
was not really an issue. There was no record company obligation,
and we had not committed to touring dates. The making of the
album could initially determine the pace of work.

The how centred primarily over David's choice of writing
and working partners. An early decision was made to bring
Bob Ezrin back in as co-producer. It was unfortunate that Bob
Ezrin had been considered as a producer for Roger's *Radio KAOS*
album, which was being recorded at the same time. Bob maintains
that he had established that he would not work on Roger's record
because they could not agree a schedule that would suit both of
them. Bob specifically wanted to avoid lengthy sojourns away
from home; Roger wanted to get on and finish the work. The fact
is that Roger felt betrayed as Bob signed with 'the opposition' –
according to Bob, Roger at this point designated the rest of us 'the
Muffins'.

In the event, Pat Leonard, who had worked with David
previously, and was in the frame for our record, eventually worked
with Roger and was delighted with the opportunity, so perhaps
honours were even. Andy Jackson was brought in as our engineer
– Andy had worked with James Guthrie on the soundtrack for

The Wall movie. Knowing James we would have expected him to choose wisely, and he did not let us down.

After the experiences of recording *The Wall* in France, Bob proved to be completely sympathetic to the spirit of the project. One of his great qualities is an ability to apply a specific mix of skills to a given situation. Now he quickly realised that on this album his primary function was to support David by acting both as a catalyst and as a kind of musical personal trainer: Bob was particularly good at exhorting David to keep on going.

As far as writing songs was concerned, David decided to experiment by working with a number of potential collaborators to see what would result. Along the way he spent some time with Phil Manzanera, the Roxy Music guitarist, Eric Stewart of 10cc, Liverpool poet Roger McGough and the Canadian musician Carole Pope. What materialised from these try-outs was that what David was really looking for was a lyricist, and that person turned out to be Anthony Moore, who had been part of the band Slapp Happy, which many moons earlier had been on the roster of Blackhill Enterprises.

The location we settled on for the early stages of recording was *Astoria*, David's houseboat studio moored on the River Thames near Hampton Court. This curious vessel had been built in the early 1910s (at a cost of £20,000 – at the time an enormous sum) for an old music hall and variety show impresario called Fred Karno – the Harvey Goldsmith of his day – who entertained the likes of Charlie Chaplin on board. The *Astoria* measures ninety feet long, and has a facility for a seventy-piece orchestra to play on the roof should one so wish (we chose not to). David had been living a couple of miles away when he bought it, almost on a whim, as an aquatic home studio.

For the late-twentieth-century musician, David, aided and abetted by Phil Taylor, had constructed a studio in the converted dining room – a shade on the small side, but with sufficient room for a drum kit, bass guitar and electronic keyboards. The control room, built in the main living room, had windows looking over the river on two sides and across the riverside garden on the third. The boat also provided enough space for all the accompanying ancillary equipment.

The recording started out with us using an analogue 24-track machine with overdubs onto a 32-track Mitsubishi digital recorder. This marked our first foray into digital recording on tape. This new technology had a number of benefits – including improved sound quality and no degradation – as did the houseboat's location. Phil Taylor remembers that during the recording for *A Momentary Lapse Of Reason*, David sailed upriver, stayed on board for one weekend and recorded the entirety of 'Sorrow' including all the guitar parts, vocals and the drum machine, so that when we reconvened on the Monday, there was only a bit of spit and polish required.

The Trout, a 1930s Thames slipper launch, was moored alongside, available for anyone needing to get away, or indeed for anyone living locally to get home should their road licence have been suspended. It still seemed quite radical to have a view of the outside world – and a particularly attractive one (within a few years, however, it had become de rigueur to record in some equally beautiful setting). It proved a successful formula, and such a pleasant environment that even if work had come to a stop no one particularly wanted to leave in a hurry.

There was the occasional unnerving motion when large boats cruised past over the speed limit, but the only other passing traffic, apart from the odd oarsman, were the hundreds of swans from the local haven. We did once have a visit from an uninvited television news crew who, having failed to gain an audience, claimed to have donned scuba outfits and, in a scene reminiscent of *Above Us The*

Waves, recorded us at work underwater. They would have had to have been there so long, and been so cold in order to get even a snippet of waterlogged sound, that I think the story can be filed alongside the one that maintains that we get our inspiration from alien beings visiting from other planets...

A more serious threat was caused when the river started rising so fast that the whole boat began to tilt as it became snagged up against one of the piers keeping it in place. The prospect of the *Astoria* disappearing into the foaming waters *Titanic*-style as the band played on was too ghastly to contemplate, although I like to think Leonardo DiCaprio could have successfully captured my boyish charm in the made-for-TV epic that would doubtless have ensued. As it was, our faithful boatman and caretaker Langley was on hand to release the offending clamp. In damp-browed gratitude, we later invited him to be a principal character (as the rower) in the tour films. Since Langley lives on the boat, and rows every day, he's the nearest equivalent to Ratty in *The Wind In The Willows* that I've ever met.

Working life on board was greatly enhanced by the new technology available since *The Wall* and *The Final Cut*. In the intervening years, computer software and equipment had become standard in the control room. Like most technological advances, the great advantage of computerisation was that all sorts of decisions could be put off while an infinite variety of options for sounds and editing were tried.

This was the album where we first incorporated significant amounts of sampling; the samples were easy to manipulate and songs could be developed out of the sounds themselves. For the drum parts, the tempo, drum fills and even bar-by-bar elements could now be altered, with a deliberate variation in the tempo dialled in to make it a little more human. Obviously a computer still can't throw a television out of a hotel window or get drunk and be sick on the carpet, so there is little danger of them replacing drummers for some while yet.

In fact, I found myself overwhelmed by the computers on this record. I hadn't played seriously for four years and didn't even like the sound or feel of my own playing. Perhaps I had been demoralised by the conflict with Roger. Certainly I ended up struggling to play some parts satisfactorily. With time pressure on, I surrendered a number of parts to some of the best session players in Los Angeles, including Jim Keltner and Carmine Appice – an odd feeling, a bit like handing your car over to Michael Schumacher. This was not only a defeatist attitude, but meant I then had to learn the damn drum part to play it live (an experience to file under 'never ever again').

The guest artists were part of a general panic when – with Bob becoming homesick, and needing a bigger studio – we shipped ourselves, somewhat against our better judgement, over to his native LA. In the A&M Studios, we were able to admire the talents not only of Messrs Keltner and Appice, but also Tom Scott's saxophone and the keyboard work of Little Feat's Bill Payne. Bob Dylan was recording at A&M too, so the whole experience felt like a return to the real world of music after the swans and cucumber sandwiches of the *Astoria*.

While we were in California, I encountered a new breed of human being: the drum doctor – not the venerable roadie who made sure the kit was set up correctly, but a magician who coaxed unheard-of sounds out of the available resources. The drum doctor would arrive with a van-load of equipment, sniffing disdainfully at my own kit, and proceed to erect an array of fabulous-sounding material: a choice of half a dozen snares, full of subtle nuances, and myriad cymbals. It was a complete eye-opener, like having Jeeves permanently on hand, laying out co-ordinated cymbals rather than ties.

Rick joined proceedings quite late in the day and was quarantined from any costs or legal repercussions from Roger. This was mainly a practical matter. There was some confusion over Rick's position within the band. When David and I first wanted to talk to Rick we discovered that buried in his leaving agreement from 1981 was a clause that prevented him rejoining the group. Consequently we had to be careful about what constituted being a member of the band; only David and I appeared on the cover of the album.

Most of the songs on *Momentary Lapse* had been complete before we started recording and as a result there really is very little filler. When I went over to Los Angeles to hear the work in progress on the initial mixes, I was slightly taken aback. It seemed as if there was too much going on aurally. We had recorded a lot of material and most of it seemed to be in the mix. Generally we had tended to lose material in the mix. We agreed that it wasn't sounding right and the final version had much more space and air.

A couple of things strike me about the finished album. In hindsight I really should have had the self-belief to play all the drum parts. And in the early days of life after Roger, I think David and I felt that we had to get it right, or we would be slaughtered. As a result it is a very 'careful' album with very few risks taken. These things together make me feel ever so slightly removed from *Momentary Lapse*, to the point that it doesn't always sound like us. However, 'Learning To Fly' does for some reason – it feels very much like a 'home' track.

We spent the obligatory three weeks agonising over the album title: each choice had to be given more than one test. Did we like it, was it suitable for the music, and would Roger and the critics use it against us? Eventually it dawned on us that there was no word or phrase in existence that someone couldn't make fun of, so, having settled on *A Momentary Lapse Of Reason*, a phrase taken from a lyric created by David with Phil Manzanera, we reverted to worrying about the other elements.

For the album cover, we turned again to Storm Thorgerson. In keeping with the river setting of much of the recording and a lyric describing a vision of empty beds, the concept evolved into a river of beds, photographed on Saunton Sands in Devon, where most of the war sequences for the film of *The Wall* had been shot. All the attendant problems of fast tides and rotten weather ensued. A bonus was that with all the alternative formats at our disposal – CD, vinyl, cassette, minidisk, versions for different territories – we could make the maximum use of good design ideas we might otherwise have had to discard, neatly avoiding lengthy arguments and difficult decisions.

By now we were preparing for a tour. Michael Cohl, the Canadian promoter, proved to be a tower of strength, at a time when we were grappling with the final stages of the album, and the legal aspects. Michael had been promoting shows since the late 1960s, concentrating initially on his native Canada and then expanding to North America. He became heavily involved with the Rolling Stones, promoting their *Urban Jungle/Steel Wheels* tour, and thereafter *Voodoo Lounge, Bridges to Babylon* and *Forty Licks* tours.

Michael was confident that a tour could happen, and taking the risk that Roger would injunct any promoter selling tickets, began advertising our shows. At a time when we did not know ourselves what would happen, support like this was priceless and ensures Michael a place in our personal Hall of Fame. Early ticket sales were strong; now all we had to worry about was whether we would be sued, whether the audience would be outraged when Roger failed to appear, and how to pay for the set-up of the sort of show we wanted to produce...

Since the early 1980s, sponsorship had become a major element in tour financing, but although attractive, this was not an option that was available to us. With all the unknown elements facing our reception – and the potential of a dramatic pratfall – there was no queue of cola or trainer shoe manufacturers outside the door. We couldn't put all the tickets on sale and use the money up front. The only viable way to do it was for David and me to fork out.

In my particular case I was a bit short of ready cash for the millions required, so I eventually went down to the upmarket equivalent of the pawn shop and hocked my 1962 GTO Ferrari. Probably my most prized possession, and an old family friend (I had bought it in 1977) this car yet again added to its distinguished competition history. Because the car market had recently gone berserk, with this model at the top of the madness – one car reputedly sold at the time for $14 million – I had little trouble in financing my half of the tour set-up costs.

As we compiled the team to work on the tour, we encountered more strains on people's sense of fair play and loyalty. To design the staging, we initially approached Fisher Park, but they turned down the opportunity since they were already committed to working on Roger's *Radio KAOS* show. It was unlikely that either side would have taken kindly to sharing their talents. Considering they were also to be involved in Roger's version of *The Wall* in Berlin two years later they were probably right to stick with his team.

I have no idea if it was the case, but I sensed that Jonathan Park in particular was loyal to Roger rather than us, whereas Mark Fisher would happily have done both projects. I mention this because it became an issue seven years later, when, mean-spirited as we are, we asked Mark alone to work for us. We may forget to give credit when it is due, but we always have no problem remembering real or imagined slights.

Steve then carried out some research into set designers and came up with Paul Staples. As soon as we had talked to him and seen some of his work we thought Paul could do the job. He brought a large dose of fresh thinking to our staging: he had extensive experience of working in the theatre as well as on innumerable exhibitions and presentations. Paul came up with a raft of ideas – as usual, some had to be scrapped, while others survived. The show was initially designed for indoor arenas but still required a roof structure to hang the screen. We wanted a large stage, and although we never seem to achieve it, we always aim for as clean a stage floor as possible.

We also required the maximum amount of darkness for projection purposes, which led to the creation of what was essentially a large black box. We have one very specific advantage over the majority of touring bands. The total inability of any of us to moonwalk, duckwalk, set fire to our hair or play guitars with our teeth means that the audience do not need a constant video monitor to show what we are doing on stage. People sometimes ask me why don't we just get computers to perform instead. I usually reply, 'No, we can't, they move around too much…'

Film is more unwieldy than video in many ways but it has such good quality and luminescence in comparison that it is still more suitable for stadium environments. The future probably holds laser, full-colour hologram projection into an artificial cloud hanging over the auditorium, but it certainly wasn't available in 1987.

Marc Brickman, who Steve had called at short notice in Los Angeles to work on *The Wall* shows, now took another call from Steve, asking him to fly over from LA. Marc remembers talking to David, and picking up the feeling that David was 'incensed' that Roger thought he had the right to shut Pink Floyd down. Marc was taken on as lighting designer, and started work with Robbie Williams and Paul Staples. Marc and Robbie went to Brussels to meet Paul, who was working with a ballet company. They had a coffee in a nearby café, and a tram trundled past. Marc and Paul looked at each other, as their cerebral light bulbs went on. In the tour, lights running on tracking were used, stopping directly over Rick's head as he played the intro to 'Wish You Were Here'. Another effect was something of an accident. Testing the Very lights and the round screen, there was a computer glitch. As Marc reset the system all the lights flipped over. He realised they could 'dance' and the technique became a major element of the show. Other new toys included the periactoids, which were the spinning sections built into the front face of the stage base. They could be set to turn at different speeds, or to flicker in pre-set patterns.

One of the fattest files in the touring department is 'The Ones That Got Away'. Much time is expended on effects that promise a great deal but always seem to end up being bloody dangerous, fabulously expensive and only work once in fifty attempts. Sometimes (viz the inflatable pyramid), despite fulfilling all these characteristics, they still slip through the net. This time we decided mid-tour to ditch Icarus, an apparently airborn figure who sprang forth in 'Learning To Fly' and flittered across the stage. He never quite worked, ending up looking like oversized washing on a line.

One idea – the flying saucer – sounded perfect. A large helium-filled device, it could be radio-controlled to hover over the auditorium, dripping with lights and effects. No wires or rigging were required. The problem was that it was a fantasy. To carry sufficient power for the proposed lighting rig it would have been about the same size, cost and approximately as safe as the *Graf Zeppelin*...

A decent model of the staging was built to show how the whole thing could be assembled, folded and trucked. One of the most important aspects of these rehearsals was working out the most efficient way to pack up and down the trucks, since saving one truck for one year of touring could save something in the region of $100,000. This was all well and good. But we also had to construct a band – and however many models we constructed, the musicians had to be at least partly human. We had used additional musicians before. Ever since *Dark Side*, additional singers had been part of the show. Snowy White had added a second guitar to *The Wall* – and for that brief period in early 1968 Syd and David had presented a two-guitar line-up. We had also used an additional drummer on *The Wall*. We obviously now needed a bass player. Perhaps the most significant change was the arrival of a second keyboard player. This was a response not only to the possibilities offered by digital technology – we needed someone who was familiar with sequencers and samplers – but also to help represent the fuller, more complex sounds we had been able to produce on the houseboat.

Our additional keyboard player, Jon Carin, had originally met David at the Live Aid show at Wembley Stadium. Jon was playing with Bryan Ferry, and since David was playing guitar in the same band he had an opportunity to view Jon's skills at first hand. Jon was also up to date on sampling techniques, which was particularly useful when we found we needed to re-create the sounds produced by long defunct keyboards now languishing in the Science Museum.

Guy Pratt arrived at the *Astoria* for an audition when I was present since David wanted a second opinion. Guy's rather less than respectful attitude to the Dinosaur Kings of Rock when asked to run through the bass parts alerted us to the fact that apart from being able to play them all with one hand behind his back – or indeed with a monumental hangover, and sometimes both – he would be an easier touring companion than someone who started in awe of us and then became bitterly depressed on getting to know us better. By coincidence, Guy's songwriter father Mike had co-written 'Rock With The Caveman' with Lionel Bart and Tommy Steele, which was a pleasing connection with my youthful visit to see Tommy in the late Fifties.

Gary Wallis was spotted playing percussion with Nick Kershaw at a charity show where David was also appearing. Neither of us had ever seen anything like it. Instead of sitting down to play Gary was working in a kind of cage stuffed full of percussion, some pieces of which were mounted so high that a three-foot leap was needed to strike the required object. With his obvious musical skills this additional showmanship seemed an ideal bonus for a stage that looked initially as though it might be occupied by the living dead.

The saxophonist Scott Page was another stage show in his own right. Our only problem here was holding him down, possibly strapping him down. With relatively few saxophone parts in the show, Scott became a *Phantom Of The Opera* figure. At the slightest excuse he'd be back up on stage, a guitar strapped around his neck, in the hope of finding himself another part to play, or doing a Status Quo along to David's guitar solos. He didn't have a radio mike, and used a standard guitar lead, so the road crew – possibly inspired by our tour manager Morris Lyda's rodeo background – would chop a few inches off the lead each night to restrict his movement and rope him in. He was lucky they didn't hog-tie him down.

On guitar, Tim Renwick had the best credentials of all. A native of Cambridge, he had been to the same school as Roger, Syd, David and Bob Klose, although some years behind. His earlier bands had been produced by David and he had also played on Roger's solo work. On the occasions David was absent from rehearsals, Tim made an excellent deputy as musical director.

The backing singers on the tour were assembled from various sources. We met Rachel Fury through James Guthrie, and Margaret Taylor was an LA-based singer who had worked on the album sessions. Durga McBroom, a former member of Blue Pearl, completed the initial trio – her sister Lorelei later replaced Margaret for the latter part of the tour.

We arrived in Toronto for rehearsals at the beginning of August 1987. This was mainly due to Michael Cohl's Canadian connections; the tour was also opening there. David was coming on later after completing the mixing of the record, while we moved into a very hot rehearsal room along with a mountain of new equipment to start work. We both wanted the feeling of a homogeneous band rather than a split between principals and sidemen. The nature of the new music was much more in this style anyway, and would not easily lend itself to being played live by a four-piece. After two weeks it was sounding roughly right, although this was at the expense of a lot of late nights from Jon and Gary as they struggled with endless disks of samples ('Everything's crashed, man, another two days without sleep should see it right').

The band then relocated to the airport to join the crew, who had been working on the set-up. This choice of locale turned out to be a bright idea and gave us a penchant for airfields as rehearsal bases: they provide excellent engineering facilities on site, as well as easy shipping for delivery of a constant stream of high-tech heavyweight items of equipment that were inevitably arriving late.

Security was easy to maintain; we lost far more tools and personal effects in the very smart hotels we stayed in than we ever did in the hangars. And insecurities were easier to avoid. We didn't have to perform for the endless stream of people who manage to find some reason to hang about at any sort of rehearsal. The fact that we also got to have a go on the 747 simulator and fly it round the CNN tower, to sit in a USAF F14 that was visiting for an air show, and generally hang around an airfield added to the general pleasure of the experience. Both David and I were doing quite a lot of flying in the period leading up to this record, and apart from 'Learning To Fly' the aviation theme was carried on throughout the tour. MTV gave away an aeroplane and flying lessons as a promotion prize, while the tour party sported aviator jackets rather than the normal embroidered satin baseball-style ones.

By now, the album was ready to be launched. David and I increased our workload by spending most of each morning doing an endless round of phone interviews. This was a better alternative than a whistle-stop tour of America visiting radio and TV stations, and we certainly couldn't do anything in Europe, so we settled into answering the same questions that we have dealt with for thirty-odd years – 'How did the band get their name?', 'Where's Syd?', 'Why has the band lasted so long?' – along with some new ones about the fight with Roger, and tried to sound surprised at the novelty of it all.

Meanwhile, out at the airport Paul, Robbie and Marc, along with Morris Lyda, were trying to assemble one hundred tons of steel into a stage and then work out how to pack it into a truck. Morris was a new personality to us, although already a legend in rock-show circles. An ex-rodeo rider, he had moved on to something more challenging as a rock tour manager. Having worked on the previous Genesis tour, along with 50 per cent of the rest of our crew, he had the necessary experience. As usual, the initial impression of a group of professional and responsible technicians began to dissolve as one French telescan operator was reprimanded for eating the contents of the ashtrays in a club for a bet...

By the time we arrived at the hangar we were the last thing the crew wanted to see. Not only would we mess up their beautifully arranged stage and demand changes, but anything they wanted to do had to be done with 50,000 watts of PA killing all conversation. Eventually we managed to come to an arrangement, with quiet periods as required, but it all felt much slower than we needed. The size of the crew was vast compared to anything we had done before. Even *The Wall* had only required some sixty people; now we had over 100. Not only was it very difficult to learn all their names, a year later it was still a struggle, particularly as some came or went or were on one show in three if they were part of the leapfrogging crew.

Among the difficulties were some special moments. Marc would often spend all night programming the lights and my first sight of his efforts was unforgettable, because it was so spectacular. On stage you have no concept of what the external view is like. For example, the circular screen with the lights attached appeared – from my drum stool – like just another lighting truss. Looking at the stage from out front I could see the full impact of its swirling patterns of light.

Apart from the quantity of crew we also had telephones in triplicate, radio systems, faxes and a drawing office. The last tour hadn't even had a production office. Morris favoured briefing sessions that had more affinity with D-Day than a rock show. After the jobs had been evaluated, allocated and criticised, a short homily on aggression in the field would have fitted in perfectly. When Morris said 'marine' he wasn't talking dolphin, he was talking Iwo Jima. We needed this sort of character.

One of the first duties assigned upon the arrival of the band was the packaging for the road of David's rowing machine. David seemed to think that the fight with Roger might be resolved in the ring rather than the courts and was training every day, using this wonder device that measured your progress electronically and could pit your rowing against any competitor you cared to dream up. The downside was that it weighed four hundred pounds and was ten foot long. The final road box looked like a coffin for the Incredible Hulk, and weighed as much. Nor had anyone allowed for it when packing the trucks. Eventually it was used as a punishment for the last truck out, which had to take it. Loading productivity increased by 30 per cent.

Meanwhile, we had asked Bob Ezrin to come in and lend us a

hand. We needed someone to have a look at the overall show. I think we had been so busy on the music that, although we had a fabulous lighting set-up, the band on stage was a mess. This was just up Bob's street. He equipped himself with a loudhailer and entertained us strutting up and down in front of the stage shouting loud but unintelligible advice while conducting drum fills with wild gesticulations at the same time. Later on we modified this communication system for something a little higher tech.

We also had to address relatively simply but vital issues: how and when we got on stage, how the numbers finished, whether we wanted to be lit between songs or simply segue into the next. And if any musician was to move we also had to ensure that they would not be lost forever by plunging down one of the trapdoors that disguised many of the more unusual lighting rigs.

The final dress rehearsal before we headed out to Ottawa was held at night. It was a warm summer's evening, and as we played the huge hangar doors were open, with large jets slowly taxiing past to the runways. As the music wafted out over the area, an uninvited audience of airport personnel arrived. Gradually the interior and exterior of the hangar filled with a wonderful collection of service and emergency vehicles, all with their revolving amber lights activated. It beat the more conventional use of swaying cigarette lighters into a cocked hat.

The atmosphere before the first show in Ottawa was electric – well, it was backstage even if not in the rather damp field out front. The new album was not even available in the shops, so we were starting off playing unfamiliar music to a probably sceptical audience. We awarded ourselves top marks afterwards for surviving, but we were well aware that, although most of the technical side worked, the performance was well below par. We steeled ourselves for more rehearsal time, and yet another revision of the set list.

With the fairly intense schedule that we had set ourselves everything began to settle in rapidly, and over the first few shows we were able to refine and change the show, rather than learn it. We were still quite short of material, and one extra encore found us with nearly nothing more to play: we plumped for 'Echoes'. We were not that familiar with performing the song, and the piece sounded a little stilted – it was the last time we ever played the number. David now observes that one of the reasons we couldn't quite recapture the feel of the original was that the younger musicians we were now working with were so technically proficient they were not able to unlearn their technique and just noodle around as we had in the early Seventies.

After correcting a few musical and technical aspects, the shows started gelling relatively quickly despite the occasional glitch. As a result the individual shows tend in retrospect to merge into a seamless flow. In fact the show was feeling so comfortable that we started trying to film the shows early on, but unfortunately, having filmed in Atlanta at the Omni, we didn't like the results. We hadn't spent enough and it showed. So to punish ourselves, along with everyone else, we tried it all over again in New York in August the next year. We ordered twenty cameras and ended up with two hundred hours of film. Someone is still probably incarcerated in an edit suite somewhere viewing the results.

Simultaneously, Roger's *Radio KAOS* tour was criss-crossing North America. We studiously managed to avoid each other, although a couple of our personnel went to see his show. I didn't want to see it – out of sight, out of mind – but in any case rumour had it we would not be allowed in, and I had no intention of being escorted ignominiously from the premises. We eventually formalised a settlement with Roger. On Christmas Eve 1987, during a break in touring, David and Roger convened for a summit meeting on the houseboat with Jerome Walton, David's accountant. Mince pies, noggin and festive hats were placed on hold, as Jerome painstakingly typed out the bones of a settlement. Essentially – although there was far more complex detail – the agreement allowed Roger to be freed from his arrangement with Steve, and David and me to continue working under the name Pink Floyd. The document was then handed over to our respective and expensive lawyers to be translated into legalese. They all singularly failed to achieve this; in the end the court accepted Jerome's version as the final and binding document and duly stamped it.

After the first leg in the States, we headed to New Zealand for our first visit: it was like being in England in a time warp, but a pleasant one. Seeing the local musicians I realised how hard it must be starting out there: even if you made it big in New Zealand you wouldn't make any money for the record company, so then you had to make it in Australia – and there would still be many rungs to climb. After the shows in Auckland, we returned to Australia after a long absence. The last time we'd played, in 1971, we had arrived at the wrong time of the year in bitter cold. This time we were determined to do it properly – and it turned out to be smooth and easy. The band would occasionally head for a club to jam led by the new recruits. They performed a number of times in Australia billed as The Fisherman's (short for Fisherman's Friend). I think they rehearsed harder for the renditions of 'Unchain My Heart' and 'I Shot The Sheriff' than they did for the main show...

After Australia, Japan was a little more difficult. There was no outdoor show, and shuttling between large auditoria, we had less time to experience the country. Even the cameras seemed more expensive this time. On the way back to the US, Nettie and I stopped over in Hawaii for a delightful couple of weeks, although the occasional burst of torrential rain was a throwback to a classic British seaside holiday.

On a professional level this tour had been the most enjoyable ever, and it had been particularly so on a personal level. Nettie had come along for the entire time, from the rehearsals in Toronto onwards, and had increased the pleasure of the whole enterprise immeasurably. She had been on theatre tours as an actress, but the scale of this and the numbers of people and amounts of logistics and material involved were something of an eye-opener for her. What I definitely appreciated was that going on tour without a partner was likely to put a strain on most relationships – I once worked out that 90 per cent of this particular tour party had left a trail of broken marriages and partnerships behind them. It seemed to be the case that you either took your wife along, or invited your divorce lawyer to accompany you.

The second leg in the States reinforced the law that all effects have the capacity for disaster: during a show in Foxboro, Massachusetts, the flying pig snagged somewhere and was ripped to pieces by an over-enthusiastic, or fanatically vegan, audience.

By the time we arrived in Europe the band had really settled into the groove: they were a hard-working group of musicians, who regularly – Jon Carin particularly – reviewed the tapes of the previous night's show to try and note any imperfections. Their professionalism was impeccable: even if Guy Pratt was the last out of the bar the night – or morning – before, his playing was faultless on stage, a tribute to his iron constitution or the fact that our music was too easy.

We had developed a comfortable way of living and working together on tour, by not dividing up into cliques and enjoying a reasonable level of fun. We would occasionally throw a Wally party after the show, the idea being to turn up dressed as appallingly as possible. The local thrift shops would be drained of shell suits; nylon was the order of the day. The tour had been, according to Phil Taylor – who had been touring with us since the mid-1970s –

great fun, with a good spirit and a sense of relief that we were back out on the road.

If any constitutions were wilting the following day, their owners could turn to Scott Page, who had become the tour's unofficial herbal tea salesman. He was nearly as good at this as playing the saxophone, and soon a fair number of the band were to be seen clutching horrible plastic bottles of urine-coloured liquid which they insisted on drinking at all times. Fortunately like most tour fads – Japanese cameras, buckskin cowboy jackets and tequila sunrises – it was short-lived, and I can only hope Scott still has vast quantities of those awful herbs stuffed in his attic.

In Europe the shows were more varied and have stuck in my mind for longer, mainly due to the venues we chose. Sometimes we could add an extra level of variety: in Rotterdam, we arranged for a pre-show air display, accompanied by 'Echoes' on the PA system by two motor gliders, flown by friends of ours whom David and I had met through learning to fly. Their graceful aerial balletics trailing smoke seemed like a good idea for other dates, but we were defeated by the complications of getting permission for them to fly in restricted air space.

Versailles was probably the grandest of the European shows. These events would come together through a combination of Steve recceing possible locations and direct approaches from interested parties. At the time, François Mitterand's Minister of Culture was the dynamic Jack Lang. He was on side for the Versailles project – which helped in the politicking to convert any doubters – and it seemed a natural meeting of minds.

The setting was magnificent, and most of the French were pleased to see us there. Certainly there were lengthy speeches from local dignitaries, one of whom seemed to have offered his support only if his name could appear above the band's on an official plaque. I was called on at short notice to deliver a brief speech –

having hastily cobbled together a few clichés, my mumbled utterance was unlikely to trouble historians of the *entente cordiale*. We had great weather, and it felt like a special occasion. This is really the aim of trying to work in unique places. A stadium is much more convenient for any large show, but it is more difficult to create such a special atmosphere. Whenever possible it does seem worth making the effort to utilise settings with a sense of history and place.

As a gesture of goodwill to our Italian fans, we accepted an invitation to perform on the Grand Canal in Venice. However, it transpired that the invitation had not been sent out by all the city fathers. There were two opposing factions, one delighted, the other convinced that we would achieve what a thousand years of lagoon waters had failed to do, and sink the city in a single afternoon. We held a press conference to reassure the council, the nation and the conservationists that we were not setting out to sack the city, not even to undertake any light pillaging. Nevertheless, we still failed to convince everyone that this was the case.

As Venice has limited access the plan had been to restrict the number of tourists allowed in on that particular day. We stayed outside the city, in the Lagoon, reckoning that life was hard enough without having to jostle past the fans and the city authorities. In the event, the mayor conspired with the police to allow everyone in, persuaded the shops to close and withdrew any previously arranged toilet or rubbish collection facilities. It is not impossible that support seemed to be withdrawn when the necessary payments were not made to all and sundry.

A representative of the Gondoliers' Union came and claimed his colleagues would all blow their whistles throughout the show if we didn't pay them $10,000 (they already had clients paying double for every boat). This was one bluff we could call – I have yet to hear any whistle rise above the noise we can make. Our stage-cum-barge was declared a seagoing vessel and liable to an extra tax if we tried to move it up the Grand Canal, the police blockading every other route out. Fortunately we were able to set sail on the high sea and make an escape in the Horatio Nelson tradition.

These distractions did not dent the success of the show, which worked particularly well as a live television special. Michael Kamen, who was due to play with us, was the only distressed face I saw. He had appeared before as an occasional guest but this time we wanted him involved in a more structured way, particularly as it was going to be televised. Alas, Michael was held up in the crowds, and thwarted by a lack of water transport at a critical moment, he only made it as far as the mixing desk, too late to take part, and had to watch from the shore two hundred metres away – a sort of bearded French lieutenant's woman.

One golden moment was when a royal barge arrived filled with the dignitaries who had caused us so much trouble. Covered in lights and serving a seven-course meal it drew up in front of the stage, mooring in front of the audience and blocking their view. The audience went mad. A hail of bottles and rubbish rained onto the barge. The waiters manfully defended their masters, shielding them, centurion-style, with their silver trays. Soon the barge was underway again, this time attempting a mooring alongside our platform. One look at our crew, who made Blackbeard's pirates seem like the Partridge Family, and off they went, never to be seen again.

If playing in Venice was problematic, a series of gigs a few weeks earlier had posed even more of a logistical challenge, when we played in Moscow. A shortage of currency meant that it was virtually impossible for a Russian promoter to pay the costs of the tour, but a deal was worked out that essentially covered all the practical aspects of playing. First, they were responsible for getting our equipment from Athens to Moscow and then on again to Helsinki afterwards. To do this they flew in the military

Antonov, the biggest cargo plane in the world. It looked fantastic and took the whole set easily. Accommodation was in the huge hotel in Red Square, which was still staffed with KGB surveillance on every floor along with samovars to provide hot tea. With the tightness of security and the sheer size of the place, it took us three days to find where we could get a drink in the evening and breakfast in the morning.

We also took our own catering, which was the most effective door opener available. An invitation to dinner for any official ensured all sorts of benefits. Through our tax adviser, Nigel Eastaway, who also happens to be a trustee of the Russian Aviation Research Trust, we were able to visit Monino, the Russian air force museum – the largest, and at the time, the least visited of Europe's aircraft museums. There we saw some of Igor Sikorsky's aeronautical inventions, some 1930s Russian monoplane bombers (from a period when the RAF was still using antiquated biplanes) and a politically correct version of the history of flight, along with parts from Gary Powers' U2 spy plane shot down in the 1960s, and the bombers that had circled Red Square during the May Day parades to convince American observers of the might of the Russian Air Force. We were particularly honoured, as we discovered that the Air Attaché at the British Embassy had been unable to acquire the same invitation.

The British Embassy gave us a good lunch and we ended up with hundreds of Russian dolls and an array of fur hats. I only wish I had not asked what they were made of; it transpired some of the fur was baby seal. We also made one visit to the university to talk about politics, art and life but it degenerated into yet another 'How did the band get its name?' session. We left, commandeering limousines to replace the ones we had arrived in, since we had been gazumped in the commandeering stakes by someone more important. The equipment was then driven non-stop to Helsinki with a police escort – by all accounts one hell of a ride (Phil Taylor remembers the experience of arriving in Helsinki as like going from 'black and white to Technicolor').

After the tour was over a live album was mixed – *Delicate Sound Of Thunder* – at Abbey Road, using Studio 3, now completely rebuilt since our last sojourn there. What was particularly gratifying was that so little repair work to the music was required. Without doubt recording towards the end of the tour had been a good idea.

Meanwhile, Roger was re-staging *The Wall* in Berlin and we couldn't help but hear about it. Not least because he made a point of inviting all our ex-wives, although of course it may be that my invitation simply got lost in the post... Confusion about who played in Berlin still rumbles on, though why that is I have no idea. It was entirely Roger's show, but people are always thanking me and telling me how fantastic it was. I still haven't worked out if it's easier to smile modestly and pretend we were there, or to embark on a full explanation that this was in fact Roger on his own with a cast of thousands. When fans continue to insist I *was* there, I respond with a weak grin and a vacant stare to avoid the confusion.

Just under a year after the last show on the tour (at Marseilles) we took part in the Knebworth open-air concert in June 1990, a charity event for the Nordoff-Robbins Music Therapy charity. With so little happening in this year after the excesses of the past three it was almost unsettling to assemble for just the one show. Rehearsals were minimal on the basis that since it was the same band who had done over two hundred shows they probably could still remember the parts. We did do a couple of days' rehearsal out at Bray studios, and brought Jon Carin and Marc Brickman over from America for the show. However, instead of using Scott Page, who I think was unavailable, we asked Candy Dulfer – the Dutch saxophonist who had recently had a UK hit, 'Lily Was Here', with

Dave Stewart – to perform with us: a nice European touch we thought. As with Scott, the only drawback for a saxophonist is that they really only get a cameo role; given Candy's abilities there was far too little time or space to reveal anything near the extent of her playing.

We had Vicki Brown on backing vocals, as well as her daughter Sam, who was to continue the Brown dynasty when she became a mainstay of the next tour. Clare Torry, the original performer of 'Great Gig', was also added.

After two years of touring in isolation it was a pleasure to see some other people playing, and to have the opportunity to hang around backstage at Knebworth in traditional rock-god style. It was a kind of geriatric afternoon on Mount Olympus in musical terms. Mark Knopfler and Eric Clapton were playing along with Elton John and Genesis. Status Quo, Cliff Richard and Paul McCartney finished up the bill. Rick introduced us to his new girlfriend, Millie, and we all arrived in giant Huey helicopters like a scene from *Apocalypse Now*, spilling out quantities of family and crew.

We had managed to secure the slot as the last band on, in return for being the first band to commit to the event. Becoming top of the bill did not pay off. The afternoon was typically English, changing rapidly from sun to rain, but inevitably as our spot came closer the weather took a turn for the worse and the rain and cold closed in.

Closing the show suited us, since in midsummer we wanted the dark, but as time went by and McCartney started playing yet another song the old love and peace sentiment began to fray at the edges. We eventually played in the pouring rain, to a crowd who seemed to enjoy the show, which was fortunate since they could not leave because all traffic was mired in the mud.

WISER AFTER THE EVENT '12

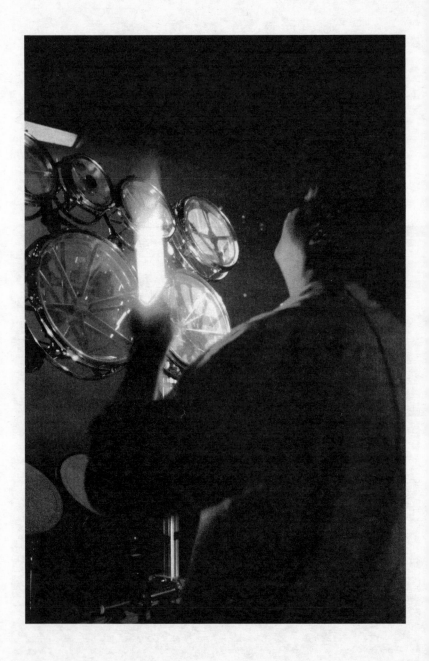

As FAR as Pink Floyd was concerned the 1990s nearly didn't happen. At the start of the decade, there was an incident that was extremely painful – and potentially fatal – and which almost put an end to any plans we might have had for the future. This was the result of a decision by Steve, David and myself to take part in the Carrera PanAmericana, which was a rerun of a wonderful 1950s race for sports cars run along the length of Mexico. The modern version, resurrected in 1988, was rather less demanding than the original flat-out race of 2,178 miles, but it still consisted of a 1,800-mile route from the bottom of Mexico to the Texas border with competition sections interspersed with long regularity elements. Rick had wisely avoided the excitement of motor racing and stuck with sailing in the Aegean.

Steve and I had driven in the event a couple of years before. However, on that occasion, when Steve had arrived in Mexico at the appointed time, casually swinging his crash helmet, the race car he had negotiated to drive failed to turn up, leaving him trailing the field for a few days in the hope that he could make a magnificent charge from the back of the grid when the car eventually showed up. As far as I remember the car arrived, but broke down terminally a few miles further on.

This time, perhaps determined to make sure there would be some positive outcome whatever happened, Steve had managed to pre-sell the rights in a film that we would make. The plan was that the film would underwrite most, if not all of the costs, up front. Here was a chance, we thought, to have a lot of fun – and get some help paying for it. I also liked the tenuous connection with my father's career. In 1953 he had driven another marathon road race, the Mille Miglia, through Italy with a camera car, and I saw myself as continuing the tradition.

We set off with two replica C-type Jaguars, roughly identical to the cars that won the Le Mans 24-hour race in 1953. We also took along two camera crews, and a couple of back-up vehicles containing the trusty mechanics who had rebuilt the cars. I was with a friend, Valentine Lindsay, in one car. The other was being driven by Steve and David. After a couple of days the event had settled down into some exciting driving, coupled with the inevitable stomach complaints as the European competitors adjusted to a Mexican diet. Fortunately I had been shown how to treat these symptoms using acupuncture. It was exceptionally effective: one quick glimpse of my box of needles and people instantly seemed to feel a great deal better.

On day three of the race Val and I arrived at one of the checkpoints to be told there had been an accident. There was nothing to be done except continue and try and find out the details further on. When we reached the evening stop we finally managed to discover that the accident had, in fact, involved the other car in our team, which had gone over the edge of a cliff at 80mph. David – who had been driving – was shaken, and seriously stirred, but essentially unhurt bar a few cuts and bruises. Steve, on navigating duties, had suffered compound fractures of one leg and was laid up in hospital: a somewhat brutal way to treat one's manager. On seeing the wreckage of the car the next day, I realised how incredibly lucky both of them had been to escape so relatively lightly.

Although Val and I managed to finish sixth, we had lost half the cast of our film, and were consequently forced to fall back on some cinematic cheating that the major Hollywood moguls would no doubt have recognised. This included recording some footage in a Mexican restaurant in Notting Hill, craftily positioning the cameras to avoid the passing Number 98 double-deckers and hiding glimpses of Steve's still plastercast-clad leg. We also had the luxury of reshooting the pre-race discussions with the benefit of 100 per cent hindsight.

After the event there was a slight twinge of embarrassment about the whole episode, especially from David (although I'm not sure if that was to do with the music or his driving). But as a visual experience it was lacking. To do justice to the event, we would have required a Hollywood budget, innumerable helicopters and Steve McQueen. To fully enjoy the low-budget version we plumped for, you really had to be a dedicated aficionado of 1950s sports cars, Mexican scenery, or cactus plants.

However, there was one bonus from all of this, in that the music for the project suggested a blueprint for recording the next album: there was no pre-studio work at all. In much the same way that we created *Obscured By Clouds*, the whole piece was concocted during sessions in the large studio at Olympic in Barnes during a couple of weeks in November 1991. It was also, for the most part, recorded with us all working in the studio together. After years of overdubbing in solitary confinement, it was great fun. We had Gary Wallis, Jon Carin and Guy Pratt from the 1987/88 tour, and fortuitously Tim Renwick, working next door on a Bryan Ferry album, was available for the odd guest moment.

Starting off with a couple of blues pieces, other pieces were simply improvised. These usually stemmed from ideas emerging from David trying something out on the guitar – and then being picked up by the rest of us in the studio. If it sounded promising enough it could then be developed into a suitable form for the film section. We think we managed to avoid slipping into becoming Hammersmith's very own Mariachi band despite the temptation of all those cactus scenes. We had experienced the odd run-in with ethnic music on our first album, as well as a guitar part on the *More* soundtrack, and I think we knew that this kind of musical colour (as well as funny hats, whether the fez or sombrero) was not our forte, not even our pianissimo.

Just over a year later we adopted the same modus operandi when we began working on the next Floyd album in January 1993. Again, the recording process proved to be extremely positive: this time there was a subconsciously conscious attempt to operate as a band. We would rule off a week in the diary and head over to Britannia Row – which now bore little resemblance to the angst-encouraging bunker of the *Animals* days. All the rooms had been remodelled to allow daylight to penetrate and, of course, there were now increased areas for rest and recreation to try and lure clients into using yet more expensive studio time.

Other than booking the time at Britannia Row, we made few preparations for a future release. Nobody had come down to the sessions with a 'Here's one I prepared earlier' fragment up their sleeves. No more hired guns; just David, Rick and myself, with the engineer at the desk, a two-track left running – and as much time as we needed. Although bitter experience had taught us to be prepared for disappointment, and though there was no pressure to come up with anything concrete at these sessions, the very fact of booking the studio was an indication of our commitment.

If nothing came of the exercise we were committed to a process of either seeking outside help or waiting for the individuals to come up with songs at their own pace, which historically had tended to be very slow. We had also spent some time maintaining that together we did create something unique. Failure now to produce anything would be deeply wounding to our egos as much as anything else and might well result in abandoning the project. While the world held its breath we sent out for more sandwiches.

After the very first day, however, we realised that we would be able to produce some good material, and after a couple more sessions we brought Guy Pratt in to play bass. This immediately added a stronger feel to the playing but we also found that an interesting phenomenon occurred, which was that Guy's playing tended to change the mood of the music we had created on our own.

Serendipity was equally important. At one point David, frustrated at being unable to get one particular idea directly out of Rick, recorded him tinkering away on the keyboard, unaware that the tape was still running. From this ad-lib session we retrieved another three possible pieces, including one piano part which we were never able to re-create quite as well in any other of the recording sessions and finally ended up using his original Britannia Row piece just as we had done with the Asdic note on 'Echoes'.

The improvisations we were coming up with were not, though, meant to be mood-pieces like the doomed 'Nothings 1–24' we'd tried to produce before *Meddle*. Instead we would sift through the results captured on the two-track for nuggets of musical ideas – the core of 'Cluster One' and 'Marooned' emerged and lingered through to the final album. But the truly significant thing was that each improvisation represented a kick-start to the creative process. That was – as we had always found – our most problematic hurdle. And by allowing ourselves to play whatever came into our heads, with no taboo or no-go areas, I had the impression that we were expanding a field of vision that had become increasingly narrow over the past two decades.

After two weeks we had taped an extraordinary collection of riffs, patterns and musical doodles, some rather similar, some nearly identifiable as old songs of ours, some clearly subliminal reinventions of well-known songs. These – which we would identify as 'Neil Young', or whoever seemed to be the originator –

were easy to knock out of contention. But even having discarded these, forty ideas were available. Given that in the past some of our records had painfully gestated from a month's work to provide a single useable note, this was a positive fund of potential pieces. At our usual work rate that was enough to keep us recording until well into the twenty-first century. We eventually ended up with enough left-over material that we considered releasing it as a second album, including a set we dubbed 'The Big Spliff', the kind of ambient mood music that we were bemused to find being adopted by bands like the Orb, although – unlike Gong's Steve Hillage – we never received any invitations to join this next generation on stage.

Led by David, but with input from Rick, the formal songs were created. My impression is that David had finally got to grips with producing music when he needed it. Perhaps some of the onus of lyric writing had been removed with assistance from Polly Samson, his new girlfriend, later his wife. Maybe the previous tour and album had proved a point, but it definitely felt less pressured, and both David and Rick seemed to produce work more easily. David was still required to lead the process, but with Bob Ezrin on board again, and the friendly face of Andy Jackson handling the engineering, it was a familiar rather than untested team.

Throughout this preparatory phase, the atmosphere was pleasantly calm. Above all it was litigation-free, as correspondence with Roger via the legal profession had come to an end. I was finding it particularly helpful to be spending so much time making music with the others, and with a real sense of purpose. I have never been the most diligent of drummers when it comes to practising technique, so the simple act of playing together regularly helped get me back in some kind of shape. Since Knebworth in 1990, my only genuinely live performance had been at the Chelsea Arts Ball in October 1992 at the Royal Albert Hall.

The Chelsea Arts Club had regenerated itself – and as part of this resurgence they mounted a ball, which was one of the biggest events they had ever done. Tom Jones was appearing, and – as a result of Gary, Tim and Guy working with Tom Jones – we had agreed to provide a guest appearance of three numbers. Inevitably this led on to Jon Carin and Tim turning up. We rehearsed for a day or so, and played a relatively low-key set with virtually no stage effects, films or fireworks.

After leaving Britannia Row we reconvened on David's houseboat to develop a core of pieces. From February 1993 through to May we worked on about twenty-five different ideas, trying to play as much as possible together in the studio. The houseboat was certainly more congenial than recording in a bunker. By now David had added a conservatory containing a kitchen, sitting and dining area. The ambience of the river and the benefits of operating in daylight worked its charms again, as did having a definite split between the workspace on the houseboat and the area on dry land where we could sit, talk and discuss progress.

The album feels much more home-made, very much as a band playing together in one space. I think that Rick in particular felt significantly more integrated in the process this time, compared to *Momentary Lapse*. It was nice to have him back.

The songs had been through a substantial sifting process. There was plenty of material and no desperation; instead we were able to simply concentrate on developing ideas. At band meetings we now started whittling down the possible songs to the probables. We set up an extremely democratic system whereby David, Rick and I would each award marks out of ten for each song, regardless of who had originally generated the piece. This should have worked smoothly, had Rick not misinterpreted the democratic principles underlying the voting system. He simply awarded all of his ideas the full ten points, and everything else got *nul points*. This meant that all of Rick's pieces had a ten-point head start, and it took David and me a while to work out why this new album was rapidly becoming a Rick Wright magnum opus. The voting system was placed under review, as we came up with various systems of electoral colleges and second preference votes that would have graced any mayoral contest.

The same issue reappeared a decade later when we were selecting tracks for inclusion on *Echoes*, the compilation album which required input from David, Rick, myself and Roger. As well as the oars being poked in by a whole galley-load of record company executives, engineers, producers and managers, this time we had to deal with the fact that Roger, like Rick before him, would only vote for his own tracks. God bless democracy.

Before the summer break we took the eight or nine favourite tracks into Olympic Studios in Barnes, recruiting the other players – apart from the backing singers – from the last tour (Gary, Guy, Tim and Jon) and recorded the lot in a week. This gave us a boost, knowing that we could spend more time developing the songs since we realised the essential elements of each song were already in place.

In fact, armed with this safety net, we eventually approached the recording after the summer in a very different way to all our previous albums. We recorded all the backing tracks on the *Astoria*, completed with no more than the three of us – Rick, David and myself – setting up the pieces during a couple of weeks in September. Advances in technology since *Momentary Lapse* meant that we could master tracks on the boat as we came towards the end of six months of recording – although there was the usual mad panic at the very end involving the use of other studios for some overdubs as the pressure mounted. Some traditions are too deep-rooted to give up completely.

Once again, it was good to have Bob Ezrin on board, sorting out the drum parts and helping with the frankly tedious process of recording and modifying the drum sounds. As the final shape of the songs emerged, Michael Kamen was brought in: he offered to provide the string arrangements we needed if we could loan him a sound system and some lights for a children's opera he was putting on in Notting Hill. This seemed like the bargain of a lifetime – an Oscar-winning composer in exchange for a couple of speakers and a few spots. What we hadn't realised was that the musical extravaganza Michael was planning would have made *Starlight Express* seem low-key...

This far into the recording process, all we needed was a deadline or two, generally anathema to all Floyd members. A salutary lesson had been learnt on the previous album, when a certain amount of dilly-dallying on our part, and shilly-shallying from the record company, had resulted in the album coming out alongside Michael Jackson's *Bad* and Bruce Springsteen's *Tunnel Of Love*. Not surprisingly, in that particular contest, our podium position in the charts was distinctly bronze.

This time the deadline was set by making a commitment to a major tour, due to start in April 1994, the thinking being that with a longer leadtime we could plan ahead and construct the most efficient routing through the vast stadiums of the US. But as none of us were avid football fans, we missed one rather important factor: the tour coincided with the 1994 World Cup in the US, which meant that certain stadiums were not only unavailable on some critical dates, but the pitches could not be used for weeks beforehand to protect the precious turf and maintain their pristine condition. Rather than the logical and elegant tour route we had imagined, the end result looked like it had been devised by a blindfolded man throwing darts at a map of the States – or worse, by the old crew at the Bryan Morrison Agency...

The final stages of the album involved the trauma of title and cover design. Yet again the choice of title turned out to be a cliffhanger. Even by January 1994 we had reached no agreement, and every day frantic discussions would take place as deadlines were approached with caution, moved and finally missed. David favoured *Pow Wow*, I liked *Down To Earth*. Everyone had a favourite. No majority could be reached (even bringing into play our by now vast range of sophisticated voting systems).

Help was at hand in the rather large shape of Douglas Adams. As well as being the author of *The Hitchhiker's Guide To The Galaxy*, Douglas was an Apple Mac genius, guitar enthusiast and – fortunately for us – a fan of Pink Floyd. He could bring a marvellous sense of humour to the most desperate moments. He became party to a lot of the discussions about the album title. We found it immensely comforting to talk about our problems with a fellow sufferer of deadline dramas – Douglas was once heard to remark that he loved the sound of deadlines whistling past his ears.

At dinner one night, we agreed with Douglas that if he came up with a name for the album that we liked, we would make a payment to the charity of his choice. He cogitated for a while and suggested *The Division Bell*. The real irritation was that it was a phrase contained within the existing lyrics: we really should have read them more carefully.

Armed at last with a definitive title, Storm Thorgerson came up with a huge variety of ideas, and we finally settled on the concept of the pair of heads forming a single head in a kind of visual illusion. Storm is famous for insisting on doing things for real rather than employing trickery, and so the heads (finally constructed, after various attempts, in both stone and metal) were installed in a suitable field somewhere near Ely.

I visited the location for the photoshoot one chilly day in

Early proposal for the *Wall* show, by Mark Fisher.

Gerald Scarfe (left) and Mark Fisher, rigging the Mother, one of the *Wall* show's inflatable characters.

The movie of *The Wall*: the troops on Saunton Sands (above), and Bob Geldof as Pink.

At Le Mans in 1984, driving in a Porsche 956 and (left) with little compunction about sporting tobacco sponsors' logos.

Steve O'Rourke at Le Mans in the Ferrari 512 BB, in its origin-al Ecurie Nationale Belge livery.

Portrait by David Bailey for the release of *A Momentary Lapse Of Reason.*

Recording session on board David's houseboat, with Bob Ezrin on bass.

Rick entertains the troops on the *Momentary Lapse* tour.

David Gilmour and Polly Samson – they married during the *Division Bell* tour in July 1994.

Performing in Venice, 15th July 1989, tethered offshore from the Piazza San Marco.

Moscow, June 1989 – the McBroom sisters and Rachel Fury do their bit for glasnost.

With my daughter Chloe before the show at Versailles, June 1988.

My sons Cary and Guy take over soundcheck duties.

Daughter Holly on the *Division Bell* tour.

Nettie and I about to embark on the *Division Bell* airship.

On the 2015 London to Brighton Veteran Car Run with Chloe, son-in-law Tim and grandchildren Oscar and Felix.

The *Division Bell* tour, 1994 – one of the pigs emerges from its sty, and the mirrorball rising up and opening in the middle of the auditorium.

The *Division Bell* tour in full swing.

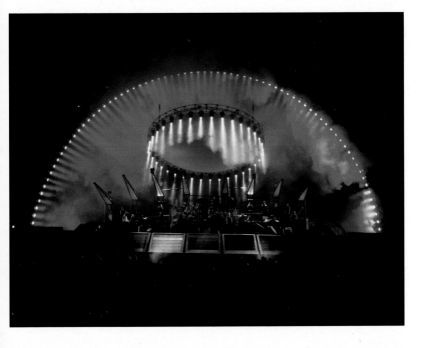

With Roger at the rehearsals for our Live 8 reunion.

The band perform at Live 8.

Live 8, Hyde Park, London, 2nd July 2005.

The Live 8 band (left to right): Jon Carin, me, Rick, Dick Parry, Carol Kenyon, Roger, Tim Renwick and David.

Rick in his happy place, on board his boat *Evrika*.

Displaying my tambourine skills alongside Roger on trumpet and David on mandolin at the O2 Arena in May 2011.

On the *Astoria* preparing for the release of *Endless River*.

Peter Wynne Willson back in control of the slide show at the *Endless River* launch, November 2014.

A nice cup of tea with Roger after unveiling the Pink Floyd plaque at the University of Westminster in May 2015.

The August 2016 press launch for the V&A's *Their Mortal Remains* exhibition.

February: it was a stunning scene, with the heads parked out in the fens. One of our biggest problems was trying to hide them from the press, who would have loved to pre-empt the album's release. Army surplus stores were raided and large quantities of camouflage netting were acquired to be draped over the heads in a rather half-hearted attempt to disguise them. The fact that the press failed to get their exclusive was, I suspect, either due to the fact that we had over-estimated the interest in our album, or that the chilly east coast winds whipping in from Siberia seemed an unattractive alternative to the creature comforts of the Groucho Club bar in Soho. Storm, who was out on the photoshoot near Ely Cathedral, remembers that the muddy conditions meant that the lowloader carrying the heads could not reach the centre of the chosen field, so a slightly disgruntled group of photographer's assistants manhandled the heavy items across the mud and set them up. They were significantly more disgruntled when Storm informed them that it was not the right field.

Meanwhile, we had been evolving the stage show. Back in 1973 we had done a show at the Hollywood Bowl, and a photo was hanging in Steve O'Rourke's office as a constant reminder of just how good a stage can look. We had in mind to try and take some of the elements of that particular show and develop them for the stadiums we would be playing. We also wanted to add a degree of flexibility into the proceedings. On the previous tour, the set had been completely nailed down, almost to the second. This time we wanted to have the option of changing the running order and substituting songs.

We again resisted the use of large video screens showing the live performance. We never have and probably never will feature close-ups of the band in that way. But we did want film pieces for some of the new music, and, having made the decision to perform some of *The Dark Side Of The Moon*, felt it was time to revisit a number of the *Dark Side* film clips. Although many had lasted very well and were included once more for the *Dark Side* suite, much of the film was very dated. In particular the politicians of two decades earlier who featured in *Brain Damage* were now so passé that half the audience were too young to know who they were. The rest had probably forgotten.

We convened a number of production meetings with perhaps our best team to date. Marc Brickman (fresh from the opening shows for the 1992 Olympics in Barcelona and having fallen out once and for all with Barbara Streisand) was back as lighting designer, armed with a bagload of new technology. He was joined by Mark Fisher as stage designer and Robbie Williams as production manager. Storm was appended to the group since he was responsible for all the additional film required – some six different pieces lasting for around forty minutes. I say appended, due to Storm's lovable inability to work in any capacity other than as a dictator.

The initial designs involved a hemisphere sitting on the ground, which then peeled back to reveal the stage. This had to be ditched as soon as it became clear that such a structure, although extremely elegant, would require the removal of the entire audience from the area in front of the stage. The final version was conceived via a number of intricate models, but even these failed to reveal some of the problems of working with the real thing.

When the stage was fully erected we found that, because of all the multiple levels, niches and alcoves we had constructed, not all the musicians could see each other, requiring visual cueing by video screens or ESP to make contact. It was also something of a health and safety nightmare, with an extraordinary number of trapdoors. I had thought the previous tour's stage was hard to navigate, but this new stage was positively labyrinthine in a

U-boat sort of way, as it was all too easy to head off into some under-stage lighting cul-de-sac in error – or have a severe accident plunging down into some uncharted hole.

Having wrestled the stage into submission, we had to turn our attention to the instruments, trying to avoid turning our nice, flat surfaces into something resembling a junkyard. Many happy hours were spent in Drum Workshops, the factory of my drum technician Clive Brooks, devising the stands for a drum kit that would work with this staging. Gary Wallis and I ended up with thirty-odd drums, twenty pads, forty-odd cymbals and innumerable other bits of junk bolted to the drum risers, an installation that should have qualified us for the Turner Prize.

We had hoped to use in-ear monitoring to avoid the unsightly wedges that clutter stage fronts. Unfortunately that didn't work out, and we were obliged to return to monitors (this was probably one of the last tours to use big wedge monitors, as earpieces have now been perfected). However, I was able to use a tiny radio pack and earpieces which meant my foldback had a volume level no louder than a moderate Walkman, and a mix consisting primarily of bass, percussion and lead guitar, not one recommended for general release.

Meanwhile, Marc Brickman was dispatched to find the best and latest developments in effects and lighting. For example, the lasers on this tour were far more powerful than anything we had been able to use before and could process the light into alternative colours, rather than the usual green. One of Marc's expeditions was to the Hughes Corporation. As one of America's largest arms manufacturers the cessation of eyeball-to-eyeball stand-offs with the USSR had left them anxious to find new uses for all the military technology they now had sculling about idle. Swords into ploughshares sounds great in principle, but it was not quite as easy as it sounds. Unfortunately in spite of the wonderfully cheap deals available we were unable to think of anything to do with a Sidewinder missile – or not during the show anyway...

Our quest for technical innovation was also thwarted when we found we could not use one particularly and enormously powerful projector – a possibility we explored as an alternative to video – since once the projector's motor, like a turbine, was started it could not be stopped or the whole thing would explode. The prospect of transporting around the globe a projector permanently running at 400,000 revs per minute daunted even the most hardy professionals on the team. Certainly none of the band was prepared to travel on the same plane.

As we looked through the back catalogue and decided to return to some older material, we reinstated our acquaintance with Peter Wynne Willson. After his involvement with us in 1967 and 1968, Peter had been working variously with a hippie theatre group touring in a bus, organising lighting for other bands, working as a joiner, manufacturing furniture for Pan's People choreographer Flick Colby, producing prisms for the disco revolution, and developing a device called the PanCam which used a controlled mirror moving in front of a spotlight.

Peter met up with Marc Brickman, having in his words 'a huge amount of fun' working with some liquid slides and re-creating the Daleks. Technical advances actually made it more difficult to re-create the feel of the originals. The level of heat generated by 6KW of light meant that instead of the original pigmented colours, the colours had to be diachronic. And whereas in the Sixties he could use the heat of the projector to do some of the work, and hairdryers to both heat and cool slides, for the new versions a whole Aircon system had to be installed to influence the gate. However, the new Daleks, larger than ever, were much better in one way: courtesy of safety elements not even considered in the Sixties, they were thankfully less life-endangering than the versions that had once threatened to decapitate us like demented Samurai warriors.

All was proceeding well on the lighting front. Over in the blue corner, however, where the new film clips were in hand, piles of storyboards were arriving as Storm tried desperately to get some kind of reactions, let alone decisions, while time slipped away. One of our problems was committing to which pieces we were going to play in the show. There was little point in making a half-million dollars' worth of film if we then decided we didn't like the song anyway. Eventually we had five different pieces of film in production – if we hadn't been finishing the record and rehearsing at the same time we might have had fun experiencing this miniature Hollywood studio.

Music rehearsals for the tour took place at Black Island studios in West London, slightly held back due to the non-appearance of the lead guitarist and main vocalist, who was once more detained on the boat working on the final mixes. Tim Renwick again deputised as Musical Director. Fortunately, since we had all played the pieces on the record we were all familiar with the new music, which was also nothing like as complicated as the music on the previous record.

We then decamped to Palm Springs, but instead of being able to work on our tennis forehands, we headed off to actual production rehearsals – at the Norton Air Force Base near San Bernardino. These events were not without drama. At one point a visibly shaken rigger who had been working twenty feet overhead at the apex of the arch descended and suggested clearing the area. The whole structure was buckling, and the thought of a hundred tons of steel work collapsing, coupled with cancelling the shows for at least three months, gave hardbitten tour personnel pause for thought. Luckily it was a rectifiable design fault detail, but proved again that myriad computer calculations and projections do not equal the final assembly.

The amount of work being generated and undertaken was enormous. We had the films in production, staging and effects being built and equipment assembled; new pieces of stage and show require a great deal of work and modification to operate properly. As is the norm, we had to produce 30 per cent more devices than we ended up with, as we discarded those that didn't make the grade or proved too expensive or dangerous.

A classic example on this tour was one particularly troublesome five-ton mechanised crane, with a lighting rig attached, that travelled on an overhead track above us. When it eventually fell off its track (fortunately not hurting anyone) Mark Fisher, Robbie Williams who had been responsible for transporting the thing, and even the band who paid for it but were playing underneath it, were all thrilled to see it disappear forever.

FOR SALE

One five-ton crane. Complete with track and all light fittings. Wd suit construction company or elderly rock band. $100. Collect from Norton Air Force Base, San Bernardino...

As usual there was the slightly awkward day or two when the band arrived to mess up everything the crew had been doing for the past two weeks. At this point, the crew also had to go through the most soul-destroying part of all, which was learning how best to pack the trucks by stripping and re-erecting the stage. This is not as mindless or military an exercise as it sounds. There is an extremely strict order of pack according to what can be dismantled first and what needs to be put in first. And since, with restricted space backstage, there is an equally strict schedule for parking the trucks in the right order, a simple, economic factor comes into play: one truck saved over a nine-month period might pay for twelve crew parties, a new car, or simply a lawyer's bill for a couple of days, or hours.

We managed to overcome most of the various teething problems. As Storm's films had by necessity been prepared against the recorded songs, we discovered there were cueing problems with the live versions. However, by now we knew some tricks of the trade – that the film should be abstract enough in the middle to give us some leeway, and Jim Dodge, our projectionist from previous tours, had become a past master at being able to adjust his projector speed to make sure the beginning and particularly the endings were in sync.

The set was a mixture of old and new, including 'Astronomy Domine', which we had not played for at least twenty years, probably longer, and which brought back memories of Syd standing there in his big-sleeved outfit. 'High Hopes' was a new addition – complete with a giant division bell, sadly operated by a trigger device rather than a bemuscled gentleman from the Rank Organisation.

The show was shaping up. Our ability finally to learn from experience came through on this tour. Whereas the initial shows of the 1987 tour had been extremely exciting, but weak in communal performance, despite the individual competence of the musicians, now we had a good idea of how to present the show. All we had to do now was pay for it.

I still have mixed feelings about tour sponsorship. Touring a big show has become a hugely expensive operation and sponsorship can be a useful ingredient in that mix. But there is always a sneaking suspicion in the back of my mind (and I think David feels this more strongly than I do) that there is a danger that sponsorship can dilute the creative strengths. The argument that without sponsorship ticket prices would be higher is usually countered by the view that the band could take less money and achieve the same effect. There is no doubt that negotiations about the size and placing of advertisements and logos can become rather fraught.

That said, I was happy to have a real tour sponsor in the shape of Volkswagen. The first item on the agenda in our new relationship with the company was the Pink Floyd car. VW had some experience of working with bands: the year before they had sponsored a Genesis tour. They had learnt from a couple of mistakes. We were told that one version had come out in a colour symbolising gay pride, which the notoriously macho car sales industry had failed to appreciate.

When discussions had begun, there was an agreement that we did not want an association with some wild ultra-fast hatchback. Instead it was decided to produce a version of the Golf that could be considered the safest and most ecologically friendly (one might think an ecologically friendly car is a contradiction in terms, like a vegetarian crocodile, but there are degrees...).

We enlisted the help of a friend, Peter Stevens. Peter is a much-respected car designer and also taught part-time as a professor at the Royal College of Art. We had met on and off over the years, and Peter had produced the graphics for cars I had raced at Le Mans with Richard Lloyd Racing. He had also been working with Gordon Murray, one of the great racing car designers (with a lifelong enthusiasm for the electric guitar) on the McLaren F1 road car. Peter's experience with car design of all sorts meant that we could at least keep our suggestions within the realms of possibility rather than suggesting changes that would take seven years to put into production. The finest moment was when we visited the huge Volkswagen factory. VW were probably expecting the meeting to be a rubber-stamping exercise, but their high-powered engineers had a shock as they realised we had turned up in the company of Herr Professor Stevens, their former tutor, to evaluate their work.

Peter found the experience educational as well. He had noted that Steve O'Rourke had carried a heavy overcoat with him for the entire journey. It was only just prior to going into the meeting that Steve put it on. Peter found this curious and asked him why. Steve explained that this was his 'mean bastard' overcoat. The extra bulk that it gave him, coupled with the fact that he would spend the entire meeting standing rather than sitting, had proved a valuable negotiating tool. Although Peter never bought a coat, he did invest in a pair of 'mean bastard' boots, which are still used for the occasional confrontational meeting. He maintains they are extremely effective.

After years of doing things our own way we were unused to dealing with another organisation that operated under very different rules, and we had a number of disagreements. But the final product was a more than worthwhile exercise – the car even sold quite well in Europe – and is certainly dearer to my own heart than even the finest of fizzy drinks.

Some climatic traditions die hard, and after rehearsals in perfectly dry conditions, the rains came down from the first gig onwards. During one show – the wettest of the wet – the equipment gradually got worse and worse. The PA was sounding distinctly soggy, monitors were dropping out, and my drums were increasingly waterlogged. We lashed ourselves to the mainsail Hornblower-style and played as long as we reasonably could, but at some point we had to abandon ship. It was a reminder that, wonderful money-spinners though they are, stadium shows are much more difficult to control. We had fabulous effects –

especially the giant mirrorball – but it was all wasted effort if the stage was going to flood.

Because of the Britannia Row sessions, David, Rick and I felt much more like a band on the road. However, with our traditional reticence, we forgot to relay this to the rest of the band – pretty much the same one as worked on the 1987 tour – and so, from their point of view, they found themselves in a rather different situation. The positive spirit David, Rick and I were enjoying threatened to dilute the overall team feel, and certainly changed the dynamic. When, shortly after the tour started, we decided to take the first bow alone, this, to say the least, did not improve matters. The rest of the band re-created their own team spirit by establishing a mobile nightclub underneath the staging, below the structure built for the lighting and sound, which they dubbed the Donkey's Knob and which became the venue for many an informal after-show performance – and even an occasional gig during the mid-show interval.

After three shows in Florida and Texas, we headed south of the border for a one-off in Mexico City. This was the first time we had played in Latin America. The atmosphere was wilder, more exuberant, and the audience considerably younger compared to the US. This audience was not only seeing a Floyd show for the first time, they seemed to be discovering the music as well. At the end of the North American leg, and after a couple of nights in New York we flew over to Lisbon and straight on to the European dates, although we took a short time out in July for David to marry Polly in London.

At the beginning of September we were in Prague (again a new venue for us). The night before playing the Strahov Stadium to 120,000 people, we had dinner with Václav Havel, the playwright and former prisoner of conscience who was now the prime minister. This was not the 'slap-up feed' that the tabloids favour (why do they insist on this Billy Bunter-speak?), but an informal buffet at a riverside café. A number of us had done our homework by reading some of his books on the way to show some knowledge of his work – and wondered if Václav had been up all night with his CD collection. Some of his ministers appeared to have been rock critics in a previous life. I did wonder if in the new regime the secret police were now doing album reviews.

The actual touring finished in Lausanne on 25th September, or at least it felt like the end of the tour as Nettie and I headed off to the South of France to recuperate following the last of the stadium shows. However, we still had a series of nights to play indoors at Earls Court in October. In 1987 we had played Wembley Arena and the Docklands, so it was fourteen years since we had performed at one of our favourite venues, a place with plenty of character, right in the heart of London. However, the home venue meant an unconscionable number of people wanting to come as guests. My daughter Chloe was working for me at the time and had handled the intricacies of tickets and seating arrangements all year. London, however, was her hardest task of all.

The subtleties of inner-sanctum passes are a degree subject in their own right. Access All Areas means about halfway in, VIP one level further. A laminate trumps a stick-on and a green dot lets you through another gate. After that it helps if you are either part of the show, a family member, or have that demented look that ensures that there are always a few lunatics who make it to where they absolutely should not be. One startled tour manager found a stranger in his office who suggested he should have knocked first before barging in.

We had decided that the income from the London shows would be given to charity, and had come up with a complex formula to ensure that the smaller charities with which we had personal ties would benefit along with the larger ones we all supported. This meant a series of photocalls with each of the individual charities, who quite rightly wanted to obtain the maximum exposure from the event. Unfortunately in the event none of them got a look-in, as just before the show started a whole section of seating collapsed.

The house lights had been dimmed and amid the hum of anticipation, I heard what sounded like a roll of thunder. Maybe one of the tapes had miscued. Word quickly came that a section of seating had sheared away. There was no alternative but to bring the house lights up immediately and to get help to people trapped and first aid for those needing it. The show that night had to be cancelled. By the following day, only a few people were still hospitalised, which was a relief to everyone, apart from those few, of course.

By chance we had built an extra rest day into the series of performances there, and so we were able to schedule the date a few days later, so that most – if not sadly everybody – had the chance to see the cancelled gig. Despite the events of that first night, the shows felt a fitting end to the tour. All the previous work ensured the shows were as good as they could be, and a little glow of charity gave some additional feel-good factor. Douglas Adams joined us on stage at Earls Court for the 28th October show, an opportunity we had offered him partly as a birthday present, but also in thanks for having come up with the title for the *Division Bell* album. My one piece of advice to him was 'Whatever you do, Douglas, don't look down…', which in the excitement of the moment he clearly forgot, as he spent the whole song staring intently at his fretboard.

During the Earls Court shows, one unexpected but very welcome backstage visitor was Bob Klose. I hadn't seen him since the Tea Set days of the mid-Sixties, although by coincidence he had married an old schoolfriend of mine from Frensham. It reminded me that a couple of years later, at the Goodwood Festival of Speed, an even more unlikely arrival from the past had been our other Regent Street Poly cohort Clive Metcalf. Somebody with a marked lack of tact made the unkind comment to Clive that, having chosen to leave the band, he must feel like somebody who'd lost the winning lottery ticket. Clive calmly replied that when he and Keith Noble had decided to jettison the rest of us, they thought they were the ones making the right career move. As Clive observed, 'We thought you were losers, anyway…'

Although at the time the Earls Court concerts were simply the end of another tour, they in fact marked a significant cessation of activity. During the following ten years we did release a live album and a video, both called *Pulse*, from the tour, as well as various anthologies and re-masters of our work in new formats. But we did not tour again or release any new material.

David would, I think, freely admit that he was the one who was the least eager to return to the fray. He seemed to have little appetite for all the ramifications of cranking up the whole machinery of touring yet again. But I did hang on to the hope that this was not necessarily the end of Pink Floyd as an active force. There were various things we had never done. We never developed the idea David had for a twist on the unplugged concept. We never released the 'ambient' tapes from the *Division Bell* sessions. And – to date at least – I have never appeared in the 'Identity Parade' round on *Never Mind The Buzzcocks*. However, the prospect of Pink Floyd recording again, let alone the likelihood of any live performances, looked decidedly unpromising following so much relative inactivity. However, out of the blue – the azure blue of the Caribbean, as it happened – events took an unexpected course.

REMEMBERING
A DAY

13

In January 2002 I was taking a holiday with my family on the Caribbean island of Mustique. At the beginning of each year a beach picnic is held to raise funds for the local school. During the party I suddenly felt a forceful pair of hands grasp my shoulders, and then my neck. Opposite me I saw Nettie's eyes widen in surprise…

It was Roger. Seeing me there he had crept up and caught me unawares. We had only seen each other a couple of times during the previous fifteen or so years. I had often wondered what the atmosphere would be like if we happened to run into each other, and how I should approach such a meeting. What a waste of all that planning.

Roger and I started talking, carried on talking a fair amount of that afternoon, and met up a couple more times during the holiday. After all the water that had flowed under the bridges of the past, it felt terrific to make peace with one of my oldest friends. A large amount of emotional baggage got dumped at Mustique customs.

Later that year I got a call inviting me to play a guest spot with Roger at Wembley Arena during his 2002 tour. I didn't say 'yes' straight away – the idea felt slightly alarming – but it did not take long to work out that to miss this opportunity would be something I would regret ever after. I had spent long enough bemoaning the split between us, so it seemed particularly stupid not to jump at this chance to give a pretty public demonstration of a rather grown-up moment of reconciliation. I played on only one number – Roger's arrangement of 'Set The Controls For The Heart Of The Sun' – but the evening was fantastic. Roger's band was enormously welcoming, and a particularly nice touch was the chance to work with Harry Waters, who was on keyboards; apart from being Roger's son, Harry is also my godson.

Working with Roger again had been a joy. I loved the rehearsals. Despite many assurances that the intervening years had mellowed Roger, I was pleased to find any imperfections in the show were met with the familiar irascible shout from the stage to the mixing desk.

And that I genuinely thought was that. When *Inside Out* was first published in September 2004, the question about the possibility of Pink Floyd playing together again – with or without Roger – was an obligatory line of enquiry in every related interview. I faced these questions with a determinedly straight bat, but still tried to offer at least a glimpse of optimism, since, as far as I was aware, our innings had not yet been declared.

When *Mojo* produced a special edition devoted to the band that autumn, Roger and I were both interviewed. Roger was asked about the possibility of a thaw in relations with David, a suggestion that he politely but determinedly squashed: 'I can't think why. We're both quite truculent individuals and I don't think that's going to change.' Elsewhere David had compared the idea to 'sleeping with the ex-wife' – it didn't look hopeful.

In my piece, the final two questions were along traditional lines: 'Will there be another Pink Floyd album?' and 'What about a one-off Pink Floyd concert with Roger Waters for the thirtieth anniversary of *Wish You Were Here*?'

I said: 'I could imagine doing it. But I can't see Roger would want to. I think David would have to feel extremely motivated to want to get back to work. It would be fantastic if we could do it for something like another Live Aid; a significant event of that nature would justify it. That would be wonderful. But maybe I'm just being terribly sentimental. You know what us old drummers are like.'

Six months later someone pointed out a comment made by Bob Geldof in a TV interview in which he had said that he had seen a quote from me about a Pink Floyd reunion being – just maybe – feasible for a big charity event. Sadly, I can't take any credit for the final outcome, but clearly a seed had been planted in Bob's brain as he evolved the idea of putting together an event similar to Live Aid twenty years on from the original.

I was so unaware of his plans that when my wife, Nettie, told me Bob was on the phone one day in June 2005, I had no idea why he might be calling. We had occasionally met at social events, and the odd charity committee for the Roundhouse Trust since his appearance as Pink in the movie of *The Wall*, but we didn't speak on a regular basis.

The first stirrings of Bob's efforts to mount Live 8 had not yet permeated my consciousness. Bob now told me about the event and said that he had spoken to David about the possibility of Pink Floyd appearing, but that David had said no. Bob, as ever, merely saw this negative response as an inspiring challenge, and said he'd take the train down to David's house to discuss it further. Bob had already reached East Croydon when David rang him to say 'Don't bother', but Bob decided that he would push on anyway. However, even a direct and personal plea from a man so famously persuasive still failed to change David's mind.

What was clear to me was that David had perfectly good reasons for not wanting to regroup for Live 8. The band was not in a working state, and he'd spent the last few years working on his own solo projects. He knew that if we did play, everybody, including the record company, the press and our fans, would be clamouring for us to release some new product and announce a tour. From his point of view, the timing was exquisitely poor – and so, in the light of subsequent events, I think that his was the greatest sacrifice.

Bob asked if I could help broker a deal with David. I said no, simply because I thought that adding my voice to the swell would not sway him – in fact, it might have completely the opposite effect. As I later remarked, you can take a horse to water but you can't make it drink; in David's case you can't even get him near the water. However, bringing the Waters to David might just work...

I felt I had to do something, at any rate mention the idea to Roger. Nevertheless, I did not want Roger to think I was using our recently re-established friendship to start calling in favours, and I was very aware that he had spent twenty years building a successful solo career. Peter Gabriel once said that if he had rejoined Genesis after so long on his own there would be so much to lose: it would be like playing snakes and ladders and sliding all the way back down to bottom along a particular lengthy boa constrictor.

Caution was called for. I e-mailed Roger and made the most diffident of references to Bob wanting us to help him in his endeavours to save the planet. If Roger didn't reply, so be it. At least I had given it my best, if rather feeble, shot.

Roger e-mailed me straight back, asking what Bob wanted us to do. 'To be honest, I'm not sure,' I replied, reverting to the same mixture of duplicity and diplomacy that had marked our first conversation in the Regent Street Poly over forty years earlier. So Roger rang Bob. Despite the distraction of Bob's domestic life rumbling in the background, Roger managed to establish that Bob wanted us to perform together again. Then the Geldof household took precedence again, and Bob said he'd have to call Roger back.

Roger was immediately positive about the idea of playing together again for an event that was politically in tune with his own sentiments, especially as Bob's intention was not to raise funds, but to hoist a massive, global rallying cry and send a clear message about needless poverty to the leaders due to attend the G8 summit at Gleneagles a few days after Live 8.

By the time Bob rang Roger back, two and a half weeks had elapsed. Roger asked Bob the date of the Live 8 concert and was suddenly struck by the fact that it was less than a month away: there was no more time for reflection. He offered to make the ultimate gesture and place a call to David. 'Hello,' Roger said when he got through, 'I think we should do this.' David was still uncertain, worried that his voice and guitar parts would be too rusty, an idea Roger was quick to counter. David asked for some time to ponder the matter. Twenty-four hours later he had successfully pondered.

Thus it was that, one Friday in June, barely three weeks before the event, David called Bob, Roger and me to say 'Let's do it.' To all of us it was clear that since Live 8 was about increasing awareness, the coming back together of the four members of Pink Floyd for a single performance would bring more attention to the event, although Roger made it adamantly clear that, whatever else, he was not prepared to be a support act for the Spice Girls or an ABBA tribute band. Despite this, Bob was moved to describe Roger as a great diplomat – this really was breaking new ground.

However, there was still one more person who had to agree. Rick had not been party to these early negotiations, since they mainly concerned Roger and David, but it was imperative that he be part of any re-forming of the band. If we were going to do it, we were going to do it properly. Rick said yes unprompted, although there may have been a slight quiver of alarm in his voice at the prospect of voluntarily re-entering what had once, for him, been something of a gladiatorial arena.

By Sunday the news had officially broken after weeks of the rumour mill working harder than an Italian waiter's pepper grinder. David issued a statement in which he said, quite rightly, that 'any squabbles Roger and the band have had in the past are so petty in this context'. Roger, responding to suggestions that this was merely an excuse for some geriatric rock musicians to promote their back catalogue said, with glee, 'The cynics will scoff. Screw 'em!'

The headline writers had a field day. Hatchets were buried. Loggerheads were prised apart. And pigs that could fly were suddenly being scrambled in formation all across the broadsheets and a tabloid or two. Richard Curtis got in touch to suggest that if the band could agree on a set list, then surely the G8 summit could agree on a practical commitment to resolving Africa's problems.

For some reason our internal difficulties, really no different from those of many other bands, had been built up into a mythical representation of rock'n'roll's greatest feud. Having lived through it, I can honestly relate (and hope that *Inside Out* has reflected this) that it was not actually World War III, or, if it was, I'd have to say I think I had quite a good war.

I was amused by a spoof piece by Toby Moore in *The Times* that gave readers an 'exclusive peek' inside rehearsals, each of us sitting in the studio as a row of lawyers conferred over whether an F sharp could or could not be included. And I liked a line that he attributed to me, saying that rock'n'roll was all about 'rows, recriminations and lawyers'. One paper also reported that Syd's sister, Rosemary, had asked him what he thought about the reunion. She remarked that he had not reacted at all. 'He's no longer Syd,' she said. For many years, he had just reverted to being Roger Barrett.

Once the decision was in place, one of our first tasks was to settle on what to play. Initially Roger and David discussed this, with some input from Bob. I did suggest that the numbers we played should be the slower ones...

With ten days to go, the four of us convened at the Connaught Hotel in London to make the final choice. As time was pressing, we got quickly down to the business of discussing what had to be done.

We had brought along a selection of video tapes – some from Roger's shows, the rest from the last Pink Floyd tours – for use in the show. Unable to break the habit of a lifetime, we felt a little extra tweaking was required, which meant I was able to sit with Roger in an edit suite selecting sequences to accompany the set. It reminded me of how much I enjoy the way Roger likes to work. Under pressure, no time was wasted, but although Roger kept a sense of clarity about what he wanted, he was still able to take on board other ideas if it looked like they would work.

We had agreed to rehearse over a three-day period at Black Island Studios in West London, and it was only natural for our stalwart sidemen Tim Renwick and Jon Carin to join us – a neat link back to the original Live Aid, when Jon had been in Bryan Ferry's band with David.

Dick Parry brought along his sax, and Carol Kenyon provided the backing vocals on 'Comfortably Numb'. We had also managed to bring together a team of long-time collaborators and crew, including Phil Taylor (our longest-serving NCO), my drum tech Clive Brooks, Roger's guitar tech Colin Lyon, Andy Jackson at the live mixing desk, and James Guthrie looking after the broadcast sound. We were all a little older and may be a tad wiser, and we even managed to have some healthily creative differences of opinion about how pieces should be played, without hitting the self-destruct button. A frisson of tension did occur when Rick was talking about a particular bass line that Guy Pratt had once used on one of the previous tours (Guy married Rick's daughter, Gala, shortly after the *Division Bell* tour). Roger, hearing this, announced, 'Rick, what you and your son-in-law get up to in private is none of my business.'

On the eve of the Live 8 show we gathered at Hyde Park. In the area immediately in front of the main stage, scattered knots of event staff, security, band members and their families watched Madonna work out her white-clad ensemble. I was also pleased to notice my two boys, Guy and Cary, up on stage, looking as though they belonged there although clearly they did not, having obviously shown early promise in the art of bluffing their way past security. As dusk fell, and with individual sound checks complete, we began to play our set. The rehearsal ran fairly smoothly, although there was, I must confess, a certain level of instability in the drum department. However, like all good dress rehearsals, this left plenty of room for improvement on the night.

Come Saturday, 2nd July, we knew we were going to be on late – it was clear that it would be a physical impossibility for the show to run to schedule – so we had planned to head down to Hyde Park for five or six o'clock. On reflection, it seemed absurd to miss the opening of such a significant occasion, and I think we all turned up in time for the kick-off.

My daughter Chloe gave me a timely reality check. Arriving in the artists' car parking area, I climbed out of the car (Damon Hill was kindly acting as chauffeur – the precursor of a particularly thrilling Uber pick-up). I think I had let the headiness of the moment get to me and was being slightly 'Here I am. Hi...' I saw Chloe, and was about to embrace her, but she brusquely said, 'Not now, Dad, I'm really busy', and carried on doing a live feed for VH1.

I quietly packed my rock'n'roll ego away and headed out front to watch Paul McCartney and U2 perform 'Sgt Pepper' and, even as a fully paid-up, jaded and jaundiced veteran of the music business, was moved by the power and strength of what was happening both onstage and in the audience.

Backstage the shortage of dressing rooms meant that each one only became free an hour or so before the next artist was due on stage, a kind of timeshare system which excluded any diva-like excesses. We found the previous occupants of ours rather reluctant to depart but when they did they left in their wake a nostalgically telltale bouquet of dope.

We were able to do some media interviews and push the message of what Live 8 was about, all of which helped me feel that we had made the right decision to reconvene; in the absence of any jugglers or fire eaters, we provided the necessary 'novelty act' that might just make the audience wonder, 'What on earth made them do it?' and reflect on the real message of the cause.

Our slot moved ever backwards, as an overcast sky gave way to a shepherd's delight sunset. By the time we hit the stage at eleven o'clock, we had drawn on all our communal experience of waiting, adrenalin bubbling underneath while nervousness crept stealthily in. But once the tape of the heartbeat for 'Breathe' started in the pitch-black arena, I was already relaxing, easing into the familiar feeling of being part of a band.

It was fantastic to be playing with the others again – Rick layering in his unique textures, David as reliable as ever, pitch-perfect and lyrical, and Roger despite the advancing years extremely animated in a way I didn't remember, probably the side-effect of two decades as a frontman. The whole set felt tight and contained and we managed to keep a lid on any over-excitement despite the importance of the event, thankfully restraining ourselves from yelling 'Hello, London!' and enquiring if the audience were 'having a good time'. However, Roger's more measured words before 'Wish You Were Here', mentioning Syd, ensured that we did make some meaningful contact with the audience.

After our final bow, we headed backstage, where there was plenty of undisguised emotion on show, but I am delighted to report that, great troupers that we are, the four of us displayed that inscrutable and dry-eyed stoicism that is part of a fine Pink Floyd tradition...

And that, I think I thought, was that. We had come together for a worthy cause, probably the only reason we would ever get back together, and performed in front of an audience that stretched not only into the Hyde Park night – some 200,000 people – but way beyond to a TV audience of several hundred million. We were definitely raising awareness on a major scale – although within days the news agenda had rollercoasted on to the announcement of London winning the Olympics on the following Wednesday, and the appalling 7/7 terrorist attacks in the city the very next day.

After the show we headed off back to our usual lives. There were the inevitable swirling rumours that we had been offered ludicrous amounts of money to go on the road together one more time. David certainly made it clear that whatever the value of appearing at Live 8, any long-term plans for a chummy comeback tour were off his personal agenda. The rehearsals for Live 8, he said, had convinced him that was not 'something I wanted to be doing a lot of'.

I understood his reasoning. I think David had found it particularly hard work on the final couple of Pink Floyd tours. He carried the weight of them on his shoulders with only minor lifting from me, simply because he was out front, with all the lead vocal responsibilities. And whereas I look forward to the details of set design, staging and visuals, those aspects probably interest him less than they do me.

And yet, like so many other things, what looked like an ending proved to be another beginning. First, however, I was finishing off a round of promotional tours and book signings for the first edition, and the foreign language versions, of *Inside Out*. During the first signings as a naive whelp I gamely asked everyone who they wanted the book dedicated to, but quickly learnt that deciphering the spelling of an East European patronymic could take up most of an evening. I soon realised that being armed with a stack of Post-Its with names prepared in advance was a much more rapid solution.

Being back out on the road – even if a somewhat more solitary and sedate version and with no more expensive kit than a freshly bought pack of Pentels – I was back in the front line talking to fans who hadn't seen a real live Pink Floyd member to chat to for some time.

In the Paris studios of France Inter for a radio interview, Serge Le Vaillant, the presenter, had the bright idea of talking me through an A–Z of Pink Floyd: 'A pour Architecture, B pour "Brain Damage"' and so on ('G pour Gong' was a pleasant surprise). When he reached V, Serge was almost choking up when he chose 'V pour la Vie – votre

vie, Nick Mason – merci énormément – mais aussi ma vie, notre vie.'
I swear there were tears welling, if not in his eyes, then possibly in
mine.

There was some nostalgia in returning to those cities we had
performed in. En route to France Inter's studio we drove past the
Théâtre des Champs-Elysées, where we first played in January 1970,
which reminded me how enthusiastically the French had embraced
us at a time when the UK seemed less than completely convinced, and
how they had been stalwart supporters ever since.

In LA I stayed in Venice Beach, evoking memories of our show
there at the Cheetah Club in 1967. The T-shirts were much the same,
but were now on sale as 'retro' rather than cutting-edge fashion, and
the anti-war, anti-Republican sentiments were now being applied to
a different theatre of war and an alarming and theatrical president.

I gradually came to realise that many of the 'fans' wanting things
signed were in fact part of a cartel of organised eBay merchants. They
always came armed with an array of guitar scratchplates and albums.
You had to admire the blend of tenacity, patience and desperation
that meant they had to stand in the queue waiting like everyone else.

In Manhattan I rather grumpily congratulated one of these
scavengers on his persistence in tracking me down to the restaurant
where I was having dinner with Roger (who was there on tour).
While Roger remonstrated with him, I said I suspected him of merely
collecting autographs in order to re-sell them online. He gave a long
New York sigh: 'A guy's gotta make a living.' I couldn't refuse to sign
the proffered item in the light of such a candid response.

Back in the UK, an appearance on *Top Gear* beckoned. They were
particularly interested in having my recently acquired Ferrari Enzo
Ferrari on the show. Initial negotiations had ground to a halt, but
over dinner with Jeremy Clarkson one evening he mentioned it again.
I suggested that if he and his team could promote *Inside Out* on the
show, I would waive any charge for using the Enzo, confident that

stringent BBC regulations about overt on-screen advertising would preclude any possibility of me ever having to deliver on the promise.

A couple of days later Jeremy was on the phone. He had had a brainwave. To circumvent the BBC's diktats, he said he would write a script that would neatly side-step the issue.

So it was that as the Enzo drove into camera shot, I was in full Shopping Channel mode. Jeremy asked me how big a thrill it had been to get the Enzo. 'Probably as exciting', I cheerfully replied, 'as the moment I got my hand on the first copy of my book, *Inside Out...*' Later, in the studio, Ginger Spice – Geri Halliwell – was on the sofa. Asked by Jeremy what her current music project was, she was on the verge of mentioning her new release. Jeremy cut in. 'Just stop,' he said sternly, 'we don't do plugging on this show.' As the camera tracked back the entire audience standing behind Jeremy and Geri were sporting T-shirts with slogans stating 'Buy Nick's book', or 'Nick is a great author'.

I later learnt that clips of that particular show were compulsory viewing for trainee BBC producers – just to show them what never to let slide through, however successful (and potentially belligerent) the presenter.

Authorial duties fulfilled, I had a sense of the looming onset of 'legacy' when, a few months after Live 8, Pink Floyd was inducted into the UK Hall of Fame in a ceremony at Alexandra Palace. Pete Townshend did the honours, reporting that the only time he had ever missed a Who show, 'apart from car crashes or illness', was skipping a gig in Morecambe to take Eric Clapton to see us playing with Syd. He also said he had been delighted that we had played with Roger at Live 8. 'I never thought it would happen. Another wall came down.'

Rick was recovering from an eye operation, and Roger was in Rome for the première of his opera, Ça *Ira*, so David and I turned up to represent the band. Above us hovered a gigantic video screen with Roger's face being beamed in live. It felt like some Orwellian or North

Korean rally, with Roger as the Eternal Leader of the Republic of Pink Floyd. 'All those eulogies,' he said, 'were rather unnerving but I have to say very touching', before revealing that Rick actually hadn't had an eye operation. 'He and I have eloped, and are living happily in a small apartment on the Via Veneto…'

I told the audience the honour was something to make up for nearly forty years of having to listen to bad drummer jokes, although I had heard one that day which summed it all up: the small boy who says to his mother, 'When I grow up, I'm going to be a drummer.' His mother laughs, looks at him pityingly and says, 'You can't do both.'

Even if these events did not yet involve leaving imprints of our hands on the pavement outside Grauman's Chinese Theatre, it still felt as if our history was beginning to be cemented into some kind of structure that might oddly survive ourselves. It was also a sign that we had perhaps passed our 'best before' date, and that we were being viewed very much in retrospect rather than as a vibrant musical force.

David added his voice to proceedings when at the start of 2006 a story appeared in the Italian newspaper *La Repubblica* stating in Pythonesque terms that 'Pink Floyd the brand is dissolved, finished, definitely deceased.' In what was rapidly becoming a regular refrain, David told them, 'I think I've had enough. It's over, è *finita*.' That was almost like a red rag, or at least a fetching crimson cravat, to me, because my immediate reaction was to think, 'BUT you never know…' I just can't help myself.

The reason David was being so emphatic was possibly linked to the fact that he had a new solo album, *On An Island*, coming out. Among his collaborators, who included Rick, David Crosby and Graham Nash, was Bob Klose, who had provided such sterling guitar work back in our earliest Tea Set/Pink Floyd Sound days, a happy link back to those first outings as a performing outfit (in another neat coincidence, I had been at school with Bob's wife, Mary). I joined David on stage at the Royal Albert Hall during the accompanying tour, a couple of days after David Bowie had appeared for a guest slot.

A year later, in May 2007, I was performing with David again, and Rick, in sadder circumstances. Syd had died the previous July, and a tribute – 'The Madcap's Last Laugh' – had been organised by Joe Boyd at the Barbican.

None of us had gone to Syd's funeral. Whatever regrets I have about how the band had dealt with Syd, I think we tried to do the right thing by the family and by Syd and the privacy he had sought for the previous thirty-odd years. Even if we had considered attending, I don't think we were invited: it was very much a private family event.

At the Barbican, David, Rick and I performed 'Arnold Layne'. Roger (with whom I had been playing from time to time on his *Dark Side* tour) played a version of his own song 'Flickering Flame' with help from Jon Carin on keyboards. Backstage there was an intriguing conglomeration of artists, including Chrissie Hynde, Damon Albarn, Kevin Ayers and not least Captain Sensible, an exuberant reminder of my own skirmish with the dark forces of punk.

The following year, there was further bad news. Rick died in September 2008. We knew he was ill, but the news was no less shocking. He had seemed fine at Live 8 and on the few occasions I had seen him since: he was not often in the UK as he spent much of his time on his boat, *Evrika*. Rick was an intrepid and skilful yachtsman, as illustrated by the fact that he had sailed across the Atlantic.

I had met him in Ibiza by chance when we were on holiday there, staying with Roger Taylor, the Queen drummer, on his boat, *Tiger Lily*. Heading to shore on a small dinghy I noticed a beautiful yacht ahead: I was sure it was Rick's boat. It did not look as if anyone was on board as we hailed it, circling round. Unexpectedly a white-haired ancient mariner rose to his feet, and luckily, just before I yelled out, '¿Hola, donde está el capitán?' I realised, 'Oh *?@*, it's Rick.' In fact he didn't seem to have aged that much, or no more than any of us, but his hair was pure white. I suggested we could have dinner together that night, and he said, 'Dave's here as well, on Formentera', so we sailed over there for an impromptu reunion supper.

Following Rick's death what I felt most was the sense of imbalance caused by his loss. Rick perhaps never received the credit – both inside and outside the band – that he deserved for his talents, but the distinctive, floating textures and colours he brought into the mix were absolutely critical to what people recognise as the sound of Pink Floyd. Musically he knitted us all together. His approach to playing was genuinely unique: he once summed up his musical philosophy by saying, 'Technique is so secondary to ideas.' Many fine keyboard players could and did emulate and recreate his parts, but nobody else other than Rick had the ability to create them in the first place.

One of Rick's interventions had a significant, unexpected impact on *Dark Side Of The Moon*. Po – Aubrey 'Po' Powell, Storm Thorgerson's partner in Hipgnosis – remembers, 'We turned up at Abbey Road to generate some ideas. On this occasion, Rick stood out from everybody else because rather than just telling us to go away and think of something, which was the normal brief, he said, "Can't you do something different? I'm sick to death of bloody cows and surreal photos. Why can't we just have something graphic like a Black Magic chocolate box?"' This all rings true: I remember Rick had a tendency to become a touch petulant when confronted with Storm.

The Hipgnosis chaps headed back to consider how best to respond. Sitting in Storm's house searching for inspiration they came across a French book about physics from the 1940s. On one of the pages was a photograph of a clear glass paperweight by a window through which the sun was creating a prism of colour. 'Storm went, "I've got it", and for some reason or other drew that triangle, just like that. We went back to Abbey Road and everybody, bar none, said, "That's it, that's it." Serendipity, a magical moment.'

Rick's memorial service was held at the Notting Hill Theatre. It was a wonderful send-off to a friend who had been part of my life for more than four decades. Rick had said he wanted a party that was not too formal, and he absolutely got his wish. It was an event that induced a feeling of enjoyment, rather than sadness, both socially, with so many familiar faces there, and musically. David and I played Rick's 'Remember A Day' for the first time in nearly forty years, and Jeff Beck's performance, a beautiful, unaccompanied guitar solo, was so sensational I tried to book him for my own funeral.

With Rick gone, any prospect of Pink Floyd re-forming was well and truly over. It would be down to the tribute bands. I now realise that somewhere every night Pink Floyd music is being performed, just not by me. The tribute band drummers have certainly mastered all my mistakes far better than I ever could. Like the James Bond franchise, my dapper, witty Roger Moore could easily be replaced by a rugged Daniel Craig, and maybe nobody would actually notice.

I had direct experience of the Bond effect. Anthony Horowitz, the writer and a good friend, was working on the new Bond novel *Trigger Mortis* (even Ian Fleming is replaceable) and wanted to set much of the action on the Norschleife, part of the original Nürburgring, considered the most testing circuits in motor racing history (Jackie Stewart called it 'Green Hell'), no longer used for Grands Prix but still available for driving on. To help his research I supplied a racing driver – my daughter Holly's husband, Marino Franchitti – who drove Anthony round the track so he could make the sequences in the book as realistic as possible.

In July 2010 Roger agreed to appear with David at a charity event to raise money for Bella Freud's HOPING Foundation, which supports and improves the lives of Palestinian children. We had all been asked to play, individually, by Jemima Goldsmith – who was hosting the event at her home, Kiddington Hall in Oxfordshire – and had all said yes. But on reflection there was a realisation that once again we would face endless questions about whether this presaged a Pink Floyd reunion, which would have been out of proportion with the relatively intimate scale of the fundraiser, which had an audience of only a couple of hundred guests.

So Roger and David took to the stage and, despite the absence of their faithful drummer and peacemaker, they played a short set including 'Comfortably Numb', 'Wish You Were Here' and 'Another Brick'. They weren't quite yet at the stage of declaring a rapprochement, but it was the closest to date.

David had wanted to do a two-part harmony version of the Teddy Bears' classic 'To Know Him Is To Love Him' as part of the set, but Roger baulked at this, as although David could easily sing either part he thought it was outside his personal vocal comfort zone. David was still keen, and offered a deal. If Roger would perform the song, then David would come and perform 'Comfortably Numb' at one of Roger's *Wall* shows.

Roger accepted, and David duly appeared at Roger's O2 concert of *The Wall* in May 2011. I joined both of them on 'Outside The Wall' as we reprised the way we had finished the original show. I had a tambourine, David played a mandolin and Roger was on trumpet. At least we were on stage together again, even if our selection of instruments might have struggled with a reworking of 'Echoes'.

That year David and I completed the long process of re-mastering our back catalogue, in a multi-disc, multi-format extravaganza. The job of re-mastering everything had fallen to James Guthrie and he had manfully tackled this immense task while I magisterially watched from the wings and allowed myself to be interviewed by the *Huffington Post*.

It felt, I said, like the last chance for us to put out physical records. At the same time, advances in digital technology had enabled us to clean up old analogue material in a way we could not have done before, but the work had been Sisyphean. I knew that there must have been hundreds of rolls of tape, two-inch multi-tracks, let alone the rough mixes and outtakes stored on ¼" tape. As I commented at the time, 'It must've been a hell of a job to go through all of this.'

A particular favourite among the various elements was our Empire Pool, Wembley, concert from 1974, which could now be cleaned up sufficiently for us to justify release. But the jewel in the crown, for me, was the rediscovery in the EMI vaults of Stéphane Grappelli soloing on 'Wish You Were Here'. I had thought this session lost forever, and worried that I might have been the one who'd unwittingly wiped the master tape or recorded over it. That it was still extant was a real joy, and if we were ever to play 'Wish You Were Here' again, I would – in the absence of Stéphane himself – ask an equally talented violinist to step in and play on it: maybe Nigel Kennedy or Vanessa-Mae.

I also placed down my own marker by saying that I personally was still up for the concept of 'reviving the dinosaur and taking it on the road', although I doubted that David ever would be and Roger couldn't even entertain the possibility, as he was touring *The Wall*.

Not having any consistent music-making on the agenda, some of my time and energy was going into music politics. The landscape of the music industry had been altered almost beyond recognition. Piracy, downloads and streaming had directly affected the way product was released. Time was when we used to tour to promote a new album; now the album was a means to promote the tour. It was my strong belief that artists needed to come together make sure they had a voice at the table – especially bearing in mind Bernie Ecclestone's comment that 'If you don't have a seat at the table, you're probably on the menu.'

I joined the board of the Featured Artists Coalition, an organisation set up to protect and fight for the rights of artists, both established and emerging, especially in the digital era and at a time when record companies are less and less like risk-taking venture capitalists than conservative private equity companies, more interested in proven propositions. We have also looked at specific aspects of legislation that affect fans – secondary ticketing for instance, working to find solutions to counteract organised ticket touting.

The FAC tries hard to involve as broad a cross-section of the music industry as possible: Billy Bragg, Mark Kelly from Marillion, Sandie Shaw and Rumer have all been board members at various times, alongside Howard Jones, Annie Lennox, Radiohead's Ed O'Brien, Master Shortie and Kate Nash. It bridges something of a gap with the Musicians Union (I am still a member of the MU after fifty years) and also back to my father's own union activities.

One long-time link was severed when we were transferred from EMI to Universal and then Warner, although this was hardly traumatic as the decision was part of various commercial manoeuvres we were not directly involved in. There was a sense of being bought and sold on the block in a Roman slave market. We had already been through the experience of the venture capitalist Guy Hands acquiring EMI as a commodity, with apparently no knowledge of the music business. It *is* a business of course, but you would like to think there was a glimmer of interest in the word 'music' that precedes it. Suffice to say that, under his stewardship, EMI was (or so it is reputed) given the nickname 'Every Mistake Imaginable'.

I never met Guy Hands, but do remember reading that he had hired the former BBC director-general John Birt to help him run EMI. They had obviously been on an awayday for a corporate thinktank and decided that what they really needed to do was increase productivity, so John Birt was dispatched to call up all the artists on the roster and tell them just to… work harder. I thought if only we could get hold of the tapes of the former BBC boss ringing Roger and telling him to work harder, what a lovely thing that would be.

I had never spend much time consorting with record company people, the honourable exception being Caryn Tomlinson, who had survived unscathed working with a string of chairmen and CEOs at EMI. I once happened to sit next to one chairman, Colin Southgate, at some function or other. 'Do you know?' he remarked, 'I don't think I have ever sat next to one of my artists before.' There seems to have been a return in recent years to high-profile music moguls, some reminiscent of Tolkien's Dark Lord, others genuine music men. I remember David Crosby once remarking that the thing about record companies is that they were all sharks and crooks, but at least there used to be someone you could scream at, whereas once Business Affairs are in charge there is no one to talk to, let alone harangue.

While the machinations of the music business were churning away, David and I finally began lubricating our own creaking Pink Floyd machinery.

With a little digital assistance we were able to dust off some demo tapes from the *Division Bell* sessions – which had been laid down not on multi-tracks but onto a simple DAT – and totally isolate Rick's keyboard parts so that we had a platform to build on. Around his parts we constructed new layers of percussion, drums and vocals with the help of a trio of producers: Andy Jackson, Youth and Phil Manzanera.

David and Phil, the guitarist of Roxy Music, had worked together before: I did not know him that well, although Phil's wife, Claire Singers, had been our publicist. Similarly I had never met Youth, aka Martin Glover, the bassist with Killing Joke, who in his guise as producer for The Orb had worked with David on the album *Metallic Spheres*.

Youth, Phil and Andy all brought something invaluable to proceedings: enthusiasm. Left to our own devices I suspect the project might never have seen the light of day. Even though Rick's death had galvanised both David and me, it was enormously helpful to have someone from outside saying, 'Nick, you should redo these drums' or 'David, you could play a fresh piece of guitar over that.' Each of them was able to come fresh to the mix, with suggestions about what to put in or take out and how to reorder what was already there.

I particularly enjoyed working with the demo tapes because it not only reminded me of the *Division Bell* days on the *Astoria*, but way back of how we used to put everything together in the studio. From the depths of the percussion storeroom we dusted off the gong, the chimes and the roto-toms, none of which had seen the light of day since I'd taken them out on the road with Roger during his *Dark Side* tour in 2006.

Afterwards it was the visuals rather than the music that caught my attention. Away from performing and recording it is unusual for me to deliberately listen to one of our tracks. But the footage from the small static cameras that had been running in the studio while we were playing brought back a host of memories.

During the reworking of the new tracks, I took a short sabbatical to perform at the closing ceremony of the London Olympics. As ever there had been much speculation about who was going to appear, both at the closing and the opening show.

Patrick Woodroffe, the lighting designer, recalls that 'Pink Floyd were always in the picture and on the list of classic English bands that should be represented and everyone wanted. But Kim Gavin' – the choreographer who was creative director for the ceremony – 'also thought there should be a modern take and so approached Ed Sheeran.' There was a brief flicker of a rumour that David, Roger and I would all perform, but in the event I was the only band member to appear.

What made the idea even more appealing was the prospect of sharing a stage not just with Ed, but also with Mike Rutherford and Richard Jones, both good friends as well as excellent musicians. And since it was only the one song ('Wish You Were Here') it required minimal homework.

I have to say I really enjoyed the Olympics. Like many people I had doubts about how well it would work, but it was a genuinely fantastic experience. As a Londoner, who had enjoyed being able to participate as a spectator or participant in some of the city's major public events like the Festival of Britain – or Live 8, come to that – it was uplifting and engaging. There were thousands of helpers, all fulfilling useful roles even if there were far too many of them: looking for the catering facility at least half a dozen Games Makers offered to show me the way.

Apart from the performance itself, which was over in a Usain Bolt-like flash, I remember two things in particular. Since there were a host of acts doing one or two numbers each, the drum changes were very quick (and extremely well handled), but I experienced a little nervousness in case I turned up on stage and found no kit. I was busy practising my Marcel Marceau mime moves backstage just in case.

Because the Games organisers had clearly signed stringent deals with anyone who was a sponsor, no other manufacturer's name was allowed to be seen on any piece of equipment. So one of the drum techs had to spend hours with various abrasives eradicating any trace of the word 'Paiste' from each of my cymbals, a company I had used for forty years.

There was as ever a lot of waiting around. All these events and festivals are hugely social because even if you are playing at eight o'clock at night, you have to turn up at ten in the morning, and consequently I spent many hours nattering with the likes of George Michael and Pete Townshend about the good-ish old days in a scene reminiscent of *The Best Exotic Rock'n'Roll Hotel*.

The residents of that particular hotel were, sadly, continuing to dwindle. In April 2013 Storm Thorgerson died, another huge loss. Storm was one of those designers who was able to imagine and create incredibly powerful, truly iconic images – if you ever see a prism you automatically think *Dark Side* – but also loved words, which is not usually a designer's forte (or even their piano). Storm loved puns and plays on words. He once intoned to me that 'There are nine letters in Nick Mason, nine letters in Pink Floyd, and nine letters in *Inside Out.*' The deeper meaning of this eludes me to this day.

Po says of Storm, 'What a madman. Pictorial genius. A lateral thinkist. A man who was difficult beyond. We were chalk and cheese. We would fight a lot: Hasselblads would fly across the studio. But we got on like a house on fire. I loved him, he was like a brother to me.'

He recalls Peter Gabriel describing the experience of working with Storm, 'fondly remembering the trepidation of walking up the studio stairs, knowing that you were going to be humiliated, put down, that your music would be torn to shreds and your lyrics laughed at, and an argument would ensue. After all that, you might get a decent album cover. But first, before that, Storm would try and fob you off with some designs he had tried to sell to somebody else.'

On one occasion, Po and Storm were presenting cover ideas to Led Zeppelin. 'We'd done several covers for them and got on well. We went over to Swan Song's offices, where the band and Peter Grant, their manager, were sitting waiting for us. I had half a dozen roughs, and on the way noticed Storm slip another one in. In the meeting I started propping the roughs up against the wall. There was the idea Storm had added: a close-up photograph of a tennis racket on a grass court. Jimmy Page said, "What's this?" to which Storm replied, "What's it look like?" "Well, it's a racket." "You got it, Jim-Bob." Jimmy said, "Are you inferring that we make a racket?" Storm looked him in the eye, "Absolutely right." We were quickly shown the door.' Po spent much of his time unruffling the feathers Storm had gleefully ruffled.

By July 2014 our new album – to be called *The Endless River* – was ready for release. The news broke unexpectedly, with social media playing a role that it could not have done, by virtue of not existing, on any of our previous albums.

Word reached our camp that a Sunday newspaper was about to run an exclusive on the release of the new album. To pre-empt that

Polly Samson took the initiative. Polly, David's wife, who had written the majority of the lyrics on both *The Division Bell* and the new album, was a former publisher and journalist and a successful author in her own right. She applied her writing talents to the 140 characters of Twitter and issued a swift, deft spoiler: 'Btw Pink Floyd album out in October is called "The Endless River". Based on 1994 sessions is Rick Wright's swansong and very beautiful.'

Durga McBroom, who had added extra vocals to the album, took this as a green light to go public with the news and created a Facebook post, featuring a photo of her in the studio with David and the message, 'YES. THERE IS A NEW PINK FLOYD ALBUM COMING OUT. AND I'M ON IT. And there was much rejoicing.' An official Pink Floyd press release followed closely on the heels of her post...

A third social media connection was directly responsible for the cover artwork, again in a way that could not have occurred before. Since Storm was no longer with us, we had asked Aubrey Powell to oversee the design. As he and Storm had not worked together for many years, Po found the prospect somewhat daunting, so he asked a range of people to submit ideas. Damien Hirst was among them, but although he came up with dozens of ideas, the problem from our point of view was that they looked like wonderful Damien Hirst artworks rather than Pink Floyd album covers.

Po had also approached an advertising agency to present some ideas. One of the images they had sourced came via behance.net, a website showcasing the portfolios of illustrators and designers. It featured a man standing on the prow of a boat, maybe an Arab dhow, floating through clouds towards the rising, or possibly setting, sun. Po, David and I all liked it – and it turned out the illustrator was a seventeen-year-old Egyptian student, Ahmed Emad Eldin, who lived with his family in the town of Rafha in the north of Saudi Arabia, close to the border with Iraq.

Via the website, Po e-mailed him, the first that Ahmed knew we were interested in his artwork. He remembers the moment precisely. 'I was in my room. It was two in the afternoon, on 31st July 2014. I was shocked: Pink Floyd contacting me about my work? I was speechless. I tried to go and tell my family what had just happened but I couldn't talk for ten minutes.'

What Po had no way of knowing – and was bowled over to discover – was that Ahmed was a fan. He had heard 'Hey You' from *The Wall* on the soundtrack of an American comedy film called *Due Date*. 'I was really curious to find out who this band was. I asked some friends and they told me it was Pink Floyd. From that moment I became a big fan of the band. A really strange thing was that I was actually listening to "Hey You" when the e-mail arrived in my inbox.'

Po agreed with Ahmed that we could use his image – which he had created when he was sixteen and was called *Beyond The Sky* – with a few tweaks, giving the boatman an oar so he could punt the boat – now a Thames skiff – through the sea of clouds. Three months later it was being unveiled as an eight-metre-high banner on the South Bank in London.

The album performed well. I never like to trumpet (or even tambourine) our successes, but it was pleasing to learn that it was the most pre-ordered album ever on Amazon at that point, and the fastest-selling vinyl release in 2014, and apparently for all of the previous seventeen years. Hearing that reminded me of another fact I had once been told, that every second house in Britain owns a copy of *Dark Side*: my theory is that actually the figure is only one in seven but quite a lot of those households contain people with very poor memories who keep re-buying the album.

We held the launch party for *The Endless River* at the Porchester Hall, with Peter Wynne Wilson reprising his 1960s role by laying on a magnificently retro lightshow, complete with slides and bubbles. The legacy aspects of being a band rapidly approaching their fiftieth anniversary were starting to stack up. In May 2015 Roger and I went along to the former Regent Street Poly, the University of Westminster as is, to unveil a plaque noting that he, Rick and I had met there.

David and I were already working on a new release, *The Early Years, 1965–1972*, which included over twenty-four hours of audio and video ('This is just the trailer,' I told one Canadian journalist. 'I'm actually living in the full-length version.') Just as *The Endless River* had been an opportunity to recognise Rick's contribution to the band, this set of mainly unreleased material allowed us all to revisit Syd's time with us.

People are always asking me completely impossible questions like, 'What would have happened if Syd had stayed?' And if you read all the histories of the band (there is a particularly good one by the drummer), you'll find a general, facile acceptance of the idea that Syd was an ill-starred genius who tripped up, quite literally, and became another sad acid casualty. But I feel more and more that perhaps we should recognise that we were the people dragging him down a path he did not want to follow, and that he actually wanted to be an artist. He had done the pop star bit for a while, and he did not particularly care for it. Even by our second *Top Of The Pops* appearance, he was already showing signs of losing interest. As Ronnie Laing had told Roger at the time, maybe Syd was not mad at all, maybe we were.

There is a truth there. Syd may have been thinking, 'All of this isn't that great', whereas we couldn't believe that anybody wouldn't, couldn't, think that it was that great.

Having listened to, and watched, all the material again, what struck me was the improvising. Our musical technique was very basic but it is still quite impressive to realise what we managed to achieve from our rather simple repertoire of skills.

Since the music straddles the time of Syd's departure I found it intriguing to see the transition from Syd's writing to Roger's writing, as well as listening to all the singles to try and understand why most of them did not trouble the Top Ten. It is as if the audience knew better than we did what we were good at, or what they liked about our music. Around the time of the *Early Years* release, I watched a documentary about the Hollies, in which they said they had released a track called 'King Midas In Reverse', which failed utterly, because it was far too sophisticated compared to what their audience thought they should be doing.

The visual material we turned up was again more interesting to me than the music. A lot of video was held by the BBC, Pathé or individual TV stations in America who still had access to video tapes of live broadcasts from the 1960s and '70s. The clips we ploughed through included our appearance on *The Dick Clark Show* with Syd vaguing out, just the way I had always remembered it, although it was disconcerting to see oneself at twenty-two scampering about in a shiny shirt and tight trousers, and shouting at the camera: for some reason we always shouted at the camera even when there was no sound. Perhaps we believed that if we were loud enough it would imprint itself on the celluloid.

Alongside all this accretion of rare material, we were beginning work with the V&A Museum for an exhibition that would follow on from their David Bowie exhibition. This really was, whether I wanted to admit it or not, full-blown legacy stuff. We had to accept that we had become of interest to not just one generation but a whole bunch of future generations. This was a very strange feeling, considering that in 1967 we all knew this rock'n'roll phenomenon was ephemeral and that we'd be back making a living in an architect's office within a couple of years, if that. Even Ringo had plans to open a chain of hairdressing salons after the Beatles.

The V&A had approached us. One of their curators knew Po and discussions were in the early stages when I nearly scuppered the whole idea. I heard, just a few days before the museum were having a critical meeting to decide whether to put the exhibition on or not, that Martin Roth, the museum's director, thought I was against the idea.

I had met Martin at a Goodwood event, and I think there had been a misunderstanding. When he mentioned the prospect of an exhibition I had been slightly bowled over by the suggestion that we might be next, after the success of their David Bowie exhibition, and I'd said something along the lines of 'The trouble is, we can't possibly…' thinking that we did not have the size of archive that David Bowie had, or the costumes, and that nothing we had was that neatly organised and pre-curated.

I had clearly sounded rather too hesitant and negative, and Martin had obviously read my reaction as 'Oh, I don't think so.' I'm not sure this perception would have stopped the exhibition from happening but certainly might have wrongfooted it. Fortunately, having heard about this I wrote to Martin and told him we would love to do it.

This was not the first Pink Floyd exhibition. In 2003 we had mounted one, called *Pink Floyd: Interstellar*, in the Cité de la Musique in north-east Paris, part of the Parc de La Villette complex out near the *périphérique*. The staging of the exhibition was overseen by Storm and had brought together some of the inflatables (pigs, pyramids and the Father from the *Animals* tour), Rick's Farfisa, a couple of my drum kits, including my Hokusai Ludwig kit, the Azimuth Co-ordinator and various other bits and pieces.

We later had the possibility of putting on a second version at Milan's Fabbrica del Vapore, a former tram factory, this time using the best of Storm's imagination when he had been in full Italian, especially Venetian, flood. One idea had been that the smaller items would be in a palazzo and a shuttle vaporetto would take you down to see the larger exhibits. Sadly it was not to be. The promoter behind the project failed to get the necessary funding and sponsorship – these things, even without Storm's involvement, are never cheap operations. In turn the collapse of that project nearly jeopardised the

V&A's exhibition because everyone who had been involved in the Italian project were still smarting from a lack of renumeration for their efforts.

So initially there was a distinct lack of interest from the Floyd camp, and the V&A exhibition got off to a decidedly shaky start. However, with the enthusiasm of Martin and the V&A team the project moved inexorably forward, and was entitled *Our Mortal Remains* – a gloomy title (a reference to a line from 'Nobody Home)' but definitely one with a suitably Floydian ring.

I was amused to discover that Johnny Rotten's 'I Hate Pink Floyd' T-shirt would feature in the exhibition, although John Lydon insisted that he not be shown in any photograph consorting with his former Sex Pistols band members. Maybe this exhibition would, asteroid-like, finally kill off this particular herd of rock dinosaurs, so we would be preserved in amber but with no latter-day Dickie Attenborough to extract our DNA.

David, following the release of *The Endless River*, had continued with his regular refrain of declaring that it was definitively, indubitably, irrefutably Pink Floyd's last album: 'This is the end.'

And in the corner a fresh-faced young drummer piped up with a quiet but insistent 'BUT you never know…'

AFTERTHOUGHTS

Before our Live 8 reunion, Roger had already made his own distinctive contribution to this book. Towards the end of its gestation, after he had finished reading the manuscript, we met up in a London hotel to talk through his comments. He had gone to a lot of trouble to make corrections, and to question some of my interpretations and emphases. These observations had been made in green ink, and as he flipped through the pages I was occasionally alarmed to see sections where the use of green ink was remarkably liberal. On one page Roger had simply scrawled 'Bollocks' across the whole text. However, after our session on the book, we were still feeling sociable enough to go out for a convivial dinner with my wife Nettie and Roger's girlfriend Laurie, where who should we run into but Gerry Scarfe, who crept up behind Roger and placed his hands… Oh no, not again.

David obviously frequented the same stationer's as Roger, as his comments were also made with a green highlighter, and he had taken equal care over the exercise. In David's case I particularly appreciated his comments as I knew he had always had reservations about any one of us attempting to write a history of the band, since none of us can have been present at every decisive or creative moment in a history, and so it can never be definitive. I have done my best to capture the mood of each period, and although I have tried to be even-handed I know that most moments are inevitably coloured by my own feelings of joy, sadness or fatigue.

Rick also added his comments, faxed from a yacht in the Caribbean. I was particularly intrigued to find that after all these years he was finally able to reveal the real reason he had refused to give Roger his cigarettes when we were at the Poly. First of all, Rick said, Roger had been somewhat aggressive in asking for them – little surprise there. But worse, having secured possession of the cigarettes, Roger had taken the packet and ripped off the cellophane protecting it, which Rick was zealous in keeping intact.

During the life of this book we have lost a number of people who were helping and supporting the project or played a key role in the story, including Syd, Rick and Storm of course. While the writing and research was underway, June Child, Tony Howard and Michael Kamen died (as did Nick Griffiths shortly after the first edition was published). In 2008 both Bryan Morrison and Mick Kluczynski died. Bryan was the archetypal music business rogue we loved to hate; even Roger had a tendency to allow a wry smile to appear at the mention of his name. And I have to credit Bryan with being enormously helpful with this book, generously supplying stories he was intending to retain for his own memoirs (as yet unpublished). Mick was a stalwart of the road crew from the early 1970s onwards – a time when the crew was small enough for us all to get to know each other well – who could provide a steadying influence whenever mayhem threatened to intervene. Norman Smith, Mike Leonard and Mark Fisher are also no longer with us.

One of the most upsetting losses for me was that of Steve O'Rourke, after a stroke in October 2003. Given that a fair amount of this book is taken up with Steve being given a rather hard time by the band I have included a few lines from a letter that I wrote after Steve's funeral.

'It's that shared experience element I miss. We can tell other people the stories, but to re-live it with someone who was present tends to be a more intense version of the comedy, humiliation or raw fear shared. I was devastated to realise just how much of my life was shared with Steve, and how irreplaceable he is.

'Not a bad description might be to suggest that I feel like I've lost a shipmate. On the good ship "Floyd" Steve and I worked together for over thirty years – mainly before the mast. We served under harsh captains. Mad Cap'n Barrett was the first; his gleaming eyes with tales of treasure and strange visions nearly led us to disaster, until mutiny put us under the domination of the cruel (Not So Jolly) Roger… Later Roger was to carelessly walk his own plank to be replaced by Able Seaman Gilmour.

'Throughout these adventures, despite endless promises of promotion (some, I regret to say, from Steve) I remained Ship's Cook. Steve, I think, was Bos'un. He was never allowed to wear the captain's uniform, but was frequently required to sail the ship through stormy seas whilst all the crew squabbled below decks about how to divide the treasure.'

Given that there never is enough credit to go around with the vast cast of egomaniacs that accumulate with a band it is unlikely that Steve's contribution would ever be properly recognised. To be fair he was wise enough to know this, and smiled at the occasional 'Thanks to' or even 'Special thanks to' that would grudgingly creep onto the odd record sleeve or programme. Inevitably there are significant contributions from Steve in this book, but I do regret the fact I wasn't able to go through it all with him while he said, 'No, no, no, Nick, it wasn't like that at all.'

Rereading this, I felt that the list of those who are no longer with us might be too morbid an ending, and if I sit back and muse on what this book represents, I am reminded of all the good times, rather than the bad or the sad ones. So I was delighted when at one of the Goodwood Revival meetings, I was reunited with an 89-year-old Joe Mayo, the year tutor at Regent Street Poly who granted me the sabbatical year I needed just as the band was taking off. Even better, Joe told me in his opinion I might have made a perfectly good architect, something I had never dared to ask, so there's still time for a career change.

And if you are wondering why this piece is at the end of the book instead of appearing as the usual foreword, preface or introduction, well, it is called *Inside Out*...

THANKS

First, thanks to David Gilmour, Roger Waters and Richard Wright. Then, for accessing their memories for me and giving encouragement: Douglas Adams, Chris Adamson, Peter Barnes, Joe Boyd, Marc Brickman, Lindsay Corner, Jon Corpe, Nigel Eastaway, Ahmed Emad Eldin, Bob Ezrin, Jenny Fabian, Mark Fenwick, Mark Fisher, Peter Gabriel, Ron Geesin, A.A. Gill, Nick Griffiths, James Guthrie, Tony Howard, Andy Jackson, Peter Jenner, Howard Jones, Andrew King, Bob Klose, Mick Kluczynski, Norman Lawrence, Mike Leonard, Lindy Mason, Lise Mayer, Clive Metcalf, Dave Mills, Bryan Morrison, Steve O'Rourke, Alan Parker, Alan Parsons, Aubrey Powell, Guy Pratt, Gerald Scarfe, Nick Sedgwick, Norman Smith, Tony Smith, Phil Taylor, Chris Thomas, Vernon Thompson, Storm Thorgerson, Judy Trim, Snowy White, Robbie Williams, Peter Wynne Willson, Patrick Woodroffe and Juliette Wright.

For helping the book to become a reality, thanks, first and foremost, to Philip Dodd, editor, amanuensis and compulsive coffee maker, who has seen this through since the really early days, and sometimes been required to get out and push when it seemed all was lost. Also Michael Dover at Weidenfeld & Nicolson whose enthusiasm for the book ensured it got finished, and all the publishing team, including Jennie Condell, Kirsty Dunseath, Holly Harley, Justin Hunt, Jenny Page, David Rowley, Mark Rusher, Alan Samson and Mark Stay; picture researcher Emily Hedges; and David Eldridge and Two Associates.

For their help along the way: the archivists and keepers of

the artefacts Stephanie Roberts and Tracey Kraft; researchers Silvia Balducci, Jan Hogevold, Jane Jackson, Lidia Rosolia, Jane Sen and Madelaine Smith; the Ten Tenths team of Victoria Gilbert, Julia Grinter, Stella Jackson, Michelle Stranis-Oppler and Paula Webb; Jonathan Green for allowing me to use his own research; and for other assistance and favours Elina Arapoglu, Jane Caporal, Christine Carswell, Sadia Choudhry, Paul Du Noyer, Vernon Fitch, Matt Johns, Suzenna Kredenser, Chris Leith, Irini Mando, Steve Mockus, Ray Mudie, Olympus Cameras, Tom O'Rourke, Shuki Sen, Rob Shreeve, Di Skinner, Paul Trynka, Sarah Wallace and Alan Williams.

Throughout the book I have been very sparing with name checks. Given that literally hundreds of people have worked with and for us over the years (we had a crew of more than 200 on the last tour) it became impossible to credit or mention everyone. Profuse apologies to all unnamed heroes or heroines. You are not forgotten.

This book is for Annette,
co-pilot, co-driver and when required perfect rock wife,
and also for the children, primarily Chloe, Holly, Guy and
Cary, but also for all the long-suffering offspring of the band,
management and crew.

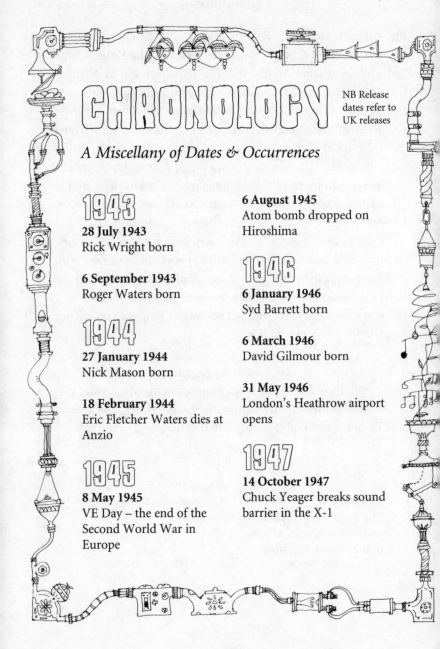

CHRONOLOGY

A Miscellany of Dates & Occurrences

1943

28 July 1943
Rick Wright born

6 September 1943
Roger Waters born

1944

27 January 1944
Nick Mason born

18 February 1944
Eric Fletcher Waters dies at Anzio

1945

8 May 1945
VE Day – the end of the Second World War in Europe

6 August 1945
Atom bomb dropped on Hiroshima

1946

6 January 1946
Syd Barrett born

6 March 1946
David Gilmour born

31 May 1946
London's Heathrow airport opens

1947

14 October 1947
Chuck Yeager breaks sound barrier in the X-1

1948

1948
First 33 $^1/_3$ long-playing
records released by
Columbia Record Co.

30 January 1948
Mahatma Gandhi
assassinated

1949

2 March 1949
First non-stop around-the-
world flight by Capt. James
Gallagher in a Boeing
B-50A

1950

1 October 1950
First credit card issued,
by Diners Club

1951

May 1951
The Royal Festival Hall,
London, is opened as part
of the Festival of Britain

July 1951
J.D. Salinger's *Catcher In
The Rye* published

1952

15 June 1952
Publication of *The Diary
Of A Young Girl*, by Anne
Frank

1953

5 February 1953
Sweets rationing ends in
the UK

April 1953
Brigitte Bardot makes a
stunning impact at the
Cannes Film Festival

29 May 1953
Edmund Hillary and Sherpa
Tenzing conquer Everest

2 June 1953
Coronation of Queen
Elizabeth II

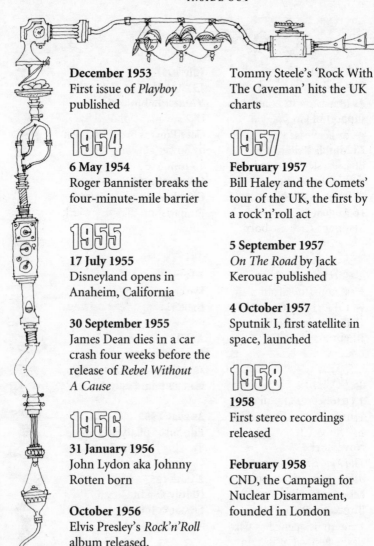

December 1953
First issue of *Playboy* published

1954

6 May 1954
Roger Bannister breaks the four-minute-mile barrier

1955

17 July 1955
Disneyland opens in Anaheim, California

30 September 1955
James Dean dies in a car crash four weeks before the release of *Rebel Without A Cause*

1956

31 January 1956
John Lydon aka Johnny Rotten born

October 1956
Elvis Presley's *Rock'n'Roll* album released.

Tommy Steele's 'Rock With The Caveman' hits the UK charts

1957

February 1957
Bill Haley and the Comets' tour of the UK, the first by a rock'n'roll act

5 September 1957
On The Road by Jack Kerouac published

4 October 1957
Sputnik I, first satellite in space, launched

1958

1958
First stereo recordings released

February 1958
CND, the Campaign for Nuclear Disarmament, founded in London

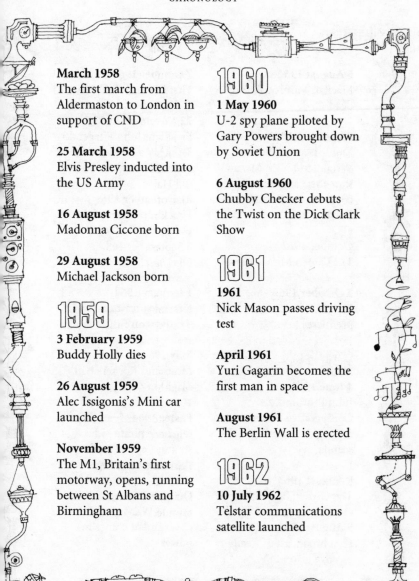

March 1958
The first march from
Aldermaston to London in
support of CND

25 March 1958
Elvis Presley inducted into
the US Army

16 August 1958
Madonna Ciccone born

29 August 1958
Michael Jackson born

1959

3 February 1959
Buddy Holly dies

26 August 1959
Alec Issigonis's Mini car
launched

November 1959
The M1, Britain's first
motorway, opens, running
between St Albans and
Birmingham

1960

1 May 1960
U-2 spy plane piloted by
Gary Powers brought down
by Soviet Union

6 August 1960
Chubby Checker debuts
the Twist on the Dick Clark
Show

1961

1961
Nick Mason passes driving
test

April 1961
Yuri Gagarin becomes the
first man in space

August 1961
The Berlin Wall is erected

1962

10 July 1962
Telstar communications
satellite launched

5 August 1962
Marilyn Monroe found dead

September 1962
Roger Waters, Richard Wright and Nick Mason start their architecture course at the Regent Street Polytechnic

October 1962
The Cuban Missile Crisis

5 October 1962
First Bond movie, *Dr. No*, premieres

1963

4 June 1963
John Profumo, Conservative minister, resigns over a call-girl scandal

8 August 1963
The Great Train Robbery

9 August 1963
First broadcast of *Ready Steady Go!* on ITV

7 October 1963
First flight of the Learjet 23

22 November 1963
President John Fitzgerald Kennedy assassinated in Dallas, Texas

21 December 1963
First appearance of the Daleks on *Doctor Who*

1964

1 January 1964
First broadcast of *Top Of The Pops* on BBC TV

May 1964
Mods and Rockers battle in Brighton

Easter 1964
Offshore pirate radio station Radio Caroline starts broadcasting

October 1964
Harold Wilson's Labour government comes to power

1965

March 1965
First US combat troops sent to Vietnam

29 July 1965
The Beatles film *Help!* released

August 1965
First outdoor Notting Hill Carnival in London

15 August 1965
The Beatles perform at Shea Stadium to a then-record audience of over 55,000 fans

October 1965
Tea Set play at Libby and Rosie January's birthday party

25 October 1965
The Beatles receive their MBEs from the Queen

1 November 1965
First concert at the Fillmore Auditorium, San Francisco

1966

17 January 1966
Simon and Garfunkel release *Sounds Of Silence*

March 1966
Pink Floyd play at the Marquee Club's Spontaneous Underground event

29 June 1966
First British credit card, the Barclaycard, is issued

30 July 1966
England win the football World Cup

8 September 1966
First telecast of *Star Trek*

30 September 1966
First Pink Floyd gig at All Saints Church Hall, Powis Gardens, London

15 October 1966
IT launch party at the Roundhouse

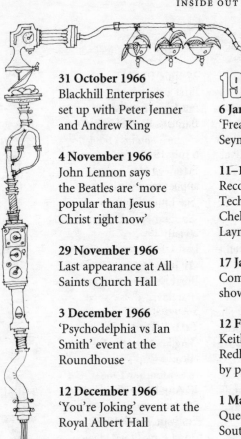

31 October 1966
Blackhill Enterprises
set up with Peter Jenner
and Andrew King

4 November 1966
John Lennon says
the Beatles are 'more
popular than Jesus
Christ right now'

29 November 1966
Last appearance at All
Saints Church Hall

3 December 1966
'Psychodelphia vs Ian
Smith' event at the
Roundhouse

12 December 1966
'You're Joking' event at the
Royal Albert Hall

23 December 1966
UFO club opening night

26 December 1966
Cultural Revolution
declared in China

1967

6 January 1967
'Freak Out Ethel' event at
Seymour Hall, London

11–12 January 1967
Recording session at Sound
Techniques Studio in
Chelsea includes 'Arnold
Layne'

17 January 1967
Commonwealth Institute
show

12 February 1967
Keith Richards' home at
Redlands in Sussex raided
by police

1 March 1967
Queen Elizabeth Hall,
South Bank, London,
opened

11 March 1967
'Arnold Layne' released

17 March 1967
Jimi Hendrix Experience's
'Purple Haze' released

1 April 1967
EMI press launch

29–30 April 1967
The '14-Hour Technicolour Dream' free speech festival at Alexandra Palace, London

May 1967
Procul Harum's 'A Whiter Shade Of Pale' enters the UK singles charts

12 May 1967
'Games For May' at the Queen Elizabeth Hall

June 1967
The Beatles' *Sgt. Pepper's Lonely Hearts Club Band* released

16 June 1967
'See Emily Play' released

16–18 June 1967
Monterey International Pop Music Festival takes place

27 June 1967
First automated cash machine installed at Barclays Bank, Enfield

6 July 1967
First *Top Of The Pops* appearance, performing 'See Emily Play'

28 July 1967
Last UFO show at the original Tottenham Court Road location

5 August 1967
THE PIPER AT THE GATES OF DAWN released

12 August 1967
7th National Jazz and Blues Festival, Windsor

30 September 1967
The BBC launches Radio 1. The first track played (by DJ Tony Blackburn) is The Move's 'Flowers In The Rain'

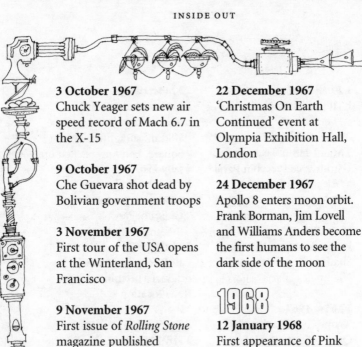

3 October 1967
Chuck Yeager sets new air speed record of Mach 6.7 in the X-15

9 October 1967
Che Guevara shot dead by Bolivian government troops

3 November 1967
First tour of the USA opens at the Winterland, San Francisco

9 November 1967
First issue of *Rolling Stone* magazine published

3 December 1967
First successful heart transplant carried out by Dr Christian Barnard

14 December 1967
Start of the Jimi Hendrix tour, at the Royal Albert Hall

18 December 1967
'Apples And Oranges' released

22 December 1967
'Christmas On Earth Continued' event at Olympia Exhibition Hall, London

24 December 1967
Apollo 8 enters moon orbit. Frank Borman, Jim Lovell and Williams Anders become the first humans to see the dark side of the moon

1968

12 January 1968
First appearance of Pink Floyd as a five-piece with David Gilmour

4 April 1968
Martin Luther King assassinated in Memphis, Tennessee

6 April 1968
Syd's departure officially announced

12 April 1968
'It Would Be So Nice' released

29 April 1968
The Broadway premiere of
Hair

May 1968
Student-led riots in Paris

28 May 1968
Kylie Minogue born

5 June 1968
Robert Kennedy assassinated
in Los Angeles, California

29 June 1968
A SAUCERFUL OF
SECRETS released.
Hyde Park free concert

8 July 1968
Second tour of the USA
starts

15–17 August 1968
Scene Club, New York City

20 August 1968
Soviet troops invade
Czechoslovakia to end the
'Prague Spring'

27 October 1968
Anti-Vietnam war
demonstration outside the
US Embassy in Grosvenor
Square, London, broken up
by police

26 November 1968
Cream's farewell concert at
the Royal Albert Hall

17 December 1968
'Point Me At The Sky'
released

1969

2 January 1969
Nick Mason marries Lindy
Rutter

9 February 1969
Boeing 747 makes maiden
flight

2 March 1969
Concorde makes maiden
flight

14 April 1969
'More Furious Madness
From The Massed Gadgets

of Auximenes' event at the
Royal Festival Hall, London

13 May 1969
Premiere of *More* at Cannes
Film Festival

26 June 1969
Royal Albert Hall, London,
final show of first major
UK tour for two years

5 July 1969
The Rolling Stones play in
Hyde Park, dedicating their
performance to Brian Jones

21 July 1969
Neil Armstrong and Buzz
Aldrin become the first
men to walk on the moon
– BBC use Floyd music for
moon landing

15–17 August 1969
The Woodstock Music and
Arts Festival

29–31 August 1969
The Isle of Wight Festival

5 October 1969
First BBC broadcast of
Monty Python's Flying Circus

25 October 1969
UMMAGUMMA released

6 December 1969
The Rolling Stones appear
at the Altamont Speedway,
California

1970

3 January 1970
Syd Barrett's *The Madcap
Laughs* released

5 February 1970
Zabriskie Point premieres

10 April 1970
Paul McCartney announces
that the Beatles are splitting
up

16 April 1970
Apollo 13 returns safely
to earth

4 May 1970
Four anti-Vietnam War

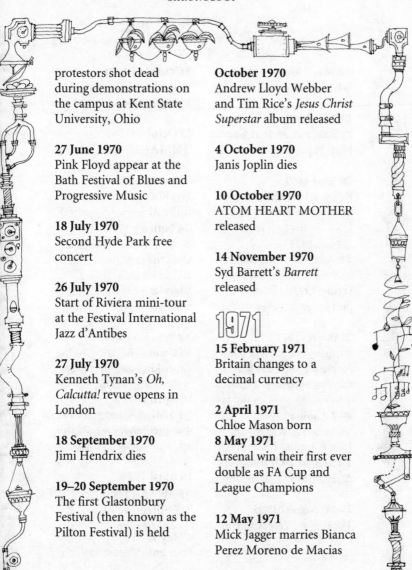

protestors shot dead during demonstrations on the campus at Kent State University, Ohio

27 June 1970
Pink Floyd appear at the Bath Festival of Blues and Progressive Music

18 July 1970
Second Hyde Park free concert

26 July 1970
Start of Riviera mini-tour at the Festival International Jazz d'Antibes

27 July 1970
Kenneth Tynan's *Oh, Calcutta!* revue opens in London

18 September 1970
Jimi Hendrix dies

19–20 September 1970
The first Glastonbury Festival (then known as the Pilton Festival) is held

October 1970
Andrew Lloyd Webber and Tim Rice's *Jesus Christ Superstar* album released

4 October 1970
Janis Joplin dies

10 October 1970
ATOM HEART MOTHER released

14 November 1970
Syd Barrett's *Barrett* released

1971

15 February 1971
Britain changes to a decimal currency

2 April 1971
Chloe Mason born

8 May 1971
Arsenal win their first ever double as FA Cup and League Champions

12 May 1971
Mick Jagger marries Bianca Perez Moreno de Macias

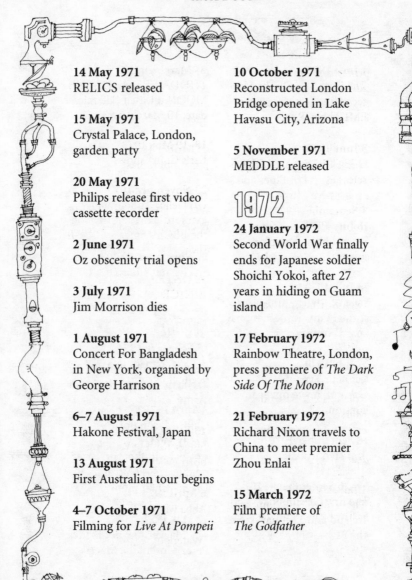

14 May 1971
RELICS released

15 May 1971
Crystal Palace, London,
garden party

20 May 1971
Philips release first video
cassette recorder

2 June 1971
Oz obscenity trial opens

3 July 1971
Jim Morrison dies

1 August 1971
Concert For Bangladesh
in New York, organised by
George Harrison

6–7 August 1971
Hakone Festival, Japan

13 August 1971
First Australian tour begins

4–7 October 1971
Filming for *Live At Pompeii*

10 October 1971
Reconstructed London
Bridge opened in Lake
Havasu City, Arizona

5 November 1971
MEDDLE released

1972

24 January 1972
Second World War finally
ends for Japanese soldier
Shoichi Yokoi, after 27
years in hiding on Guam
island

17 February 1972
Rainbow Theatre, London,
press premiere of *The Dark
Side Of The Moon*

21 February 1972
Richard Nixon travels to
China to meet premier
Zhou Enlai

15 March 1972
Film premiere of
The Godfather

1 June 1972
The Dark Side Of The Moon
recording sessions start at
EMI Abbey Road

3 June 1972
OBSCURED BY CLOUDS
released

1 September 1972
Bobby Fisher becomes
world chess champion,
beating Boris Spassky

September 1972
Olga Korbut captivates the
Munich Olympics

November 1972
Live At Pompeii film
premieres.
Roland Petit Ballet de
Marseille performances at
end of European tour

1973

1 January 1973
The United Kingdom, with
Ireland and Denmark, joins
the EEC

24 March 1973
THE DARK SIDE OF THE
MOON released (US release
date: 10 March 1973)

18–19 May 1973
Earls Court shows

23 November 1973
Uri Geller, spoonbender
extraordinaire, appears on
the BBC's *Dimbleby Talk-In*
show

15 December 1973
A NICE PAIR released

1974

4 February 1974
Patty Hearst kidnapped by
the Symbionese Liberation
Army

13 February 1974
Singer Robbie Williams
born

6 April 1974
Abba win the Eurovision
Song Contest with
'Waterloo'

26 July 1974
Robert Wyatt's *Rock Bottom* released

9 August 1974
President Richard Nixon resigns following the Watergate affair

1 October 1974
First UK franchise of McDonald's opens in Woolwich, South London

4 November 1974
British Winter 1974 Tour opens at the Usher Hall, Edinburgh

1975

24 March 1975
Holly Mason born

8 April 1975
Wish You Were Here tour opens in Vancouver

30 April 1975
The Vietnam War formally ends as Saigon falls

20 June 1975
The pyramid balloon breaks free in Pittsburgh

5 July 1975
Knebworth Festival

17 July 1975
Soyuz 19 and Apollo 18 dock. The end of the space race

20 July 1975
Voyager I probe lands on Mars

5 September 1975
WISH YOU WERE HERE released

1 October 1975
'The Thriller in Manila': Muhammad Ali vs Joe Frazier

20 December 1975
Video for 'Bohemian Rhapsody' shown on *Top Of The Pops*

1976

18 February 1976
Controversy over Carl Andre's bricks at the Tate Gallery, London

3 December 1976
Algie the pig escapes at Battersea

November 1976
The Sex Pistols' 'Anarchy In The UK' released

1977

1977
Nick Mason buys Ferrari 250GTO with '250 GTO' numberplate

28 January 1977
ANIMALS released. *Animals* world tour opens in Westfalenhalle, Dortmund

19 May 1977
The Sex Pistols appear on the *Bill Grundy Show*

25 May 1977
First *Star Wars* film, *Episode IV: A New Hope*, goes on release

2–7 June 1977
Queen Elizabeth II's Silver Jubilee celebration

18 June 1977
The Sex Pistols' 'God Save The Queen' reaches UK Number One

6 July 1977
Olympic Stadium, Montreal show on the *Animals* tour

16 August 1977
Elvis Presley dies

16 September 1977
Marc Bolan dies

November 1977
The Damned's *Music For Pleasure* released

16 December 1977
Release of *Saturday Night Fever*

1978

1978
'Space Invaders' launched

January 1978
Kate Bush's debut single
'Wuthering Heights'
released, goes to Number
One in the UK

25 July 1978
Louise Brown, world's first
'test tube' baby, born

7 September 1978
Keith Moon dies

27 December 1978
Forty years of military
dictatorship in Spain end

1979

1979
Sony Walkman released

2 February 1979
Sid Vicious dies

April 1979
The Wall recording sessions
begin in France

4 May 1979
Margaret Thatcher becomes
Britain's first woman prime
minister

9–10 June 1979
Nick Mason's first drive at
the Le Mans 24-Hour

12 June 1979
First man-powered
flight across the English
Channel by Bryan Allen in
'Gossamer Albatross'

30 November 1979
THE WALL released

22 December 1979
'Another Brick In The Wall,
Part 2' becomes Number
One in the UK

1980

5 February 1980
US launch party for Rubik's
Cube

7 February 1980
The Wall tour opens at LA
Sports Arena

22 March 1980
The Dark Side Of The Moon has the longest run of a contemporary album on US charts, after 303 weeks

17 July 1980
Saddam Hussein becomes president of Iraq

21 November 1980
'Who Shot J.R.?' episode of *Dallas* airs

8 December 1980
John Lennon shot dead in New York City

1981

1981
'Pac-Man' video game released

9 February 1981
Bill Haley dies

12 April 1981
First space shuttle launched

13–17 June 1981
Five performances of *The Wall* at Earls Court – the last live performance by David, Nick, Roger and Rick for 24 years

29 July 1981
Wedding of Prince Charles and Lady Diana Spencer

7 September 1981
Shooting for *The Wall* movie begins

23 November 1981
A COLLECTION OF GREAT DANCE SONGS released

1982

1982
Trivial Pursuit launched

January 1982
Erika Roe streaks at Twickenham during an International rugby match

April 1982
Sinclair ZX Spectrum released

2 April 1982
Start of the Falklands
war, as Argentina and
Great Britain fight over
ownership of the Falkland
Islands/las Malvinas

23 May 1982
The Wall film premieres at
Cannes

1983

1 January 1983
The Internet created

21 March 1983
THE FINAL CUT released

29 October 1983
*The Dark Side Of the
Moon* becomes the longest
running chart LP of all time
after 491 weeks

1984

1984
Nick Mason joins the
Rothmans Porsche team for
the filming of *Life Could Be
A Dream*

January 1984
The now-classic 128K
Apple Macintosh launched

30 April 1984
Roger Waters' *The Pros
And Cons Of Hitchhiking*
released

June 1984
Douglas Adams' *The Hitch-
hiker's Guide to the Galaxy*
published

16 September 1984
First broadcast of *Miami
Vice*

November 1984
Band Aid's 'Do They Know
It's Christmas?' released

1985

19 February 1985
First BBC broadcast of
EastEnders

March 1985
Mikhail Gorbachev
succeeds Chernenko as
Soviet President

May 1985
The Groucho Club in
London's Soho opens

13 July 1985
Live Aid concerts at
Wembley Stadium, London
and the JFK Stadium,
Philadelphia.
David Gilmour plays with
the Bryan Ferry band at the
Wembley show

19 August 1985
Nick Mason and Rick
Fenn's *Profiles* released

1 September 1985
Wreck of the *Titanic*
located

1986

23 January 1986
First inductions to the Rock
and Roll Hall of Fame,
including Chuck Berry,
James Brown and Elvis
Presley

30 April 1986
Chernobyl fire

16 May 1986
Top Gun released

22 June 1986
Diego Maradona scores
his 'hand of god' goal for
Argentina vs England in the
World Cup

1987

January 1987
Mikhail Gorbachev
launches *glasnost* followed
by *perestroika*

1 February 1987
DAT tapes launched by Aiwa

April 1987
Roger Waters press release
confirms his departure
from Pink Floyd

29 May 1987
Matthias Rust lands his
Cessna plane in Moscow's
Red Square

15 June 1987
Roger Waters' *Radio KAOS*
released

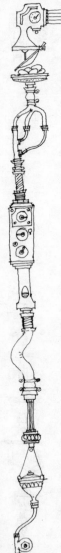

August 1987
Pink Floyd rehearsals for
Momentary Lapse tour start
in Toronto

8 September 1987
A MOMENTARY LAPSE
OF REASON released

9 September 1987
*A Momentary Lapse of
Reason* tour opens in
Ottawa

1988

23 January 1988
*A Momentary Lapse of
Reason* world tour opens
in Western Springs, New
Zealand and runs through
to 23 August 1988 at Nassau
Coliseum, Long Island

30 April 1988
The Dark Side Of The Moon
drops out of the US album
charts after 724 weeks in
Top 200

21–22 June 1988
Chateau de Versailles shows

10 November 1988
Lockheed's F-117A stealth
bomber unveiled

22 November 1988
DELICATE SOUND OF
THUNDER live album
released

1989

14 February 1989
Fatwa issued against
Salman Rushdie for writing
The Satanic Verses

13 May 1989
Another Lapse tour starts in
Werchter Park, Belgium

June 1989
The Tiananmen Square
student demonstration is
put down in Beijing, China

3–4 & 6–7 June 1989
Olympic Stadium, Moscow,
shows

15 July 1989
Venice show

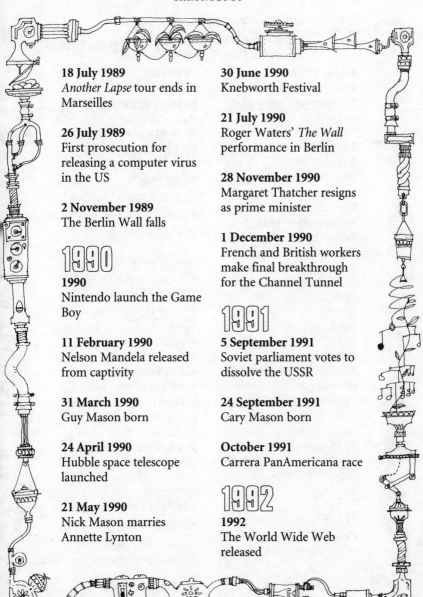

18 July 1989
Another Lapse tour ends in Marseilles

26 July 1989
First prosecution for releasing a computer virus in the US

2 November 1989
The Berlin Wall falls

1990

1990
Nintendo launch the Game Boy

11 February 1990
Nelson Mandela released from captivity

31 March 1990
Guy Mason born

24 April 1990
Hubble space telescope launched

21 May 1990
Nick Mason marries Annette Lynton

30 June 1990
Knebworth Festival

21 July 1990
Roger Waters' *The Wall* performance in Berlin

28 November 1990
Margaret Thatcher resigns as prime minister

1 December 1990
French and British workers make final breakthrough for the Channel Tunnel

1991

5 September 1991
Soviet parliament votes to dissolve the USSR

24 September 1991
Cary Mason born

October 1991
Carrera PanAmericana race

1992

1992
The World Wide Web released

13 April 1992
Video of *La Carrera Panamericana* released

1993

23 June 1993
John Wayne Bobbitt bobbitted

13 September 1993
Yasser Arafat and Yitzhak Rabin shake hands, standing on the White House lawn with Bill Clinton

1994

30 March 1994
THE DIVISION BELL released.
The Division Bell tour opens at Robbie Stadium, Miami

29 October 1994
Final Earls Court show ends *Division Bell* tour

1995

30 May 1995
PULSE live album released

1996

17 January 1996
Pink Floyd inducted into Rock & Roll Hall of Fame by Billy Corgan

5 July 1996
Dolly the sheep, the first mammal cloned from an adult cell, is born

November 1996
DVD machines launched by Toshiba in Japan

1997

1 May 1997
The UK general election gives Tony Blair and Labour a landslide victory

31 August 1997
Diana, Princess of Wales dies in Paris car crash

1998

10 April 1998
Good Friday Agreement, first stepping-stone

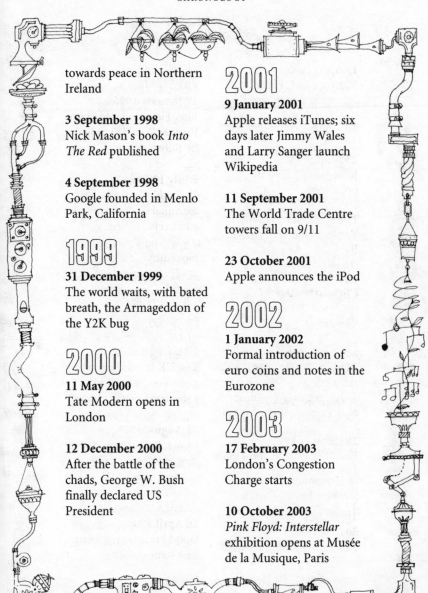

towards peace in Northern
Ireland

3 September 1998
Nick Mason's book *Into
The Red* published

4 September 1998
Google founded in Menlo
Park, California

1999

31 December 1999
The world waits, with bated
breath, the Armageddon of
the Y2K bug

2000

11 May 2000
Tate Modern opens in
London

12 December 2000
After the battle of the
chads, George W. Bush
finally declared US
President

2001

9 January 2001
Apple releases iTunes; six
days later Jimmy Wales
and Larry Sanger launch
Wikipedia

11 September 2001
The World Trade Centre
towers fall on 9/11

23 October 2001
Apple announces the iPod

2002

1 January 2002
Formal introduction of
euro coins and notes in the
Eurozone

2003

17 February 2003
London's Congestion
Charge starts

10 October 2003
Pink Floyd: Interstellar
exhibition opens at Musée
de la Musique, Paris

24 October 2003
Concorde's final
commercial flight from JFK
to LHR

30 October 2003
Steve O'Rourke dies

22 November 2003
England win the Rugby
World Cup

2004

4 February 2004
Facebook launched at
Harvard

7 October 2004
Inside Out publication date

31 October 2004
Nick Mason and the Enzo
Ferrari appear on BBC's
Top Gear

14 December 2004
Norman Foster's Millau
Viaduct inaugurated

26 December 2004
Tsunami devastates
countries bordering the
Indian Ocean

2005

23 April 2005
First YouTube video clip
uploaded

9 April 2005
Charles, Prince of Wales
marries Camilla Parker-
Bowles

2 July 2005
Nick, Roger, David and Rick
reform for Live 8 at Hyde
Park

7 July 2005
The day after London
is awarded the 2012
Olympics, terrorists kill 52
civilians on the city's tube
and bus network

16 November 2005
Pink Floyd inducted into
the UK Music Hall of Fame
by Pete Townshend

17 November 2005
Roger Waters' opera *Ça Ira* premieres in Rome

2006

6 March 2006
David Gilmour's *On An Island* released

21 March 2006
First ever tweet posted by Twitter co-founder Jack Dorsey

7 July 2006
Syd Barrett dies

17 July 2006
President George W. Bush greets PM Tony Blair with 'Yo, Blair'

2007

10 May 2007
'The Madcap's Last Laugh' tribute to Syd Barrett, at the Barbican, London

1 July 2007
Smoking is banned in all enclosed public spaces in England

14 November 2007
High Speed 1 railway opens, linking London and the Channel Tunnel

2008

15 September 2008
Lehman Brothers bank collapses.
Rick Wright dies.

5 November 2008
Lewis Hamilton becomes youngest-ever Formula One World Champion

2009

20 January 2009
Barack Obama inaugurated as 44th President of the United States

25 June 2009
Michael Jackson dies

2010

15 April 2010
Dust from the eruption of Icelandic volcano Eyjafjallajökull causes closure of much of European airspace

6 May 2010
Caroline Lucas becomes the UK's first Green Party MP

10 July 2010
Roger Waters and David Gilmour appear together at Hoping Foundation fundraiser, Kiddington Hall, Oxfordshire

2011

4 January 2011
Death of Tunisian street vendor Mohamed Bouazizi catalyses the 'Arab Spring'

2 May 2011
Osama bin Laden killed by US special forces

12 May 2011
David and Nick join Roger to perform during Roger's *Wall* show at the 02 Arena

2012

12 August 2012
Nick Mason performs 'Wish You Were Here' with Ed Sheeran, Mike Rutherford and Richard Jones at the closing ceremony of the London Olympics

21 September 2012
Sale of EMI to Universal confirmed

21 December 2012
Predicted to be the 'End of the world' based on the Mayan calendar. However, world keeps turning

2013

8 April 2013
Margaret Thatcher dies

18 April 2013
Storm Thorgerson dies

7 July 2013
Andy Murray wins
Wimbledon singles title,
first UK man to do so for
77 years

2014

29 March 2014
First same-sex weddings in
England and Wales

19 September 2014
Scotland votes 'No' to
independence

7 November 2014
ENDLESS RIVER released

2015

25 March 2015
BBC confirms it has
dropped Jeremy Clarkson
from *Top Gear*

18 September 2015
David Gilmour's *Rattle
That Lock* released

13 November 2015
Terrorists kill 89 at the
Bataclan concert venue in
Paris as part of coordinated
attacks in the city

2016

23 June 2016
Brexit: the UK votes to
leave the European Union

8 November 2016
Donald J. Trump wins the
US presidential election

11 November 2016
THE EARLY YEARS
1965-1972 released

2017

13 May 2017
'Their Mortal Remains'
exhibition at V&A opens

PICTURE CREDITS

The publishers would like to thank the following sources for their kind permission to reproduce the photographs in this book. We are particularly grateful to Nick Mason for access to his picture archive (NMA = Nick Mason Archive). Every effort has been made to trace the copyright holders but should there be any omissions or errors we would be happy to correct them in future editions of the book.

SECTION 1

Page 1 NMA Page 2 NMA (both pics) Page 3 (top) Clive Metcalfe; (bottom) NMA Page 4 Mike Leonard (both pics) Page 5 NMA Page 6 NMA (both pics) Page 7 (top left) Peter and Sumi Jenner/Graham Keen; (top right) NMA; (bottom) NMA Page 8 Graham Keen Page 9 (top) Adam Ritchie; (bottom left) NMA/Wendy Gair; (bottom right) Adam Ritchie Page 10 (top) Dave Mills; (bottom) Redferns/Andrew Whittuck Page 11 (top) Rex Features; (bottom) NMA Page 12 (top) NMA; (bottom) Colin Prime/ www.rocharchive.com Page 13 NMA (all pics) Page 14 NMA (both pics) Page 15 NMA (both pics) Page 16 Peter and Sumi Jenner

SECTION 2

Page 1 Storm Thorgerson Page 2 Strange Things Archive Page 3 (top) Jill Furmanovsky's Archive; (bottom) NMA Page 4 NMA Page 5 NMA (both pics) Page 6 Pictorial Press/Jeffrey Mayer Page 7 (top) NMA; (bottom) The Collection of Steve O'Rourke Page 8 Mick Rock Page 9 Ron Geesin/Richard Stanley Page 10 (top) Juliet Wright/Gerard Bousquet; (bottom) NMA Page 11 Rex Features/Crollanza Page 12 NMA Page 13 Repfoto/Robert Ellis Page 14 (top) Jill Furmanovsky; (bottom) NMA Page 15 NMA (both pics) Page 16 Rex Features/Everett Collection

SECTION 3

Page 1 NMA Page 2 NMA (both pics) Page 3 NMA (both pics) Pages 4 and 5 pyramids, Hipgnosis; band, Jill Furmanovsky Page 6 (top) The Collection of Steve O'Rourke; (bottom) NMA/Jill Furmanovsky Page 7 (top and middle) NMA/Jill Furmanovsky; (bottom) NMA   Page 8 Phil Taylor (both pics) Page 9 (top) Phil Taylor; (bottom) NMA   Page 10 (top) Jill Furmanovsky; (bottom) NMA/Jean Cazals Page 11 Robbie Williams Page 12 Phil Taylor Page 13 NMA (both pics) Pages 14 and 15 (both pics) NMA Page 16 NMA/ Bob Jenkins

SECTION 4

Page 1 NMA/Mark Fisher   Page 2 NMA   Page 3 (top) NMA; (bottom) NMA/VA courtesy The Kobal Collection   Page 4 LAT (all pics) Page 5 (top) NMA/David Bailey; (bottom) Jill Furmanovsky Page 6 (top) Robbie Williams; (bottom) NMA Page 7 (top) NMA; (bottom) NMA/Dimo Safari Page 8 NMA (all pics) Page 9 (top) NMA/Dimo Safari; (bottom) Alan Davison Page 10 NMA (all pics) Page 11 NMA (both pics) Page 12 (top) Jill Furmanovsky; (bottom) Brian Rasic/Rex Features Page 13 (top) Brian Rasic/Rex Features; (bottom) Jill Furmanovsky Page 14 (top) Gala Wright/ Rick Wright Archive; (bottom) NMA Page 15 (top) Harry Borden; (bottom) NMA Page 16 Jill Furmanovsky (both pics)

CREDITS FOR PART TITLES

Chapter 1 NMA   Chapter 2 Redferns/Andrew Whittuck   Chapter 4 NMA Chapter 5 Ron Geesin/Richard Stanley Chapter 6 NMA   Chapter 9 NMA Chapter 10 NMA   Chapter 11 NMA/Dimo Safari   Chapter 12 NMA/Dimo Safari   Chapter 13 Ahmed Emad Eldin/Jill Furmanovsky

INDEX